GEOGRAPHICAL INDICATIONS OF INDIAN HANDLOOMS

This book presents a comprehensive analysis of Geographical Indications (GI) in the Indian context with particular reference to the handloom sector. It discusses themes such as the rationale of GI as IP (intellectual property); the domestic position on GIs; GI protection under various international instruments; handlooms from Gujarat and their GI journey; the efficacy of GIs; and GI structure for handlooms. The volume fills the gap between law and policies and recommends the implementation of an efficient legal system. It highlights the status of Indian handlooms, a sector that represents the country's cultural heritage and supports a range of livelihoods. We examine India's GI protection system with its diverse cultures and explore how GI can help recognize, support and promote these products to bring socio-economic benefits. The work documents policy measures undertaken for the revival, restructuring and promotion of Indian handlooms and handicrafts, and will serve as an important intervention in Indian law on GI.

An investigative study that evaluates the current law and policy on GI protection through detailed case studies and empirical research on select Indian handlooms, this book will be useful to scholars and researchers of geography, economics, development studies, sociology, law and public policy. It will also interest policymakers, legal practitioners, textile and handloom professionals, design and business administration institutes, media, arts and crafts museums and civil society organizations working on handlooms or in intellectual property.

Nidhi Buch is assistant professor of Law and Head, Centre for Intellectual Property Rights at Gujarat National Law University, India. She holds a Ph.D. in intellectual property (IP) laws from Gujarat National Law University. She also teaches and trains at institutions such as the Ahmedabad Management Association, various business schools and the State Judicial Academy. She has worked in the field of IP rights for nearly two decades, with her initial experience being as an IP consultant with National Institute of Design, Ahmedabad.

Hetvi Trivedi is senior research assistant, GUJCOST-GNLU Centre of Excellence in IPR at the Gujarat National Law University, India. She researches on intellectual property rights, with a special interest in advancing the understanding of the merger between law and society through traditional knowledge and geographical indications. She holds an LL.M. in Intellectual Property and Information Law from King's College London, UK. She has previous experience in law practice and is interested in designing implementation strategies for research outcomes.

GEOGRAPHICAL INDICATIONS OF INDIAN HANDLOOMS

Between Legal Right and Real Right

Nidhi Buch and Hetvi Trivedi

Routledge
Taylor & Francis Group
LONDON AND NEW YORK

First published 2022
by Routledge
2 Park Square, Milton Park, Abingdon, Oxon OX14 4RN

and by Routledge
605 Third Avenue, New York, NY 10158

Routledge is an imprint of the Taylor & Francis Group, an informa business

British Library Cataloguing-in-Publication Data
A catalogue record for this book is available from the British Library

Library of Congress Cataloging-in-Publication Data
A catalog record has been requested for this book

ISBN: 978-0-367-43091-7 (hbk)
ISBN: 978-1-032-18776-1 (pbk)
ISBN: 978-1-003-00214-7 (ebk)

DOI: 10.4324/9781003002147

Typeset in Sabon
by Deanta Global Publishing Services, Chennai, India

TO THE WEAVERS OF INDIAN HANDLOOMS

CONTENTS

LIST OF ILLUSTRATIONS AND APPENDICES

Figures

Maps

Tables

Appendices

PREFACE

The immensity of a subject remains unravelled until it is travelled through. And the journey of a thousand miles begins with a single step forward, empowered by conviction. Yet if words are to describe the gradual formation of this work, which now lies solidified in print, it has been nothing short of thrilling. While it started when being socially active in the physical realm was a popular means for man to achieve the end called "life", by the time it was finished, mankind had learnt how to isolate in a bid to survive. Devoured by a single virus, the world urgently moved online and newer terms became part of the human vocabulary. These sudden transitions added to the challenges of this research pursuit. Thus, on a scale of *that* normal to *this*, the work you now hold formed, flourished and was finished.

Talking of Geographical Indications, the subject central to this research, although previously linked in one form or another with traditions underlying agriculture and food cultivation, handlooms and handicrafts, it was thrust into the limelight in its current international status only with the Agreement on Trade-Related Aspects of Intellectual Property Rights, aka TRIPS. In those footsteps, India followed to recognize and unleash the potential of its tremendously rich culture and traditions by enacting the Geographical Indications of Goods (Registration and Protection) Act, 1999. Cutting to the chase, a decade later we embarked on this journey, first to understand whether and to what extent the law has been successful in recognizing and protecting the countless practices that flaunt the badge of India's collective, age-old culture and traditions. In particular, handlooms were our study target.

We moved further with a preliminary understanding of the difficulties faced by handlooms despite their recognition as Geographical Indications of India. The objective was to connect the dots to learn why Indian handlooms, ranging from the regal and well-known Banarasi and Kancheepuram silks to the simple-looking yet equally intricate weaves like Kota Doria, have not received their share of post-registration GI benefits. However, the Indian handlooms' condition is but a maze of many factors coming into play.

Parameters like socio-economic conditions, educational background, specific and general awareness and many other dynamics interface with this *sui generis* law, making their inclusion in the evaluation of the law inevitable. Then again, considering major role-players like the government, non-governmental organizations (NGOs) and other external agencies were required for a complete assessment. The handloom sector has held a significant place in India's policy measures. Unique initiatives for the revival and restructuring of the sector were taken through the erstwhile 5-year plans and in the current policy actions by NITI Aayog, the Handloom Census being one such measure devised to understand the overall health of the sector. Thus, gradually the research became an amalgamation of law and policy evaluation with a single objective to appreciate the situation of handlooms and their recognition as Geographical Indications.

The distinctiveness of this work is reflected in the blend of both doctrinal and empirical approaches of research employed to study the handlooms with an identical goal: to assess the efficacy of their "GI tag". Through case studies, the severity of handlooms' deteriorating condition is highlighted, which is then backed with empirical evidence from weavers of Kutch and Tangaliya shawls in Gujarat. The results are eye-opening, to say the least, and they call for a prioritized action. Handlooms are torchbearers of the Indian traditional legacy. Their healthy survival is imperative to build a *Shining India* for the generations to come.

So, in a blink, 4 years passed, and the research not only increased in size and matter but also developed from a mere idea into its current form. We embarked upon this research journey with a humble vision of making a valuable contribution to the growing ecosystem on Geographical Indications of India and to comprehend the law's efficacy on the ground for its better reach to the primary stakeholders. Now, we remain sincerely hopeful that this resultant work is beneficial to fellow enthusiasts among bureaucratic circles, research communities, academia and young minds, all of whom can come together for the betterment of India's handlooms. Lastly, we pray for the ailing humanity to overcome this time and emerge victorious.

ACKNOWLEDGEMENTS

Research cannot thrive in isolation. It is an amalgamation of ideas, theories and experiences spanning years, sometimes decades or even more, in a contemporary fashion. This research too gathered inspiration from countless such works. Needless to say, the initiation of this research and its journey to its conclusion was due to several contributors who in one way or the other propelled its different aspects. The idea to measure the success of Geographical Indications (GI) law in India was first gathered from a modest newspaper article about Tangaliya shawls, which would have gone unnoticed if not for the search for related news for *IP Weekly*, a newsletter circulated among Gujarat National Law University staff and students. The seed for a potential research project thus sown was given the go-ahead by the university's Research & Publications Division, then led by Dr. Ranita Nagar and members of Research Council, Dr. Vikas Gandhi, Dr. Viral Pandya and Dr. William Nunes. The idea, in its infancy, was selected for presentation as a working paper at the 3rd Works-In-Progress Conference "IP Scholars Asia" organized by the Singapore Management University in March 2018. Many thanks to Professor Irene Calboli, Delphine Marie-Vivien and Dr. Gargi Chakrabarti, who wholeheartedly engaged in intellectually stimulating discussions in the GI session at the conference. Further, as the pace and intensity of this research increased, we buried ourselves deeply within the work. Our heartfelt gratitude to Prof. (Dr.) S. Shanthakumar, Director and Dr. A. N. Rao, Dean, Research & Publications Division, Gujarat National Law University for being with us throughout the lengthy research journey. Of course, we cannot thank enough the GNLU library, both physical and digital, and other online resources that became our chief sources of knowledge for this work.

The research moved forward significantly with the help of field investigator Rajendrasinh Khant and data analysts Rahil Mathakia and Dr. Vikas Kumar. Student members of the Centre for IPR at GNLU enthusiastically aided with the research for which we are extremely thankful, especially the Centre's Student Research Associates Sayan Chandra and Lakshay Garg.

We are also thankful to Ms. Shaiva Shah from Y. J. Trivedi & Co. for helping us with the nuances of GI Application and Registration procedure under Indian law.

The research in its preliminary report form would not have reached this point if not for the endless support of Ms. Shoma Choudhury, commissioning manager at Routledge India, Taylor & Francis Group. Her belief in the work and understanding approach during the COVID-19 lockdown strengthened us a great amount in planning some features of the book from scratch as the pandemic derailed us from the original track. Similarly, Ms. Rimina Mohapatra, our publishing manager, and her team guided us extensively during the publication process. We thank the entire team at Routledge India for standing by us.

This section of the book would be incomplete without acknowledging the sincere efforts of Ms. Vaishali Singh, our deeply regarded colleague at GNLU and our team-member when the idea was generated. Her gusto gave this idea its much-required foundation.

The weavers of Kutch and Tangaliya shawls of Gujarat deserve a special mention and applause. Their co-operation during the entire empirical investigation was commendable. Trusting strangers from a university they were not aware of with details of their professional and personal life was a brave feat indeed. Our earnest gratitude goes to Baldev Bhai, a weaver from Surendranagar, for talking with us freely about the art of Tangaliya weaving and bringing us close to the people from his community.

Any potential research builds its base on prevailing/previously generated research. Ours too was inspired by the ground-breaking works on GI by the late Dr. Dwijen Ragnekar, Dr. Dev Gangjee and Professor Irene Calboli. These works made us appreciate the long-standing history of GI along with its contemporary significance for developing countries.

A four year research experiment is impossible without the ceaseless encouragement of friends and beloved family members, especially this research, which started and was completed in what seem like two different eras: pre- and post-COVID. They supported us with unwavering faith, not just as we spoke about this promising idea but also as we nurtured it in a rather difficult phase through 2020–2021. If not for each one of them, we would have lost strength and sanity. An acknowledgment of their direct and indirect involvement sounds uncomfortably formal, but in the end we can only offer words of love and gratitude for the immensity of their trust in our determination. This work belongs to all of you as much as to us. Thank you!

ABBREVIATIONS

AO	Appellation of Origin
BIRD	Bankers Institute of Rural Development
COP	Code of Practice
GI	Geographical Indication
IHB	India Handloom Brand
IP	Intellectual Property
IPR	Intellectual Property Rights
IS	Indication of Source
NABARD	National Bank for Agriculture and Rural Development
TRIPS	The Agreement on Trade-Related Aspects of Intellectual Property Rights
GI ACT	The Geographical Indications of Goods (Registration and Protection) Act, 1999
GI RULES	The Geographical Indications of Goods (Registration and Protection) Rules, 2002
GI RULES	The Geographical Indications of Goods (Registration and Protection) Amendment Rules, 2020
TK	Traditional Knowledge

INTRODUCTION

Geographical Indications of Indian handlooms: The gap between legal right and real right

This book is the culmination of a contemporary idea in the field of intellectual property laws with particular reference to Geographical Indications (GIs), as examined with the help of empirical and doctrinal methods of research. In less than a few years, intellectual property, or IP, as it is popularly known, has become a buzzword globally and has been brought into focus through multiple challenges in the two worlds that we now know, pre- and post- pandemic.

The theme of Geographical Indications within the vast universe of intellectual property came as a choice-by-chance. It sounds about right to say that instead of us choosing the focus area, it chose us. The use of the term *GIs* has grown exponentially, and nowadays one will find the topic regularly featured on the front pages of national dailies. Hence, just like IP suddenly becoming a topic for casual conversation, GIs too have breached the boundary of legal academia and research to intrigue the common man. But what are Geographical Indications? Apart from the available definitions, to understand this term rather simply, one needs to recall any locally grown or made item of food or clothing. Such item or good is required to carry a mark of the territory in which it is produced. One of the indisputably famous examples is that of Darjeeling Tea, known worldwide for its characteristic flavour. A product of north-east India, this tea cannot be found elsewhere in the world as it grows only in a specific region with certain climatic conditions coupled with local agricultural knowledge, which makes it hard to replicate anywhere else. Such features of taste and colour are so unique to Darjeeling Tea, they cannot be found in other varieties of tea. The tag of Geographical Indications thus awarded to the tea recognizes that the good is produced only in a marked geographical territory and carries certain unique features which are attributable to that area only. In one way or the other, each of us have come across goods that are suitable to be recognized as GIs; however up until now, the issue has never so vividly come to individual attention, especially in the Indian context.

DOI: 10.4324/9781003002147-1

To boost the positive efforts made to channel the existing domestic IP structure especially in the context discussed here, we picked up this rather modern theme of Geographical Indications to analyze the effectiveness of the law and related policy initiatives by surveying the grass-root stakeholders. India has walked a distinct path by implementing a law on Geographical Indications that not only recognizes its unique agricultural products but also categorizes handicrafts and handlooms as prominent value-additions in making the country what it is today. However, as researchers, we took on the responsibility to evaluate and analyse the current scheme of law and policy in the context of Geographical Indication (GI) protection in order to suggest suitable modifications to increase its efficacy. This book presents an outline of the international and domestic position of Geographical Indications as a form of IP and evaluates the effectiveness of the GI regime from the viewpoint of selected handloom products from India that have had the GI tag for a decade or more.

The uniqueness of this work is reflected in the fact that India has produced very little literature on its law on Geographical Indications, suggesting a significant gap in its understanding from an academician-researcher's point of view. The reach of the GI law is increasing in the quantitative sense, with registration applications for products pouring in from each State on a monthly basis; however, the qualitative investigation of the law and related policies is hugely deficient. Thus, this book builds on an ambitious plan to begin a dialogue on the GI law and kick-start a fruitful discussion.

Considering the scope of the book, which focuses on the efficacy of Geographical Indications, it is pertinent to note that efficient and effective utilization of a GI protection system can garner socio-economic benefits, as is acknowledged by several nations across the EU and Asia. Though the global IP system introduced the term "Geographical Indications" for the first time through TRIPS, the value of origin-based goods was not completely unknown. Previous systems such as Appellations of Origin (AO) and Indications of Source (IS) are proof that products like Champagne and Darjeeling Tea have attained global popularity due to their unique geographical origin-bound characteristics. However, the status of Geographical Indications has been the subject of legal treatments varying from nation to nation. In view of such distinctive treatments given to GIs by developed and developing nations in their domestic legislative framework, the protection of GI and its efficacy has emerged as one of the most contentious issues in the field of IPR. In India, prior to the 1999 legislation,[1] GI was protected under common law and Indian courts recognized the existence of GI through the action of passing off in absence of any statute.

The legislative framework in form of the Geographical Indications of Goods (Registration and Protection) Act, 1999 (hereinafter the GI Act) provides for a *sui generis*, distinct and broad system of protection. Unlike TRIPS, the GI Act does not restrict itself to wines and spirits only, thus treating various categories of goods equally. In fact, one of the distinctive features of this Act is that it covers protection for names, symbols and words other than geographical names, such as "Blue Pottery" for a type of traditional craft from Rajasthan and "Phulkari" for a type of embroidered craft from Punjab. India being a country of cultural diversity, the significance of GI protection is more than in other countries. GI in its present form also serves the purpose of protecting traditional knowledge such as Patan patola[2] from Gujarat as well as traditional cultural expressions such as Kathputlis[3] from Rajasthan.

Speaking further about the significance of GI for India, it is not just a form of IP used for economic gain but also can be viewed as a tool for rural development. A common feature among all GI registered goods is their origination in rural areas where the majority of the population can be categorized as socially backward and have limited means of livelihood. Thus, GI has the ability to contribute towards the support of skilled and inter-generational artisans, weavers, farmers and so on. To date, India has identified and registered 370 GIs divided among several categories of goods such as agriculture, handicrafts (including handlooms), foodstuffs, manufactured goods and natural goods. Out of these 370 registrations, 214 goods are registered under the handicrafts category, followed by 112 registrations from the agriculture category. Of the 214 registrations in the handicrafts category, 74 are granted to handloom products. These statistics sufficiently convey the significance of two majorly unorganized but highly employment-yielding sectors of the Indian economy. Specifically speaking, India is a textile-rich country which has been recognized for her handlooms since time immemorial. Each State in India boasts of communities working wonders through the art of weaving, which gradually became a part of their cultural heritage, passed on through the generations. In this context, GI can be viewed as the only legal instrument with a power to preserve cultural heritage along with the rights of communities involved in this sector. However, this law cannot have the expected effects in the absence of appropriate policies, which makes it essential to study both these tools of development together.

Arriving at the focal point of this work, the question of pertinent importance is whether the combination of law and policy has achieved the desired protection of Geographical Indications relating to goods. To answer this, we, while conducting the literature review, identified that though various studies recognized GI as a component of critical value and investigated it from the perspective of market economics or social impact, there is space for GI to be probed from a law and policy perspective in order to understand their combined efficacy for the stakeholders involved. The law, in order to stay truthful to its objective, must place both registration and its enforcement on an equal footing, which is possible only by undertaking appropriate policy measures. With such reasons in consideration, this work aims to fill the gap in law and relevant policies in relation to the handloom sector in India. We take a unique approach to discern the law on Geographical Indications as implemented in India, but not without a thorough understanding of the earlier terms like Appellations of Origin and Indications of Source in order to set a base for creating a background for the distinct Indian approach to GIs. The weakness in the implementation of the GI law in the handloom sector of India sets the premise for this book. To substantiate the premise, this work is divided into two parts, applying both doctrinal and empirical research methodologies. First, we studied the GI journey of 12 selected handlooms from 10 States in India: Rajasthan, Madhya Pradesh, Maharashtra, Karnataka, Telangana, Assam, Jammu and Kashmir, Uttar Pradesh, Himachal Pradesh and Gujarat through available secondary resources. Statistically speaking, this covers approximately 50% of States whose handlooms are registered as GIs. It is pertinent to mention that the efficacy of any law can be assessed only after a considerable time has elapsed since its enforcement, and hence only such handlooms that have completed one cycle of registration i.e., 10 years, were made part of this study. In the latter part of the work, we present results from an empirical study that was carried out on two handlooms in Gujarat. The State of Gujarat is immensely vibrant and has a unique forte in handloom and handicrafts which is truly reflected in the lifestyle, culture and spirit of the State, especially the Kutch-Saurashtra region. Post scrutiny into attributions that make them unique, some products from this region have been accorded recognition and protection under GI. As is known, GI recognition can ensure an enhanced level of safeguarding of a traditional and cultural ethos from piracy and add value to the goods so they can access a wider international market. While initiating the empirical study (October 2017), Gujarat had 15 GI registrations, of which 4 (Tangaliya shawls, Kutch shawls, Patan patola and Rajkot patola) were from the handloom category. From these registered handlooms, only Tangaliya and Kutch shawls had completed one cycle of registration. Meanwhile, we learnt an interesting fact about the Tangaliya handloom, which was rescued from the brink of extinction by intervention from the National Institute of Fashion Technology, Gandhinagar (Gujarat), which also provided required assistance for its GI recognition, while even then the condition of the craft continued to remain dire. This served as an inspiration for the we to evaluate the status of GI protection with reference to Tangaliya shawls as well as Kutch shawls.

Despite having Geographical Indications status for a decade and a half, the Kutch and Tangaliya handlooms lack the desired strength. With the present law on GI and welfare schemes in place, doubts arise as to why this primary and secondary assistance has not aided the required development of the handlooms. The investigative study, through empirical research, that forms a major part of this book makes an attempt to find out the root causes of the poor marketability of these crafts, especially Tangaliya shawls, even after the legislative protection and to understand how far government support through various schemes has helped them in sustaining and extending the life of their work. Thus, the overall framework of the book revolves around analyzing the hurdles pre- and post-GI registration with an emphasis on the handlooms of India in general and of Gujarat in particular.

The evaluation here is undertaken from a socio-legal perspective to understand the practical difficulties faced by the stakeholders. Further, as mentioned, it identifies existing policy initiatives by the government in order to support the handloom sector. It is believed that there is adequate and efficient amalgamation between the policies and the GI Law, however, the research has challenged this belief by seeking answers from grass-root level stakeholders. This book is therefore a result of an extensive, planned doctrinal-empirical study which provides a unique take on the GI law and related policies as implemented in the handloom sector of India.

We, through this work, look at the problem regarding the Geographical Indications of Indian handlooms from three perspectives: 1) the legal context, 2) its current status and 3) the existing policy scenario. Post an understanding of the reality on the ground, the work moves on to analyze policies in place and suggest measures towards the betterment of the recognized goods. These measures pertain to amendments in law and policy as well as strategies that may be adopted such as awareness, marketing and branding. This work offers a glimpse of the structure of law and policy to open a dialogue on the existing issues of implementation and enforcement while making suggestions for adopting measures for a better GI system in India.

CHAPTER 1: *Geographical Indications as intellectual property: Evolution and rationale*

Chapter 1 provides an in-depth understanding of the journey of GI as a form of intellectual property (IP). This form of IP has an extensive history, which needs to be examined in order to learn why it is treated uniquely by many nations. This chapter aims at understanding GI through various international instruments, the most recent being TRIPS, before and after the introduction of which the regulation of Geographical Indications underwent a remarkable transformation. Relevant provisions on GI from other international instruments such as the Paris Convention for the Protection of Industrial Property, 1883; the Madrid Convention for the Repression of False Indication of Origin, 1891; and the Lisbon System are highlighted. Further, in order to understand GI as a concept, comparisons are drawn with other widely accepted concepts like Indications of Source, Appellations of Origin and Trademark to mark the distinctive characteristics of GI. In order to appreciate the rationale and significance of GI, its role as a tool for rural development and the protection of traditional knowledge are briefly highlighted. Lastly, through the salient features of the Geographical Indications of Goods (Registration and Protection) Act, 1999 and the Geographical Indications of Goods (Registration and Protection) Rules, 2002 (hereinafter the Rules), the Indian legal treatment of GI is discussed.

CHAPTER 2: *Legal recognition of Indian handlooms: Recounting the challenges through case studies*

The objective of this chapter is to discuss and analyze the concept of "legal right" and the process of acquiring the same in the case of Geographical Indications in India. As set out in the premise of this work, we attempt to understand the efficacy of GI law which is dependent on the realization of the legal right granted under the law. To achieve this objective, we go through the "legal right" acquisition journey of certain handloom products through doctrinal research, mainly relying upon secondary resources. Further, the chapter lays down the registration requirements and procedure for acquiring GI under the Act. This discussion is required to set the tone of this as well as the next chapter. While dealing with the case studies, the present status of GI registrations has been statistically analyzed.

As the focal point of this work is to assess the effectiveness of GI in the handloom sector of India, the chapter – with the help of case studies – then carries on to discuss handlooms of India and their unique identities attributable to a specific geographical area, due to which their registration under the GI law was found appropriate. It concludes by drawing observations on certain debatable issues such as the registration of authorized users, absence of functional inspection bodies, sparsity of infringement cases etc. in order to explain the gap between legal right and real right, which forms the framework of the concluding chapter.

CHAPTER 3: *Evaluating the success of GI status: Tangaliya and Kutch shawls of Gujarat*

The rationale of this book is developed further under Chapter 3 through empirical evidence from a study conducted on two handlooms from Gujarat – Tangaliya and Kutch shawls, both of which are the earliest handlooms in the State to be recognized as GIs and have completed a decade of registration. The empirical study was divided into two parts wherein in the final phase, 254 weavers from 11 talukas in the two districts participated. Weavers' responses were recorded through a questionnaire designed to assess their awareness and understanding of GI law, their right under the same and governmental policy initiatives targeted towards the handloom sector. Other aspects such as education, product marketing and branding, time and capital investment into weaving etc. were also studied to broadly understand their socio-economic status. Data analysis of the collected responses was carried out to substantiate the hypothesis on the effectiveness of the GI law – whether it is a collective right in the true sense or a right merely on paper.

CHAPTER 4: *Policies for revival of handloom sector in India: Tapping the lost potential*

As mentioned earlier, in order to assess the overall impact of GI registration on the handloom sector in India, mere deliberation on the GI law cannot prove sufficient. The discussion must also extend to policy initiatives and other programmatic interventions directed towards supporting handlooms and their weavers. For this, Chapter 4 elaborates on policy initiatives and other interventions in this sector by the government. Recognizing handlooms as the second largest unorganized sector after agriculture, several studies have been commissioned over the years to survey the health of the sector and understand its primary challenges so that appropriate policies can be formulated for its sustenance and gradual growth. It is essential to understand these schemes and policies together with the data collected empirically and the doctrinal case studies to verify the work's sub-premise of whether there lies a gap between legal right and real right due to weaknesses in implementation and enforcement. The analysis in this chapter offers a definite structure to the idea of this book, from which we draw important conclusions and recommendations for the betterment of the condition of the handloom sector.

CHAPTER 5: *Conclusions: Mapping the road ahead*

Chapter 5 concludes with a suggested framework of measures that can be implemented from legal and policy perspectives. Here the aim is to complete the inquiry into the effect and efficacy of the Geographical Indications law together with relevant policy measures by detailing the findings from the doctrinal and empirical studies. At the end of this chapter, we present recommendations in order to strengthen the enforcement structure of the law on Geographical Indications and its alignment with sectoral initiatives of the government for the effective enforcement of the GI law for the handloom sector in India.

Notes

1 The Geographical Indications of Goods (Registration and Protection) Act, 1999.
2 An example of the finest ikat known to the world, Patan patola is created using a double ikat technique – counted as one of the most complicated crafts in the world – whereby the warp and weft are tied and dyed before they are woven. The term *ikat* originated from Indonesia, which, depending on context, can mean the nouns cord, thread, knot and the finished ikat fabric, as well as the verbs "to tie"

or "to bind". It has a direct etymological relation to the same word in Javanese. Patan patola is a product of exquisite workmanship adorned with gorgeous colours and striking designs. Although different types of handloom products are woven using the ikat technique in many parts of the country, Patan patola is the only Indian handloom product created using the double ikat technique. More technical and factual details about Patan patola are available at <https://craftatlas.co/crafts/ikat> and in the Statement of Case filed along with GI Application No. 232 in 2011 at <http://ipindiaservices.gov.in/GIRPublic/Application/Details/232>.

3 Marionettes or string puppets, famously known as Kathputlis, represent an ancient traditional art of Rajasthan. Practitioners of this art have used it for purposes such as entertainment, social commentary and passing on inter-generational tales. Originating in Nagaur, Rajasthan, the practitioners of this art (puppeteers) mainly belong to a caste of hereditary bards or genealogists. These string puppets are perhaps the only example of their kind in the world where a control or cross is not used for manipulation. In other words, all the strings are attached to the puppeteers' fingers directly, which demand a great deal of virtuosity. These puppets are operated with strings that vary in number from two to eight; the larger the puppet, the more the movement and agility the character has. Statement of Case filed along with GI Application No. 62 in 2008 at <http://ipindiaservices.gov.in/GIRPublic/Application/Details/68>.

1

GEOGRAPHICAL INDICATIONS AS INTELLECTUAL PROPERTY

Evolution and rationale

1.1 GI: Meaning and evolution as a form of intellectual property

Geographical Indication (GI), which was once considered a sleeping beauty, has gained immense popularity, especially in the recent past. The value of branding products with their origin has been recognized worldwide. From the Indian perspective, GI is a unique form of intellectual property (IP) which is not just trade and development-centric but has an inevitable socio-cultural heritage perspective. Post TRIPS (the Agreement on Trade-Related Aspects of Intellectual Property Rights), GI is considered to be an important and emerging dimension of IP for developing countries as it is capable of making significant contribution to the development of rural areas. The ability of GI to garner socio-economic benefits has been recognized since the Paris Convention, which led many nations, especially from the EU and Asia, to acknowledge legal protection of GIs prior to TRIPS. However, the kind of extensive and comprehensive protection as prescribed under TRIPS never existed before. In view of the distinct treatment given to GIs by member nations in their domestic legislative framework, the protection of GI and its efficacy have emerged as among the most contentious issues in the field of intellectual property rights (IPR). In India, prior to the 1999 legislation,[1] GI used to be protected under common law, and Indian courts recognized the existence of GI through the action of passing off in absence of any statute.

GIs are not only a form of intellectual property but are also tools for development. Adequate protection of GI can serve various objectives such as rural development, availability of quality-based products, the expansion of tourism, creation of livelihood and employment opportunities and, most importantly, preservation of cultural heritage and traditional knowledge. GI is identified to be a unique product which has its origin in a specific place, area or locality. The genesis of the GI can be explained through the uniqueness of products which is rooted in the geographical place of their production.

The uniqueness of a product protected with a GI tag is attributable to its geographical origin, which is due to the typical climatic conditions of that

DOI: 10.4324/9781003002147-2

place, as in the case of Darjeeling Tea,[2] or the uniqueness inherent in the skill of the people who belong to that geographical region, such as Pochampally ikat[3] or Patan patola.[4] Such unique features serve as the identity of the product and are deeply connected with the place of its origin. Some products are from very small places but they have proved to have global appeal due to such unique characteristics.

It is a source of identity like trademarks. However, it is substantially distinct from other forms of IP. The formal definition of GI is provided by TRIPS as an indication of a product having a strong link with its geographical origin.[5] Further, protection is provided to this form of IP through specific and elaborative provisions under this most comprehensive international instrument.[6]

The legislative framework in form of the Geographical Indications of Goods (Registration and Protection) Act, 1999, provides for a *sui generis* system of protection in India which is distinct as compared to the protection prescribed under the US and EU jurisdiction. TRIPS accords special protection to wines and spirits, whereas the GI Act does not include such special protection provisions. In order to serve the purpose of adopting a *sui generis* system, it was considered necessary to bring the vast variety of products of handloom and handicrafts that are a part of the domestic cultural heritage under the ambit of legal protection. India being a country of cultural diversity, the issue of GI protection is more significant than in other countries. Hence, the definition of GI as provided under the Act is broad enough to cover protection of names/symbols/words other than geographical names, such as "Basmati". GI in its existing form also serves the purpose of protecting traditional knowledge, as many GIs are based on centuries-old arts and crafts like Kutch and Tangaliya shawls.

1.1.1 GI – meaning and nature

It is essential to understand the terminology used for GI as the concept is wide and extensive. It is categorized as an industrial property[7] and is a sign that signifies a product's uniqueness, attributable to its geographical origin. Such characteristics stand as a link between the product and its place of origin. It is sine qua non to elucidate the terms *Appellations of Origin* and *Indications of Source* for a comprehensive understanding of GI. In fact, Geographical Indications can be considered an offshoot of both these terms.

A brief sojourn into the historical evolution is essential to understand the timelessness, so to speak, of the Geographical Indications and similar early concepts that evolved gradually as a necessary means to preserve cultural heritage and agricultural traditions. We know from the discussion in previous paragraphs here that the term *Geographical Indications* is a fairly recent addition to the group of terms that preceded through early multilateral treaties and/or the diverse national practices regulating the idea of goods and their place of origin. Among the terminologies, Indication of Source (IS) and Appellation of Origin (AO) featured in international instruments before TRIPS, and it is only practical to understand the terms and the difference between these and GI.

Though the formal use of Indication of Source was made initially in the Paris Convention,[8] a subsequent international instrument, i.e. the Madrid Agreement on Indications of Source[9] along with this Convention, remains silent on its definition. A sign that refers to the place or origin of a product signifies an Indication of Source. It can be a country or a specific place of origin of a product such as 'Made in India', 'Swiss Made' etc. It is noteworthy that IS merely conveys a product's geographical origin but does not refer to an inherent quality in it. Thus, a major distinction between IS and GIs is that the former provides no indication of any specific quality attributable to a product.

Appellation of Origin must be a geographical name which is attached to the product. The term Appellation of Origin is defined under Article 2(1) of the Lisbon Agreement for the Protection of Appellation of Origin and their International Registration adopted in 1958.

> "Appellation of Origin" means the geographical denomination of a country, region, or locality, which serves to designate a product originating therein, the quality or characteristics of which are due exclusively or essentially to the geographical environment, including natural or human factors.

Further, the TRIPS Agreement defines the expression "geographical indication" under the Article 22.1 of the TRIPS Agreement, which states:

> Geographical indications are, for the purposes of this Agreement, indications which identify a good as originating in the territory of a Member, or a region or locality in that territory, where a given quality, reputation or other characteristic of the good is essentially attributable to its geographical origin.

From a quick glance at the definitions of AO and GIs, the reader may pick up a hint of similarity between the two in terms of the prominence given to the geographical origin of the product. However, a significant distinction lies in the fact that for a product to gain protection as AO, such as Champagne, a geographical name must be attached to it, whereas GIs need not always have a geographical name attachment like Phulkari of Punjab or Blue Pottery of Jaipur. Thus, the scope of Geographical Indications is broader than Appellations of Origin and Indications of Source.

1.1.2 Historical evolution

As mentioned earlier, what was once considered a neglected form of IP has now become a crucial right in the bid to develop rural zones and, most importantly, to identify and recognize the traditional knowledge which resides in arts, crafts, food and agriculture techniques, and is unique to a geographical locale. However, it has not been a smooth transition for Geographical Indications to mark its territory under the vast umbrella of Intellectual Property Rights. Even with an international acknowledgement upholding the status of GI, it continues to be a chaotic subject because the nature, scope and institutional forms of protection available vary across jurisdictions.[10] Hence in this sense, the law governing GIs will remain debatable unless a massive consolidation of viewpoints and policies takes place among the three categories of nations. Today, Geographical Indications stand at the intersection of three hotly debated issues in international law: international trade, intellectual property and agricultural policy.[11]

While the modern recognition of GIs is comparatively recent, its evolution is not. Connections between places and goods have been around for a long time but the idea of protecting goods based on their place of origin found initial recognition in European countries, especially in France, the first country to introduce a comprehensive system of GI protection. However, a reader will come across several terms in a quest to understand the concept of GIs. Long before the emergence of the latest terminology, i.e. Geographical Indications, other concepts surrounding the recognition and protection of origin-based products were in place. From Indication of Source and Appellation of Origin to Protected Designation of Origin and Protected Geographical Indication, the GI journey is quite an overwhelming mix of terminologies. This is not All in fact, the most comprehensive World Trade Organization (WTO) survey of national laws to date reveals – a piece of GI trivia – 23 distinct definitions applied in this area![12] This indeed puts GIs in stark contrast to other IP domains.

Advancing the discussion on the epistemology, we find it both interesting and important to take a look at *Appellation d'Origine Contrôlée* (AOC) or the Controlled Appellation of Origin – the French foundation established to extend protection to goods originating from a specific place. Its *Code de la Consommation* or Consumer Code defines an AOC as the designation of a country, of a region, or of a locality that serves to indicate that a product originates from that place and owes its quality or characteristics to its geographic surroundings. The definition extends protection to both natural and human factors, thus protecting "nature" and "culture".

The regulations are applicable to production methods of certain fine foods and beverages through AOC. The most popular examples of AOC regulated goods are sparkling wine from Champagne and Roquefort cheese, producers of which are given the right to produce select wines and cheeses provided the production is undertaken within the designated geographic region associated with the goods. The law moves a step further to ensure more control over the production of AOC regulated goods by adding a requirement for these products to be processed in the same region where the raw agricultural commodities – grapes in the case of wines and milk for cheeses – are produced. Thus, wines and cheeses produced in consonance with the stipulated regulations may be legally marketed under the geographically significant appellation of origin.

Exploring the internal control measures that are in place to regulate the quality of wine produced in Champagne, we are intrigued to dive into the events that led to adoption of heightened regulations around wines, cheeses and similar products in France. A law regulating the protection of wines against false designation was introduced in the year 1824.[13] Under this, labelling of the regulated products was not made obligatory; however, if a trader chose to label the origin of the product, whatever was conveyed through the label description had to be true, thus prohibiting false designation. The regulations or laws in place then were not strongly implemented, leading to a rise in fraudulent practices of wine production. Further, from the late 1800s to the early twentieth century, phylloxera, a plant louse that destroys vine roots, attacked grape vines throughout Europe, including the vines of Champagne, resulting in major losses of vine crops and leaving several vignerons bankrupt.[14] The European vines were destroyed and replaced with plantations of American vines immune to phylloxera.[15] This, coupled with the importation of wine from other countries to meet the market demand at the time, left the sprawling wine industry in a catastrophic condition.[16]

To combat the situation of degrading practices in wine production, France introduced a law on 1 August 1905, bringing in the concept of appellations of origin; the law made provisions for protection of the appellations and gave French authorities the power to delimit winegrowing regions.[17] The delimitation arrangement received a sour welcome, thus paving the way for a new legislation post World War I. With the law introduced in 1919, the French courts were empowered to consider the question of appellations of origin and established criteria for the judiciary to use in determining if such designations were warranted.[18] This much touted law also came under scrutiny, facing many technical hurdles; meanwhile there was the other matter of overproduction, bringing forth new concerns which finally paved the way for the decree-law of 1935, through which the creation and management of *Appellation d'Origine Contrôlée* (AOC) were introduced.[19] It brought together various market operators, such as producers, processors and merchants, in addition to government authorities, including what was later to become the *Institut national de l'origine et de la qualité* (INAO).[20]

Principle of terroir *is at the heart of GI protection*

A classic debate surrounding GIs has interestingly divided the entire international community into defenders and critics. Central to this debate is the concept of *terroir* – a deep traditional connection to the land. Defenders or the "old world" nations have rigorously advocated the existence of GIs as they protect uniquely identifiable products possessing qualities attributable to the place of origin.[21] On the other hand, the "new world" nations differ significantly, arguing against the principle of *terroir* by asserting that modernization has upgraded human skills to an extent that products from any place can be replicated at any place.[22] There is no clear winner to this classic debate, and nations have moved forward to treat GIs as per their beliefs. India certainly falls into the former category of an "old world" nation as it is home to several products with characteristics that are intrinsic to natural phenomena or human skills found only within a specific geographic territory.

Historically, France has led the propaganda relating to *terroir*, which is derived from the Latin term *terra*, meaning land or earth. This term was coined in order to convey the unique characteristics of wine, which are attributable to climatic conditions arising in the product's geographical origin. The notion of *terroir* is rich in meaning and has evolved over time. Additionally, having been conceptualized in a well-defined socio-cultural context, translating the French word *terroir* into other languages is not an easy task.[23] In its narrowest sense, *terroir* refers only to the physical environmental aspects of the geographical origin of a foodstuff or wine: the soil, lay of the land, elevation, climate, and related factors.[24] Expanding the scope of *terroir* to include socio-cultural contexts, it is referred to as "a defined geographical area in which a human community builds, along its history, a collective production knowledge based on a system of interactions between a physical and biological environment and a set of human factors".[25] Due to the attached socio-technical factors, a good produced in such a defined geography benefits from an originality, a specificity and a reputation unlike others produced outside the territorial extent.[26] *Terroir* has thus earned international recognition and momentum from like-minded nations lending their unwavering support to the French belief. However, this concept has become a contentious issue of debate in negotiations on adequate protection of GIs at the global level.[27]

Sharing a French couple's heart-warming tale, this piece by Steven Erlanger aptly explains the *terroir* concept and how it sounds alien to a person at the other end of understanding.[28] Illustrating the use of *terroir*, this article reflects "new world" disbelief in the concept by saying "The importance of terroir to the French psyche and self-image is difficult to overestimate, because it is a concept almost untranslatable, combining soil, weather, region and notions of authenticity, of genuineness and particularity – of roots, and home – in contrast to globalized products designed to taste the same everywhere".[29] Further, it says, "Though related to the farm-to-table and locavore movements of a new generation, *terroir* is not about proximity, but about honesty and community, an idea even more important to a France that fears losing its identity in a larger Europe and a competitive world".[30] Hence, although massively contested, the concept of *terroir* nevertheless remains at the heart of GIs, supporting the belief system that GIs exist as a unique form of intellectual property recognizing and preserving the traditional knowledge and cultural heritage which remain innate valuable assets for several nations.

1.1.3 Characteristics of GI

What makes GI unique is the nature of the right granted to a community as a whole, which is not exclusively legal or commercial. Though similar in nature, the marketing and protection systems for GIs differ from country to country. Most GIs originate in developing and underdeveloped nations where its potential for serving as an essential tool for livelihood is well established, as most of the products for which GI is granted come from agricultural, natural or human-skilled based products like handicrafts. GI products are unique not only because of the concept's intrinsic distinctiveness but also due to its ability to recognize and support the concept of "local".[31] Alternatively, GI facilitates not only local development by tying producers to the land, but also producers' cooperation to maintain the quality of the products for collectivity.[32] A product with a GI tag has an added potential to incentivize its marketability. GI-protected products also serve as an instrument to reduce consumer confusion by way of assuring uniformity in quality. Thus, GI, as an intellectual property right, aims to protect both farmers and artisans alike.[33]

Another unique feature of GI compared to other forms of IP is that it cannot be created; it can only be recognized. It legally recognizes an already existing product having uniqueness as enshrined in the law of GI. The products protected under the GI are unique and ubiquitous at the same time. The legal right granted is limited to the use of the name, which is a link between the product and its origin; however, the product itself is not protected. The making or manufacturing of such product by an entity outside the recognized community is not prohibited, but associating such a product with the same geographical origin is not permitted. For example, enhanced protection is available only to producers within the association that is recognized along with the GI tagged Darjeeling Tea from North-East India. However, this does not prohibit anyone from manufacturing or selling of other teas in the market. Thus, what is protected is the uniqueness of the tea as grown in Darjeeling, and only those producers who are a part of the association to which the right is granted can make use of this tag.

1.1.4 Functions of GI

GI performs various functions, such as indicating origin, advertising the unique attributes of the product and assuring its quality. An unmissable functional aspect of GI is that it serves as a tool for socio-economic development of rural areas, especially by way of protecting and preserving traditional knowledge. These functions are of tremendous significance as they form the core of the GI protection system both nationally and globally.

The origin function of GI here refers to its ability to indicate the source. Through this function, information regarding the origin of the product is shared with the customers. A product through this function is identified as "originating or manufactured in the territory of the country or a region or a locality in that region".[34] As mentioned in the definition of GI, it also ensures that the goods to which GI tag is granted are also of unique quality and have characteristics essentially attributable to its geographical origin.[35] Alternatively, it can be said that the GI tag guarantees certain unique features which are of a specific quality. Thus, quality assurance is implied through the origin function. Darjeeling Tea[36] and Pochampally Ikat[37] are apt illustrations of products that are well known and preferred due to such unique features.

Another key function of GI is to advertise the product, which is also known as its investment function. Advertising of products with GI tags not only promotes the product among consumers but also influences their buying preferences. Consumer preferences in favour of such products, in turn, attract increased investment in their further production. The advertisement function also helps in resolving the issue of asymmetric information between sellers and buyers of GI products.[38] A brand for a GI product can be created through advertisements, which can create a global market for local products. Strategic advertising of GI provides protection from duplication and misappropriation of such products, which consequently translates into an intangible asset for producers.[39]

The last function of GI is crucial to developing and underdeveloped nations for whom GI is one of the most suitable forms of IP, identifying and recognizing their traditional knowledge, which in turn can facilitate the preservation of such knowledge. The involvement of local human skills behind the production of many real products is in fact the unique attribute available only within a specific geographical region, such as Patan Patola, Chanderi Sari and Kullu Shawl. Thus, the historical, cultural and economic threads are woven together in the operation of the marketplace for goods protected by GIs.[40]

1.2 GI: Rationale and significance

1.2.1 GI and TM – Conflicts and coexistence

GI and trademarks (TM) serve an identical function as forms of IP by indicating the origin of the products to which they are attached; however, their rationale differs significantly. This difference between GI and TM is well addressed by TRIPS, wherein TRIPS highlights the difference by distinctly defining the two terms. Article 15.1 of the TRIPS Agreement states that,

> Any sign, or any combination of signs, capable of distinguishing the goods or services of one undertaking from those of another undertakings, shall be capable of constituting a trademark.

Article 22.1 of the TRIPS Agreement defines the expression "Geographical Indications", which states:

> Geographical indications are, for the purposes of this Agreement, indications which identify a good as originating in the territory of a Member, or a region or locality in that territory, where a given quality, reputation or other characteristic of the good is essentially attributable to its geographical origin.

From the above definitions, it can be concluded that TM and GI are two distinct sets of right, where the former can be considered an exclusive private property right as compared to the latter, which is a community right. Rights granted under GI are non-transferrable, i.e. a GI cannot be licensed/assigned/mortgaged/otherwise transferred, which is not the case with TM. While a trademark essentially indicates the commercial origin of a product or service, GIs indicate the geographical origin of the product. Whereas, for consideration of legal protection for a mark, it must be distinct, a GI tag can be granted to a product for its uniqueness and strong association with its geographical origin. Lastly, a significant difference lies in the treatment given under various bilateral and unilateral international instruments to TM and GI, which is a recognition of their distinct natures.

1.2.2 GI – A legal vehicle for rural development

GI can become an alternative progressive system for socio-economic growth in rural India for the following reasons. Most of the GI products registered in India to date[41] come from agriculture and handicrafts, which are the two most important unorganized sectors providing livelihood opportunities to most of the population of rural India. Further, most such products are from small and medium size ventures that form part of rural sectors and have a potential to contribute towards rural development goals.[42] Such local products, being the cultural assets of a region, can vanish easily from the market if not given an adequate push. Hence, GI is not a magic formula for rural development. Nevertheless, it can contribute towards socio-economic development when utilized adequately and enforced effectively, for which legal structure and its governance must go hand in hand.

1.2.3 GI: A tool for protection of traditional knowledge

Traditional knowledge (TK) and Geographical Indications share a common component of protecting community rights. TK protects local and indigenous knowledge, knowhow, skills and practices, whereas GI protects such knowledge by way of linking it to geographical origin. The contemporary system of protecting intellectual property rights was developed in the context of industrialization and essentially to protect human innovations, keeping in mind technological advancements. However, it was observed that there are numerous innovations that are based on traditional and indigenous knowledge which need to be brought under the umbrella of legal protection. Such protection is of immense significance, especially for developing countries. Traditional knowledge lies at the intersection of multiple issues of international governance and is, therefore, being discussed in multiple forums.[43] Given the growing significance of protecting TK, GI can be considered the most suitable form of IP for protection of TK for two reasons. Firstly, GI protects those products which are based on human knowhow in the form of TK. Secondly, the nature of such protection allows the TK to remain in the public domain, and the same can be protected in perpetuity.

1.2.4 GI in developing countries

Geographical Indications can play a pivotal role in the holistic growth of developing countries. It is a tool not only to protect traditional and cultural wealth and expressions but also to tap into the economic potential of local products and capture a global market. The marketability of such products can contribute towards realizing rural development goals for developing countries like India. Thus, the main purpose of according adequate protection to GI is to preserve origin-based products and to improve consumer welfare by providing reliable information about the qualitative attributes of such products.[44] GI through legal protection and efficient enforcement ensures dual advantage for developing countries by not only generating economic benefits but also influencing people to be more integrative and innovative. The legal, social, cultural and historical traditions of various developing nations have played a vital role in defining the nature, scope and degree of GI protection globally. GI is one of the most important forms of IP for developing countries due to its potential in contributing towards economic, socio-cultural and rural development objectives along with protecting and preserving traditional knowledge and biodiversity. However, marketing and legal enforcement of GIs remain constant challenges for these countries.

1.2.5 GI and handicrafts: An inseparable bond

Culture, traditions and colours have been synonymous with India for as long as anyone can remember. She is truly blessed, with each State of hers being home to unique and well-known products, either natural or manmade, and the country derives a strong cultural identity from these locally rooted products, whose growth spans across time and generations. Indeed, Indian history stretches back thousands of years and is laced with stories of creative treasure troves or products from nature's bounty that add to its prestige on the global platform. In fact, India defends the idea that the Indian tradition in the area of "material knowhow" is as legitimate as any other tradition and can play a major role in nation building.[45] Interestingly, this nation carries a mix of "traditional-modernism", that is, it is resourceful enough to keep pace with the advancing strides of fellow developing as well as some developed nations, yet at the same time wants to stay true to its cultural and traditional legacy. So, as rightly put by the World Intellectual Property Organization (WIPO), cultures and traditions embedded in the idea of traditional knowledge[46] aren't so called due to the antiquity inherent in them but for the living body of knowledge that is developed, sustained and passed on from generation to generation within a community, often forming part of its cultural or spiritual identity.[47]

In the economic context, having suffered and survived colonization, India's approach turned interventionist, where the State played a major role. Development in India was not initiated from outside but was the result of a slow restructuring of the private sector industry, especially around the domestic market.[48] Such gradual evolution away from a prolonged period of colonization has aided India in sustaining its true essence inherent in the various traditions in each corner of its massive geographical area. Data from the GI Registry, which show that out of 370 registered GIs, 214 belong are handicrafts, is sufficiently suggestive of this inseparable bond.

1.3 Protection of GI through international instruments

Recognizing the need for and significance of commonly accepted standards for the protection of GIs, efforts to this end have been undertaken through various international conventions and treaties. Adequate and effective regulation of GI through international and domestic legal framework has paved the way for the creation of a distinct niche for GI in the IP canon. TRIPS is the latest attempt at such harmonization. In order to appreciate TRIPS, it is necessary to analyze its background along with detailed provisions concerning GIs. The journey of GI from Indication of Source to Appellation of Origin and finally to its present form is well illustrated by international instruments. This section will make an attempt to analyze the following relevant international conventions, treaties and agreements in this context:

a. Paris Convention for the Protection of Industrial Property[49]
b. Madrid Agreement for the Repression of False or Deceptive Indications of Source on Goods[50]
c. Lisbon System including Agreement for the Protection of Appellations of Origin and their International Registration and Geneva Act[51]
d. The Agreement on Trade-Related Aspects of Intellectual Property Rights[52]

1.3.1 Paris Convention

The Paris Convention is one of the most comprehensive international instruments on industrial property. The convention applies to industrial property in the widest sense, which includes patents, trademarks, industrial designs, geographical indications and the repression of unfair competition. It is one of the oldest international instruments in the field of intellectual property rights. The Paris convention was signed on 20 March 1883 and revised on several occasions – 14 December 1990 at Brussels, 2 June 1911 at Washington, 6 November 1925 at The Hague, 2 June 1934 at London and 14 July 1967 at Stockholm. It was last amended on 28 September 1979. The Paris Convention neither defines the rights it purports to protect nor prescribes any minimum standard of protection for these rights.[53] The member nations are at liberty to provide for their own legal framework for the scope and the quality of rights prescribed under the convention. The Paris Convention for the first time recognized terms like Appellation of Origin and Indication of Source through Article 1(2).[54] Interestingly, these terms are not defined in the text of the convention. It does not lay down comprehensive and extensive provisions in this regard; however, inclusion of Appellation of Origin and Indication of Source in the objects of protection of industrial property can be considered to be the first formal initiative under any international instrument. In the absence of any specific provisions on the minimum standards of protection, member countries opted for different levels of protection as per their domestic requirements.

The Paris Convention prohibited unlawful Indications of Source as well as false Indications of Source. Article 9 provides that goods bearing an unlawful Indication of Source are subject to seizure upon importation into Paris Convention countries, within the country where the unlawful use of the Indication of Source occurred, or within the country of importation. Article 10(1) provides protection against the use of a false Indication of Source, and applies the remedies prescribed by Article 9, including seizure upon importation and seizure inside the country; prohibition of importation or other domestically available mechanisms can be used instead. In addition, Article 10b is prohibits the use of a false, misleading or confusing indication that constitutes an act of unfair competition.

Thus, it was through Paris Convention that the world was made aware of GI as a form of industrial property.

1.3.2 Madrid Agreement for the Repression of False or Deceptive Indications of Source on Goods

While the Paris Convention was successful in getting a huge response from the Member State countries, it did not provide for effective protection in the case of GIs. However, it provided sufficient freedom to Member State countries to make agreements between themselves for the further protection of industrial property.[55] In furtherance of this provision, two more agreements i.e., the Madrid Agreement and the Lisbon Agreement, were duly concluded. The Madrid Agreement prescribed for provisions while focusing on the term Indication of Origin, under Article 1(1):[56]

> all goods bearing a false or deceptive indication of source, by which one of the contracting states, or a place situated therein, is directly or indirectly indicated as being the country or place of origin, must be seized on importation, or such importation must be prohibited, or other actions and sanctions must be applied in connection with such importation.

Prohibiting the commercialization of products with such false and deceptive Indication of Source is the main objective of this instrument. Though the agreement prohibits use, in connection with sale, display or offering for sale of any goods, of all indications in the nature of publicity capable of deceiving the public as to the source of the goods, it remains silent on the definition of the term *Indication of Source*. Through Article 2, it prescribes for the cases and the manner in which seizure may be requested and effected. The Courts of each contracting State can decide what appellations, on account of their generic character, do not fall within the provisions of this Agreement.

Looking at the structure of this international instrument, we have preferred not to deal in detail with further provisions and found it pertinent to restrict the discussion to the relevant parts.

1.3.3 Lisbon System

The Lisbon Agreement for the Protection of Appellations of Origin and their International Registration of 1958 and the Geneva Act of the Lisbon Agreement together form the Lisbon System. In order to make it more convenient for readers, the agreement is discussed first and the Act later.

Lisbon Agreement

Considering the narrow scope of protection provided by the Madrid Agreement and the lack of protection against free riders on the reputation of goods, the Revision Conference for the Paris Convention gave serious consideration to a wider and stronger international protection of GIs. Eventually on 31 October 1958, the Lisbon Agreement was concluded to provide for a higher level of protection. However, the agreement did not even use the term GI; instead, Appellation of Origin was the formal term defined under Article 2(1), as mentioned here, according to which the appellation must be the geographical name of a country, region or locality and there must be a qualitative link between the product and its geographical origin. A noticeable part of the definition is that such a link must be due exclusively to the geographical environment, including natural and human factors. In order to fight against unfair competition and misappropriation of indications, many countries developed a special system. However, securing protection through such a system was found to be complex due to the differences in legal treatment that existed in the systems of various nations. The Lisbon agreement provided a well-founded system for the protection of Appellation of Origin through an international system for registration compared to the level of protection provided under the Madrid Agreement to Indications of Source. As per Article 3,

> Protection shall be ensured against "any *usurpation* or imitation, even if the true origin of the product is indicated or if the appellation is used in translated form or accompanied by terms such as 'kind,' 'type,' 'make,' 'imitation,' or the like."

Thus, Lisbon agreement was concluded in order to meet the need for a system of international registration and to facilitate the protection of a special category of Geographical Indications, i.e. Appellations of Origin, in countries other than the country of origin. It protected AO by means of their registration with WIPO through a single procedure, involving a minimum of formalities and expenses.[57] Once protected in the country of origin, an application for registration under this agreement can be filed by the holder of the right to use such an Appellation of Origin through its government.[58] In principle, an internationally registered Appellation of Origin must be protected in all countries subscribing to the Lisbon system. However, during the process of registration, the member nations do have the right to refuse such protection, for example, on the grounds that, in their territory, the Appellation of Origin corresponds to a protected trademark or to a generic indication of a particular product. In absence of any such refusal, the appellation of origin will be considered automatically protected for as long as it is registered, provided the same is not declared invalid by the court of such a country.

The Geneva Act

Considering the low number of nations joining the Lisbon Agreement, WIPO decided to revise the agreement by making it more flexible and broader in scope. The Geneva Act is the result of the revision of the Lisbon Agreement, which was initiated by WIPO in 2009. The main feature of the Geneva Act is its extensive scope, which covers all GIs, in contrast to the Lisbon Agreement, which covered only AOs. Thus, the Act is more comprehensive and wider than the Lisbon Agreement, providing a broader ambit of protection. The Geneva Act was adopted on 20 May 2015 and was officially enforced on 26 February 2020.

Being appreciative of the diverse system of GI protection as it exists among various nations, contracting parties are permitted under the Act to use any type of legislation to protect products registered under the Lisbon Agreement. Further, the Act not only extends to the GI and AO but also covers trans-border Appellations of Origin and Geographical Indications. The contracting parties in cases may file a joint or separate application.

Being mindful of the significance and rationale of GI protection under the Indian System, we are of the opinion that India must seriously consider joining the Lisbon System. The register of GIs in India clearly indicates that the majority of them come from the handicrafts and agriculture sector. Many such GIs have the potential to be premium export products. Talking about an effective system of GI in the age of globalization, one cannot restrict its scope of protection to the national register only. International registration of such products will certainly help bridge the gaps in overall protection.

1.3.4 The Agreement on Trade-Related Aspects of Intellectual Property Rights (TRIPS)

GI as a form of intellectual property lacked an effective international protection mechanism even with the Paris Convention, Madrid Agreement and Lisbon System. GI is considered to have been a complex area during negotiations in the Uruguay Round of Multilateral Trade Negotiations, which took place between 1986 and 1994 among trading partners under the auspices of the GATT (General Agreement on Tariffs and Trade).[59] It was through TRIPS that GI got elaborate and precise provisions for appropriate protection. Clear provisions under Articles 22, 23 and 24 of part II, Section III of TRIPS generated wider interest on the protection of GIs across the globe. TRIPS, being a significant step towards international protection of GIs, defined the concept under Article 22(1). Along with prescribing minimum standards of protection for all GIs, Article 23 deals exclusively with GIs related to wines and spirits. Article 24 deals with exceptions as well as few unresolved issues for future negotiations. The structure of these three articles precisely and clearly encompasses an elaborate system of international protection for GIs.

Article 22 Basic Protection

The definition of GIs as given under TRIPS has enlarged the scope of the definition of Appellation of Origin as prescribed under the Lisbon Agreement. Article 22.1 of the TRIPS Agreement defines Geographical Indications as follows:

> Geographical indications are, for the purposes of this Agreement, indications which identify a good as originating in the territory of a Member, or a region or locality in that territory, where a given quality, reputation or other characteristic of the good is essentially attributable to its geographical origin.

As per this definition, GI is a sign that serves as an identity of the product. It does not, however, specify the nature of that sign, being a word or combination of it or any symbol. Further, there is no requirement that the GI must be a geographical name. It can be a noun or an adjective, provided it is sufficiently recognized to be associated with the geographical area or territory. Blue pottery (of Jaipur)[60] and Phulkari (of Punjab)[61] are examples of this.

Article 22.1 clearly conveys that GIs refer to the indications which identify a good originating in a region, limiting the scope of protection to only goods; this is not restricted to any specific category of goods and can be identified as a GI by the Member State as per its domestic legal framework for GI protection. For example, under the Indian legal framework, a GI tag can be granted to goods falling under agricultural, natural, manufactured, goods of handicraft, and foodstuff categories.[62] Another striking feature of the definition of GI under TRIPS is its broader scope of protection compared to the Lisbon agreement. TRIPS added "reputation" as another parameter in addition to quality and other characteristics that are in essence attributable to a product's geographical origin. It is interesting to note that TRIPS is silent on who may own a GI tag as well as who may become an eligible user of it. It is left to the Member State to define the eligibility of GI owner and user.

Article 22(2)[63] deals with the substantive protection to be prescribed by the Member State in terms of any "legal means" in case of "misleading use" of GI, including any use which may constitute "an act of unfair competition".[64] In this way, the protection prescribed here is not absolute. In case of use which does not fall into any of these categories, it will not be prohibited. Terms like "legal means" and "interested parties" remain undefined. There existed diversity in legal means for the protection of GI among Member States before TRIPS, such as conventional protection through trademarks, collective marks, certification marks and the *sui generis* system. TRIPS has allowed the same to be continued. Article 22(3) deals with protection against use as trademark. The origin of this article can be found in the initial proposals in the year 1990 submitted by the European Communities, Switzerland and Australia,[65] which clearly prescribed for protection within the domain of trademarks. According to this provision, the member country is under an obligation to refuse or invalidate a trademark which contains or consists of a geographical indication with respect to goods which do not originate in the territory or area as indicated. Further, if such an indication would mislead the public about the true origin of the goods, then in that case the member country must have legal means for such refusal or invalidation of such a trademark. This provision is incorporated in Section 25(a) of the Indian GI Act.[66]

Article 22(4) prevents the use of Homonymous Indications. Such indications are those that are spelled or pronounced alike, but which identify products originating in different places, usually in different countries.[67] According to Article 22(4), such GIs are refused protection in case of their being identified as misleading the public about the geographical origin of the goods. Ideally such GIs should be allowed to coexist with adequate and conditional protection. As per Indian law, it is permissible to protect homonymous GIs.[68]

Article 23: Additional Protection for Wines and Spirits

GIs that are used to identify wines and spirits are accorded a higher level or additional protection under Article 23 of the TRIPS. This is considered to be a higher level of protection as compared to Article 22 as the protection is not conditional to the use being misleading or constituting an act of unfair competition. The scope of Article 23 is limited as it is applicable to only wines and spirits, in contrast to Article 22, which relates to any type of goods. Further, under Article 23.1, each Member State by providing legal means is under an obligation to prevent the use of GI identifying wines for wines not originating in the place indicated by the GI in question. This prohibition applies even where the true origin is indicated or a GI is used in translation or is accompanied by expressions such as "kind", "type", "style", "imitation" and the likes. It is pertinent to note that this Article, unlike Article 22.3, does not impose a requirement that such a use of GI must mislead the public. This obligation is fulfilled by way of Section 22(a) and (b) of the GI Act, 1999. Similarly, Article 23.2, unlike its counterpart under Article 22.2, allows refusal or invalidation of registration of a trademark regardless of the requirement of the public being misled.

The issue of homonymous GIs for wines (not spirits) is the subject of Article 23.3, according to which, in case of homonymous GIs for wines, the use of which is not misleading or deceptive under Article 22.4, both indications have to protected. Practical conditions for differentiating such homonymous GIs must be determined by each Member State by ensuring that consumers are not misled and that producers of both GIs are treated equitably.

In order to establish an international notification and registration system for GI exclusively to facilitate the protection in those member countries participating in such a system, finally Article 23.4 requires negotiations to be undertaken within the TRIPS Council.

Article 24: International Negotiations and Exceptions

Article 24 of TRIPS deals with international negotiations and also includes a series of exceptions, most notably in relation to continued and similar use of GIs for wines and spirits, prior "good-faith" trademark rights and generic designations.[69] Inclusion of these exceptions is owing to the concerns raised by few WTO members on "already acquired rights". Article 24, being the lengthiest, consists of nine sub-paras, of which six deal with exceptions. It is noteworthy that through such exceptions, TRIPS not only reinforces but also limits GI protection.[70] Further, this Article essentially provides for a platform for members to undertake negotiations for enhancing the protection of individual GIs protected under Article 23.[71] Article 24.2 provides for review of the application of the provisions under Part II, Section 3, on the built in agenda of the TRIPS Council.[72] Article 24.3 prescribes that "Member shall not diminish the protection of GI that existed in that Member immediately prior to the date of entry into force of the WTO Agreement".[73] Thus, the

Members are prevented from taking advantage of the inherent flexibility available under Section 3 which might be of detriment to the parties claiming GI protection.[74] Parallel use of GI for wines and spirits is addressed by Article 24.4.

The exception from the scope of Article 23 as carved out under this provision is prospective in nature. It states that, under certain circumstances, the "continued and similar" use in one Member State of a GI that corresponds to a GI of another Member State shall not be prevented.[75] In order to apply the exception, there must be continued and similar use of a particular geographical indication of another Member identifying a wine or a spirit in connection with goods or services by nationals or domiciliary of that Member. Further such use must have been for at least 10 years preceding 15 April 1994[76] or for any period before that date, provided the use has been in good faith. Prior rights in respect of trademarks vis-à-vis Geographical Indications are highlighted by Article 24.5. This protection in favour of trademark, often known as the "grandfather clause",[77] would apply where the trademark rights are acquired through registration in good faith a) before the date of application of these provisions in that Member as defined in Part VI; or b) before the Geographical Indication is protected in its country of origin. Article 24.6 of the TRIPS Agreement merely states that there is no obligation to protect a GI where "the relevant indication is identical with the term customary in common language as the common name for such goods or services in the territory of that Member".[78] Article 24.7 deals with certain procedural aspects for claiming rights in Geographical Indications over trademarks and requesting the invalidation of such trademark rights.[79] A request regarding trademark under this Article for the use or registration of it must be made within the prescribed time limit of 5 years after the adverse use of the protected indication has become generally known in that Member country. Alternatively, the request may be made after the date of registration of that trademark in that Member, which is conditional to the fact that such a trademark has been published by that date. In case of such date being earlier than the date on which the adverse use became generally known in that Member.[80] Article 24.8 addresses the situation where a personal name is also used as a business or product and such name is also a GI.[81] A person's right to use his or her name in such a manner is protected under this Article provided the same is not misleading. Article 24.9 clearly expresses that the Members have no obligation to protect a GI which is a) not protected in their country of origin, b) ceases to be protected in that country or c) has fallen into disuse in that country.[82]

In short, under TRIPS, any product having GI tag is protected against any illegal use that is misleading to people or in any way constitutes an act of unfair competition.[83] While considering the drafting history of TRIPS, one cannot get convinced with the two levels of protection provided for GIs in general and GIs for wines and spirits in particular. The journey of GIs through TRIPS has been anything but smooth as member nations continue to debate the differential levels of protection.

1.4 Indian legal treatment to GI protection

Where did India's law on Geographical Indications come from? What are the logic blocks that put the law in place? In the 1990s, India realized that there were usurpations of many of its products that had not only to do with denomination of geographic origins but also involved genetic resources and traditional knowledge that were objects of patent filings – the most popular cases being of dilution of the patents for Darjeeling Tea, Neem, Basmati Rice, and Turmeric, where, with the help of academic and research institutes as well as activists, India successfully defended its rights over the knowledge bank which is in fact ages' old. However, a lesson from these sour experiences was that in the absence of any specific IP protection in the countries where the alleged infringement was taking place, the only action available was against unfair competition. Additionally, not going as far as foreign jurisdictions, and with an unprecedented rise in power looms, India itself became a hub for the mass duplication of saris made from synthetic fabrics,[84] thus infringing upon the originality that was painstakingly established by generations of handloom weavers. In the Darjeeling Tea case, the tea is uniquely grown in the Darjeeling district of the State of West Bengal, but the tea being sold under the name of Darjeeling Tea by several companies internationally was neither produced nor grown in that region.[85]

Several international instruments were already in place before the TRIPS Agreement was formalized; these instruments mentioned the concepts of Appellations of Origin (AO) and Indications of Source (IS), but TRIPS formally launched the term Geographical Indications (GIs) and gave it a connotation different to those earlier terms. Before TRIPS could be finalized, the negotiating stage on the subject of GIs exposed an ideological gap between old-world and new-world countries concerning the antiquity of their history.[86] The issue between the old world and new world gradually boiled down to a point in the development of cultural and legal differences where the old world was headed by the EU and the new world by the United States. The new-world countries thus argue that GIs are "historical and geographical accidents", as opposed to the old-world countries, for whom GIs are not historical accidents but reflect history continued and reinvigorated ceaselessly by producers who have remained in their country of origin.[87] The reputation of a product may be based on decades or even centuries of creativity through which traditional knowledge has not only been maintained but also adapted and improved. It is not an accident of geography but rather a characteristic of ecosystems, which can certainly change and call into question a GI that does not produce the same special qualities it did before, and of other places that might prove capable of creating it.[88]

India gladly fell into the old-world category and in order to achieve maximum protection for those of its products fit to be recognized as GIs adopted a *sui generis* legal framework. With much fervour, India enacted The Geographical Indications of Goods (Registration and Protection) Act, 1999 along with The Geographical Indications of Goods (Registration and Protection) Rules, 2002, with a three-fold objective to 1) Adequately protect the interest of the producers of GI goods and add to the prosperity of the producers of such goods, 2) Protect consumers from deception and 3) Promote goods bearing GI in the export market.[89] According to some opinions, the GI Act is a step forward to the minimum requirements of the TRIPS Agreement, which can serve as a model for other countries.[90] Thus, with a single legislation, India not only complied with its obligations under the TRIPS Agreement but also established a domestic system to accord protection and registration to a wide range of goods that form part of its overall identity on the global platform.

In bringing into existence a *sui generis* system for GIs, India included a broad definition of the term Geographical Indication as follows:

> Geographical Indication, in relation to goods, means an indication which identifies such goods as agricultural goods, natural goods or manufactured goods as originating, or manufactured in the territory of a country, or a region or locally in that territory, where a given quality, reputation or other characteristic of such goods is essentially attributable to its geographical origin and in case where such goods are manufactured goods one of the activities of either the production or of processing or preparation of the goods concerned takes place in such territory, region or locality, as the case may be.[91]

The explanation[92] added to this definition clarifies that for the purposes of this clause, any name which is not the name of a country, region or locality is also eligible to be protected as a GI provided the conditions laid are satisfied, thus taking into consideration the protection for symbols other than just geographical names such as Pashmina or Alphonso.

Additionally, the Act classifies the goods into four categories:

1) Agricultural
2) Natural
3) Manufactured
4) Goods of handicraft or of industry, including foodstuffs[93]

This categorization of potential goods that may be registered and protected as GIs also goes a step further than the TRIPS definition of "goods", which does not include such bifurcation. It provides for a broad spectrum which makes the Act unique and comprehensive. Considering the scope of this work, provisions relating to *Proprietorship* and *Authorized Users* are most relevant. The Act under Section 11(1) mentions "Any association of persons or producers or any organization or authority established by or under any law for the time being in force representing the interest of the producers of the concerned goods".[94] Further the Act defines the term *producer* under Section 2(k), meaning "any person who in relation to i) agricultural goods, produces the goods and includes the person who processes or packages such goods; ii) natural goods, exploits the goods; iii) handicraft or industrial goods, makes or manufactures the goods".[95] Further, the definition includes any person who trades or deals in such production, exploitation, making or manufacturing, as the case may be, of the goods.[96] Some observations from these provisions are: the term *producer* as used under Section 11(1) is defined as mentioned above but the term *association of persons* remains undefined, leading to an open interpretation of the provision. As further provided under the Section, only those representing the interests of the producers of the concerned goods are eligible for application. With the open interpretation of an association of persons, which may include legal or natural persons, combined with the pre-condition of interest representation, a doubt is created that the actual purpose of serving producers' interests may not be achieved. As can be seen from statistics provided by the GI Registry, various governmental departments and quasi-governmental bodies have filed for GI registration, but their overall contribution to the actual realization of the legal right granted through GI is negligible. A discussion on this along with relevant data is provided in Chapter 2. Thus, proprietorship is an essential component of the legal right, the non-possession of which acts as an impediment to effective implementation of the right. The term *Authorized User* as defined under the Act means the authorized user of a Geographical Indication registered under Section 17.[97] To clarify this, "any person claiming to be the producer of the goods in respect of which a geographical indication has been registered under Section 16 may apply in writing to the Registrar in the prescribed manner for registering him as an authorized user of such geographical indication".[98] This is a uniquely developed legal provision to give a broader scope of recognition to any person so related to a GI, but the same is currently under-utilized, which is also highlighted in Chapter 2.

The GI registry is established in Chennai with an all-India jurisdiction to administer the registration procedure. The Act is administered by the Controller General of Patents, Designs and Trademarks, who is the Registrar of GI. The comprehensive legislative framework under the Act is structured into nine chapters with 87 sections. Major provisions consist of five parts i.e., interpretation clause, registration procedure, effect of registration, special provisions relating to trademarks and offences-penalties. The registration procedure under the Act is technical and lengthy due to the requirements of forming a consortium of producers, submitting statement of fact along with proof of origin for the product to be registered. The Act prescribes for both civil and criminal remedies in case of infringement. These remedies are not only restricted to the registered GIs only but also extend to unregistered GIs.[99] It has been almost two decades since the Act and Rules have been enforced in India. Despite the fact that wider protection is accorded through this Act to the products of handicrafts in comparison with wines and spirits as prescribed in the TRIPS, the efficacy of this legislation has been questioned even though there are no striking deficiencies in it.

1.5 Concluding observations

The conceptual analysis of GI as it exists in the present legal framework leads us to believe that place brings physical and human, tangible and intangible, diverse and intense, experience and emotions together.[100] In order to understand and examine the core issues under discussion, an attempt is made in this chapter to highlight how GI holds a unique place under the wide umbrella of IP. It is evident from the discussion on the meaning, nature, characteristics and functions of GI that it differs in every sense when compared to other forms of IP. While exploring the significance of GI for the developing countries, its role as a tool for rural development and protection of traditional knowledge have been delineated. The discussion on the evolution of GI and its place in the international regime reveals how it is not a novel concept. It has been recognized as a legal right for over a century. However, its identity as a specific form of IP has only been recently recognized through TRIPS, whereby minimum standards of protection for all Member States have been defined. In light of the international instruments, the Indian legal treatment of GI is discussed in brief, providing a basis for further analysis of the subject in the next chapter.

Notes

1 The Geographical Indications of Goods (Registration and Protection) Act, 1999.

2 "Application Details" (*Geographical Indications Registry,* 2021) <http://ipindiaservices.gov.in/GIRPublic/Application/Details/1> accessed 9 March 2021.

3 "Application Details" (*Geographical Indications Registry,* 2021) <http://ipindiaservices.gov.in/GIRPublic/Application/Details/4> accessed 9 March 2021.

4 "Application Details" (*Geographical Indications Registry,* 2021) <http://ipindiaservices.gov.in/GIRPublic/Application/Details/232> accessed 9 March 2021.

5 Trade-Related Aspects of Intellectual Property Rights (World Trade Organization). <https://www.wto.org/english/docs_e/legal_e/27-trips_04b_e.htm> accessed 9 March 2021.
6 Ibid.
7 "What Is Intellectual Property (IP)?" (*World Intellectual Property Organization*) <https://www.wipo.int/about-ip/en/#:~:text=Intellectual%20property%20%28IP%29%20refers%20to%20creations%20of%20the,financial%20benefit%20from%20what%20they%20invent%20or%20create> accessed 20 July 2020.
8 Paris Convention for the Protection of Industrial Property (World Intellectual Property Organization) <https://www.wipo.int/treaties/en/ip/paris/> accessed 9 March 2021.
9 Madrid Agreement for the Repression of False or Deceptive Indications of Source on Goods (World Intellectual Property Organisation) <https://www.wipo.int/treaties/en/ip/madrid/> accessed 9 March 2021.
10 Dev Gangjee, *Relocating the Law of Geographical Indications* (Cambridge University Press 2015) 1.
11 Kal Raustiala and Stephen Munzer, "The Global Struggle Over Geographic Indications" (2007) 18 (2) EJIL <https://academic.oup.com/ejil/article/18/2/337/361981> accessed 9 December 2020.
12 Gangjee (n 10) 3.
13 N. S. Gopalakrishnan, Prabha S. Nair and Aravind K. Babu, "Exploring the Relationship between Geographical Indications and Traditional Knowledge – An Analysis of the Legal Tools for the Protection of Geographical Indications in Asia" (2007) ICTSD Programme on IPRs and Sustainable Development Working Paper, 10. <https://www.iprsonline.org/ictsd/docs/Gopaletal%20-%20GIs_TK.pdf> accessed 2 January 2021.
14 Gangjee (n 10) 93.
15 Ibid 94.
16 Ibid 94–95.
17 Pierre Mérel, Ariel Ortiz-Bobea and Emmanuel Paroissien, "How Big Is the 'Lemons' Problem? Historical Evidence from French Wines" (2020) 5–6 <https://dx.doi.org/10.2139/ssrn.3444625> accessed 2 January 2021.
18 Ibid 7.
19 Gangjee (n 10) 108.
20 Ibid 109.
21 Irene Calboli, "Of Markets, Culture, and Terroir: The Unique Economic and Culture-Related Benefits of Geographical Indications of Origin" in Daniel Gervais (ed), *Research Handbook in International Intellectual Property* (Edward Elgar 2014) at 1.
22 Additionally, "new world" countries have underscored that several GIs are generic terms on their soil – Champagne, Chablis, and Feta are some contested examples – and that a shift towards preventing the public from using these terms would damage businesses, which could no longer describe products using those terms.
23 "Key-Concepts of GIs" (*Organization for an International Geographical Indications Network*, 2021) <https://www.origin-gi.com/your-gi-kit/key-concepts-of-gis.html> accessed 12 January 2021.
24 Tomer Broude, "Taking 'Trade and Culture' Seriously: Geographical Indications and Cultural Protection in WTO Law" (2005) 26 (4) U. Pa. J. Int'l Econ. L. 623–692 at 651.
25 "Key-Concepts of GIs" (n 18).

26 Ibid.
27 Martijn Huysmans and Johan Swinnen, “No Terroir in the Cold? A Note on the Geography of Geographical Indications” (2019) 70 (2) Journal of Agricultural Economics 550–559, 550.
28 Steven Erlanger, “Vive le Terroir” (*New York Times*, 31 August 2013) <https://www.nytimes.com/2013/09/01/sunday-review/vive-le-terroir.html> accessed 20 June 2020.
29 Ibid.
30 Ibid.
31 Daniele Giovannucci, Timothy E. Josling, William A. Kerr, Bernard O’Connor and May T. Yeung, *Guide to Geographical Indications: Linking Products and Their Origins* (International Trade Centre 2009) 3 <https://www.origin-gi.com/images/stories/PDFs/English/E-Library/geographical_indications.pdf> accessed 20 July 2020.
32 Irene Calboli and Wee Loon Ng-Loy, *Geographical Indications at the Crossroads of Trade, Development, and Culture: Focus on Asia-Pacific* (Cambridge University Press 2017) 19.
33 Raustiala and Munzer (n 11).
34 The Geographical Indications of Goods (Registration and Protection) Act, 1999, s 2(e) [“geographical indication”, in relation to goods, means an indication which identifies such goods as agricultural goods, natural goods or manufactured goods as originating or manufactured in the territory of a country, or a region or locality in that territory, where a given quality, reputation or other characteristic of such goods is essentially attributable to its geographical origin, and in cases where such goods are manufactured goods, one of the activities of either the production or of processing or preparation of the goods concerned takes place in such territory, region or locality, as the case may be].
35 Ibid.
36 Darjeeling Tea (n 3) [Specification: Tea produced in the said region has the distinctive and naturally occurring organoleptic characteristics of taste, aroma and mouth feel which has won the patronage and recognition of discerning consumers all over the world].
37 “Application Details” (*Geographical Indications Registry*, 2021) <http://ipindiaservices.gov.in/GIRPublic/Application/Details/232> accessed 9 March 2021.
38 Cerkia Bramley, Estelle Biénabe and Johann Kirsten, “The Economics of Geographical Indications: Towards a Conceptual Framework for Geographical Indication Research in Developing Countries” (2009) The Economics of Intellectual Property 114 <http://www.wipo.int/ip-development/en/economics/pdf/wo_1012_e_ch_4.pdf> accessed 20 July 2020.
39 Ibid.
40 Irene Calboli and Daniel Gervais, “The Socio-Economic Aspects of Geographical Indications of Origin” (Worldwide Symposium on Geographical Indications, Budapest, October 2015) <https://ink.library.smu.edu.sg/cgi/viewcontent.cgi?article=3902&context=sol_research> accessed 20 July 2020.
41 “State-Wise Registration Details of G.I. Applications” (*Geographical Indications Registry*, 2021) <https://www.ipindia.gov.in/registered-gls.htm> accessed 09 March 2021.
42 G. Belletti, A. Marescotti, J. Sanz-Cañada and H. Vakoufaris, “Linking Protection of Geographical Indications to the Environment: Evidence from the European Union Olive-Oil Sector” (2015) 48 Land Use Policy 94–106 <https://doi.org/10.1016/j.landusepol.2015.05.003> accessed 30 May 2020.
43 UNCTAD Secretariat, Systems and National Experiences for Protecting Traditional Knowledge, Innovations and Practices (UNCTAD,TD/BCOM.1/

EM.13/2, 2000) 6 <https://unctad.org/system/files/officialdocument/c1em13d2.en.pdf> accessed 24 June 2020.

44 Keith Maskus, *Private Rights and Public Problems, The Global Economics of Intellectual Property in the 21st Century* (Peterson Institute Press 2012).

45 Marie-Claude Mahias, "Les Sciences Et Les Techniques Traditionnelles En Inde" (1997) 142 *L'Homme* 37, 105.

46 The term *traditional knowledge* is only incidental and does not mean that Geographical Indications are governed under it, but what cannot be ignored is that some essence of TK does lie in the body of GIs.

47 World Intellectual Property Organization, "Traditional Knowledge and Intellectual Property – Background Brief" <https://www.wipo.int/pressroom/en/briefs/tk_ip.html> accessed 09 March 2021.

48 Delphine Marie-Vivien, *The Protection of Geographical Indications in India: A New Perspective on the French and European Experience* (SAGE LAW eds., 2015) 14.

49 Paris Convention (n 8) It was adopted on 20 March 1883, and revised at Brussels (1900), Washington (1911), The Hague (1925), London (1934), Lisbon (1958), and Stockholm (1967), and as amended on September 28, 1979 <https://www.wipo.int/treaties/en/ip/paris/> accessed 20 June 2020.

50 Madrid Agreement (n 9) It was adopted on April 14, 1891 and revised at Washington (1911), The Hague (1925), London (1934), and Lisbon (1958) II; Additional Act of Stockholm of July 14, 1967 <https://www.wipo.int/treaties/en/ip/madrid/> accessed 20 June 2020.

51 Lisbon Agreement for the Protection of Appellations of Origin and Their International Registration <https://www.wipo.int/treaties/en/registration/lisbon/> accessed 9 March 2021. It was adopted on 31 October 1958, and revised at Stockholm (1967), and amended in 1979 (Lisbon Union) <https://www.wipo.int/treaties/en/registration/lisbon/> accessed 20 June 2020.

52 TRIPS Agreement (n 6).

53 Seth M. Reiss, "Commentary on the Paris Convention for the Protection of Industrial Property" <http://lex-ip.com/Paris.pdf> accessed 01 August 2020.

54 Paris Convention (n 8) art 1(2).

55 Paris Convention (n 8) art 19.

56 Madrid Agreement (n 9).

57 The Lisbon System-International Protection for Identifiers of Typical Products from a defined Geographical Area (WIPO) <http://www.wipo.int/edocs/pubdocs/en/geographical/942/wipo_pub_942.pdf> accessed 20 June 2020.

58 Ibid.

59 Matthijs Geuze, "The Provisions on Geographical Indications in the TRIPS Agreement" (2009) 10 (1) Estey Centre Journal of International Law and Trade Policy 50–64, 51 <https://www.peacepalacelibrary.nl/ebooks/files/ECJIL_Geuze10-1.pdf> accessed 20 February 2021.

60 'Geographical Indications Supplementary Journal No. 1, GI Application Numbers 66' (*Geographical Indications Registry*, 24 March 2008) <http://ipindiaservices.gov.in/GIRPublic/Application/ViewDocument> accessed 20 June 2020.

61 "Geographical Indications Journal No. 12, Application Number 27" (*Geographical Indications Registry*, 1 January2006) <http://ipindiaservices.gov.in/GIRPublic/Application/ViewDocument> accessed 20 June 2020.

62 The Geographical Indications of Goods (Registration and Protection) Act, 1999, s 2(f) ["goods" means any agricultural, natural or manufactured goods or any goods of handicraft or of industry and includes foodstuffs].

63 TRIPS Agreement, (n 6), art 22(2) [In respect of geographical indications, Members shall provide the legal means for interested parties to prevent:

(a) the use of any means in the designation or presentation of a good that indicates or suggests that the good in question originates in a geographical area other than the true place of origin in a manner which misleads the public as to the geographical origin of the good; (b) any use which constitutes an act of unfair competition within the meaning of Article 10b is of the Paris Convention (1967)].

64 Irene Calboli, "Expanding the Protection of Geographical Indications of Origin under TRIPS: Old Debate or New Opportunity?" (2006) 10 *Marquette Intellectual Property Law Review*, 181, 191 <https://ssrn.com/abstract=893193> accessed 10 August 2020.

65 "Draft Agreement on Trade-Related Aspects of Intellectual Property Rights" (1990) <https://ipmall.law.unh.edu/sites/default/files/hosted_resources/lipa/trips/W68.pdf> accessed 11 March 2021; "Draft Amendment to the General Agreement on Tariffs and Trade on the Protection of Trade-Related Intellectual Property Rights" (*World Trade Organization* 1990) <https://docs.wto.org/gatt-docs/q/UR/GNGNG11/W73.PDF> accessed 11 March 2021.

66 The Geographical Indications of Goods (Registration & Protection) Act, 1999, s 25.

67 "Frequently Asked Questions: Geographical Indications" (*World Intellectual Property Organization*) <https://www.wipo.int/geo_indications/en/faq_geographicalindications.html> accessed 10 August 2020.

68 Geographical Indications of Goods (registration and Protection) 1999, s 10 [10. Registration of homonymous geographical indications: Subject to the provisions of Section 7, a homonymous geographical indication may be registered under this Act, if the Registrar is satisfied, after considering the practical conditions under which the homonymous indication in question shall be differentiated from other homonymous indications and the need to ensure equitable treatment of the producers of the goods concerned, that the consumers of such goods shall not be confused or misled in consequence of such registration].

69 Kasturi Das, *Socio-Economic Implications of Protecting Geographical Indications in India* (Centre for WTO Studies 2009) <http://wtocentre.iift.ac.in/Papers/GI_Paper_CWS_August%2009_Revised.pdf> accessed 7 August 2020.

70 Johan Flodgren, "Geographical Indications in the 21st Century – What, When and How? A Critical Review of the Legal Framework for GI Protection and GI-Related Trade in the International Community" (Masters, University of Lund 2010) accessed 10 August 2020.

71 Prabuddha Ganguli, *Geographical Indications: Its Evolving Contours* (2007) <https://www.wipo.int/edocs/mdocs/sme/en/wipo_smes_hyd_07/wipo_smes_hyd_07_www_91823.pdf> accessed 10 August 2020.

72 UNCTAD-ICTSD, *Resource Book on TRIPS and Development* (Cambridge University Press 2005).

73 TRIPS Agreement (n 5), art 24.3.

74 Kasturi Das (n 66) at 303.

75 TRIPS Agreement (n 5), art 33.

76 This is the date of Ministerial Meeting concluding the Uruguay Round of Multilateral Trade Negotiations.

77 It is a legal regulation that permits older rights to persevere, even when such older rights conflict with newer rights that are usually better protected.

78 Dev Gangjee, "Genericide: The Death of a Geographical Indication?" in Dev S. Gangjee (ed), *Research Handbook on Intellectual Property and Geographical Indications* (Edward Elgar Publishing 2016) 508–548.

79 "Geographical Indications: Historical Background, Nature of Rights, Existing Systems for Protection and Obtaining Protection in Other Countries" (*World Intellectual Property Organization,* 2002) <https://www.wipo.int/edocs/mdocs/sct/en/sct_8/sct_8_4.pdf>accessed 5 August 2020.
80 TRIPS Agreement (n 5).
81 Kasturi Das(n 63), 307.
82 TRIPS Agreement (n 5), art 24.9.
83 Teshager W. Dagne, *Intellectual Property and Traditional Knowledge in the Global Economy: Translating Geographical Indications for Development* (Routledge 2015) 31.
84 Shefalee Vasudev, "Ground Report – The Banaras Bind' (*Livemint,* 2013) <https://www.livemint.com/Leisure/5h1lnyORjhtn9Pr0Z4wiXL/Ground-Report–The-Banaras-bind.html> accessed 9 March 2021.
85 Sudhir Ravindran and Arya Mathew, "The Protection of Geographical Indications in India – Case Study on Darjeeling Tea" (*International Property Rights Index,* 2009) <http://nbcgib.uesc.br/nit/ig/app/papers/1035442708158048.pdf> accessed 1 July 2020.
86 Dev Gangjee (n 10).
87 Delphine Marie-Vivien (n 40) at 5.
88 Delphine Marie-Vivien (n 40) at 5.
89 "Manual of Geographical Indications Practice and Procedure" (*Office of the Controller General of Patents, Designs and Trademarks & Registrar of Geographical Indications*, 2011) <https://ipindia.gov.in/writereaddata/Portal/IPOGuidelinesManuals/1_31_1_manual-of-geographical-indications-practice-and-procedure.pdf> accessed 1 July 2020.
90 Suresh C. Srivastava, "Geographical Indications and Legal Framework in India" (2003) 38 (38) EPW <https://www.epw.in/journal/2003/38/special-articles/geographical-indications-and-legal-framework-india.html> accessed 9 March 2021.
91 The Geographical Indications of Goods (Registration and Protection) Act, 1999, s 2(e).
92 Ibid.
93 The Geographical Indications of Goods (Registration and Protection) Act, 1999, s 2(f).
94 Ibid s 11(1).
95 Ibid s 2 (k).
96 Ibid.
97 The Geographical Indications of Goods (Registration and Protection) Act, 1999, s 2 (b).
98 Ibid s 17 (1).
99 Ibid s 20.
100 Anu Kapur, *Made Only in India* (Routledge 2016) 180.

2

LEGAL RECOGNITION OF INDIAN HANDLOOMS

Recounting the challenges through case studies

2.1 General introduction

The objective of this chapter is primarily to recognize the issues prevalent in context of the legal right acquired through the registration of a Geographical Indication. As is known, registration is merely a formal recognition of the legal right, the translation of which into an actual right is possible only through effective enforcement, thus allowing all stakeholders to reap the maximum benefit. GIs deal with the legal recognition of origin-bound products. This recognition grants several legal rights. Therefore, the term *right* requires some consideration here. Rights are at the heart of human civilization as a prominent consequence of any legal promulgation. According to Holland, an exponent of the Analytical School of Jurisprudence, a right is "Capacity residing in one person of controlling, with the assent or assistance of the State, the action of others".[1] A right comprises these essential elements, as Salmond expounded: i) the person of inherence, i.e. the possessor of the right; ii) the person of incidence, or the person who is duty-bound to adhere to the former's rights; iii) the content or subject-matter of the right; iv) the object of the right, i.e. the thing or object over which the right is possessed; and v) the title, through which a right is vested in its owner.[2] The course of the legal vehicle runs smoothly in terms of the enforcement of rights in favour of the right-holder and necessarily obliges the duty-bound to abide by the limitations drawn by the former's rights. Thus, with efficient invocation and sufficient realization, a right is a benchmark of human growth and prosperity.

The efficacy of any law is dependent on the realization of the right granted under it which is known as "legal right". It is acquired by following the procedure prescribed under the legislative framework. This legal right, unless realized in real life, fails to attain the objectives for which it has been acquired. Unfortunately, in most real-life situations, there is a gap between the "legal right" and the "real right". Intellectual property rights (IPR), and especially GI, being one of the most evolving branches of the law, are no exception to this. In this book, we have made a humble attempt

DOI: 10.4324/9781003002147-3

to shed some light on the efficacy of the GI law in the handloom sector of India by probing the gap between the "legal right" and the "real right" as it exists.

As mentioned by Delphine Marie,[3] "the Indian Tradition in the area of material know how is as legitimate as any other tradition and can play a major role in nation building". GI is not just a form of IP over which a set of legal rights can be acquired. It is a vehicle for rural development through the protection of traditional and collective knowledge. Thus, GI protection can certainly play a vital role in unlocking the commercial potential inherent in handloom products.

GI as a legal right establishes a nexus between product, quality and origin. The success of the legal right is contingent on effective enforcement. However, factually, various challenges are being faced by stakeholders in realizing the potential benefits of the registered GI.[4] The legal right in a true sense would only become a real right when a GI tag could add value to the age-old products and create a better market, or develop a market, in some cases, for the products protected. Numerous products after acquiring GI status are struggling even today to get takers for their products.

The legislative framework in the form of the Geographical Indications of Goods (Registration and Protection) Act, 1999 provides for a *sui generis* system of protection in India. Compared to US and EU jurisdictions, the protection prescribed by the Indian legislative framework is distinct in that it recognizes various products under a broad category of goods such as agriculture, handicrafts, natural goods, manufactured goods and food products, which is unlike Article 23 under TRIPS. The definition of GI as provided under the Act of 1999 broadly covers protection of symbols other than geographical names, such as "Basmati" for rice. India being a country of cultural diversity, the significance of GI protection is more than in other countries. GI in its present form also serves the purpose of protecting traditional knowledge as well as traditional cultural expressions, as many GIs are based on centuries-old arts and crafts like Kutch and Tangaliya shawls.

GI registration is not a mandate under the Indian legislative framework, but it is a Pre-requisite for effective and efficient enforcement. The registration provides legal protection for the unique products, which prevents unauthorized use by others and also helps consumers to get quality products of assured authenticity. Above all, it promotes economic prosperity for genuine producers of goods produced within a geographical territory. In a nutshell, a registered GI can accomplish its functions, such as identifying goods with a specific geographical origin, informing the consumers about their authentic quality and promoting their sale successfully. Thus, registration is the first step towards acquiring the "legal right".

2.2 "Legal Right": Essentials and procedural requirements under the GI Act, 1999

Registration of a product as GI is the first step towards realizing its economic potential. Registration, though not a mandatory requirement, is still a *prima facie* evidence of its validity.[5] The Act protects a registered GI for a term of 10 years in the first instance, which can subsequently be renewed in perpetuity.[6] As per the provision of the Act, such renewal is required every 10 years.[7] It is worth mentioning here that considering the nature of the right granted on registration of GI i.e., the community right, non-renewal after a period of 10 years does not invite cancellation as it does for trademarks. The GI can be registered under 34 different classes as prescribed under the fourth schedule attached with the GI Rules 2002. A quick look at the Act brings out the salient features of GI protection in India, which can be classified into three broad categories, i.e., an interpretation of important terms, the registration process and protection against infringement. In order to appreciate the nature and structure of the right acquired through registration, the process as prescribed under the Act is essential to understand.

2.2.1 GI registration

Definitions of terms like *GI*,[8] *goods*, *indication*, *registered proprietor* and *producer* carry a lot of significance as part of GI registration. The definition of GI perspicuously conveys that only those products that have a quality, reputation or other characteristic which is essentially attributable to their geographical origin can be recognized as a GI. Flexibility for accommodating those symbols or terms that are not geographical names is created through explanation. GI is broadly defined by the Act to include definitions under TRIPS as well as the Lisbon Agreement.[9] The term *good* as generally referred to by TRIPS[10] is defined by the Act with a specific categorization into i) agricultural goods; ii) natural goods; iii) manufacturing goods; iv) goods of handicraft or of industry; and v) foodstuffs. Again, this definition is illustrative and not exhaustive, further broadening the scope of what can be protected under the law. Once the product belonging to any of these categories fulfils the requirement laid down in the definition of GI, its registration procedure along with other legal requirements can be initiated. Application for registration of GI can be initiated only by an association of persons or producers or any organization or authority established by or under any law representing the interest of the producers of the concerned goods.[11] The applicant has to be a legal entity representing the interests of the producers of the product applied for. Any such organization or association being not that of the producers may have to prove that it represents the interest of producers. Thus, the representation of producers' interests is a vital necessity when applying, reflecting the idea that GI registration must bring benefits for primary stakeholders by adding value to their product. This brings us to the definition of *producer*,[12] which means any person who i) in the case of agricultural goods, produces the goods and includes the person who processes or packages such goods; ii) in the case of natural goods, exploits the goods; iii) in the case of goods of handicrafts or industrial goods, makes or manufactures the goods; and iv) any person who trades or deals in such production, exploitation, making or manufacturing, as the case may be, of the goods.

Not all indications are granted a GI tag by the registry. Only those indications that do not fall within the purview of Section 9 can be considered for registration. The registration of an indication is prohibited if it is deceptive or likely to cause confusion; if it is contrary to any law in force; if it comprises or contains scandalous or obscene matter that may hurt the religious susceptibility of any class of Indian citizens; in case of such indication being disentitled to protection in a Court; if it is generic or misleads the people about its origin; or if it has ceased to be protected in the country of origin or if it has fallen into disuse in that country (the last two grounds are relevant for a foreign GI).[13] These grounds are considered at the time of preliminary scrutiny and examination of the GI registration application. The registrability of homonymous GIs is discussed in Section 10 of the Act. The Indian Act permits the registration of such GIs if the registrar is satisfied after considering the practical conditions under which a homonymous indication can be differentiated from other such indications.[14] Further, the registrar will also consider the need for equitable treatment of the producers of such goods and ensure that consumers shall not be confused or misled in consequence of such registration.[15]

Application for registration as mentioned earlier can be filed by a group of producers or persons. The act also permits those organizations who represent the interests of such producers to file an application for GI registration in India. Three categories of people can apply under this Act, i.e., the group of actual producers, as in the case of Kutch and Tangaliya shawls;[16] the group of persons associated with producers as an association, as in the case of Darjeeling tea;[17] and any other government or non-government entity representing the interests of such artisans, farmers or producers[18] as in case of Kullu shawls and Muga silk.[19] Each application for GI registration must be submitted along with the following documents.[20] The *Manual for GI Practice and Procedure* provides details for the same.[21]

1. Specification – A brief statement describing the special characteristics and quality parameters of the goods in about 50 to 100 words.
2. Description of goods giving its uniqueness and geographical linkage – A detailed description of the GI shall clearly indicate its special characteristics, unique features, linkage to the specific geographical location

including human creativity involved. Environmental factors such as soil, water and climatic condition may be clearly brought out. This part shall also contain the standard benchmark set by the producers of the GI. Fixing such a standard may be necessary for quality control, inspection and enforcement of the GI. (Classification of Goods) Fourth Schedule.

3. Method of Production – This part shall describe in detail the method of production, including the process involved, raw materials and tools, packaging specialty if any, etc.
4. Uniqueness of the product – This part may contain the comparison with other similar products, so as to establish its uniqueness of the goods for which registration is applied. This part may be described in not more than 100 words.
5. Proof of Origin – Historic proof in the form of documentary evidence, shall be submitted, to prove the existence of the Geographical Indications such as, gazetteers, published documents, news articles, advertisement materials, for clearly bringing out the historic development of the Geographical Indications.
6. Inspection Body – This part may contain details of the Inspection Body set-up by the Applicant to monitor the production in respect of quality, integrity and consistency of the product as well as the genuine use of the GI.
7. Present scenario of the GI product – This part shall elaborate the present market of the GI product with the details of exports, if any, total turnover of the product, and the activities undertaken by the applicant association in development and promotion of the GI.

The stage-wise application process as prescribed under the Act is graphically presented in Figure 2.1.

On successful completion of the registration process and granting of the GI tag, legal rights consisting of the exclusive right to use it along with the right to obtain relief in case of infringement are conferred on the registered proprietor.[22]

2.3 Status of GI registration in India

The interface between culture and economy is an essential aspect to be considered under the law of GI.[23] The majority of the products accorded GI protection in India to date have come from agriculture and handicrafts. Both these sectors, though unorganized, form pillars of livelihood for the rural population of India. The idea of GI goes much beyond mere legal protection, it deals with the framework of holistic development.[24] When reviewing the legal rights created under the GI Act for handloom products

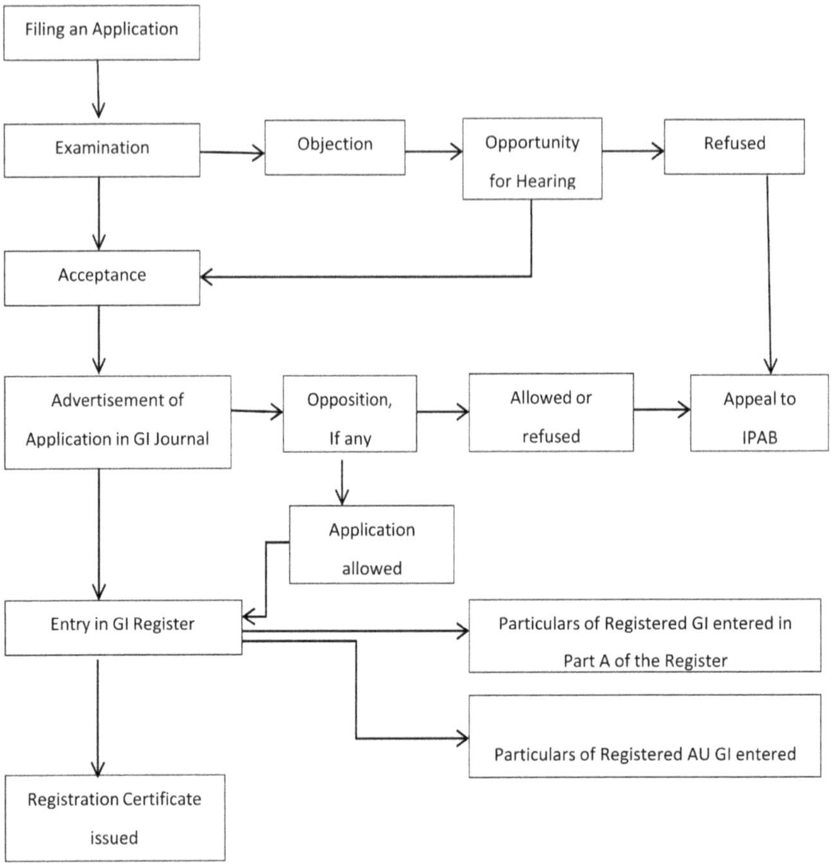

Figure 2.1 Flow chart of GI registration process. (Source: Courtesy of IP Office India <https://www.ipindia.gov.in/gi.htm>)

from India, it is essential to discuss the current status of it. The legal regime created under the Indian legislative framework is unique as it recognizes products under five different categories for protection: agricultural goods, manufactured goods, foodstuffs, natural goods and handicrafts.[25]

Figure 2.2 shows the status of all GI applications that have been filed to date with the GI registry. Out of the total 735 applications filed, 370 applications were registered; however, 25 applications stood withdrawn, 28 applications were abandoned and 53 applications were refused. A further 259 applications are pending with the GI Registry, waiting to be granted the GI tag, thus conveying its popularity. While the data shows the active approach of the GI Registry along with the high acceptance rate of GI applications in comparison to rejections, the same has to be studied based on

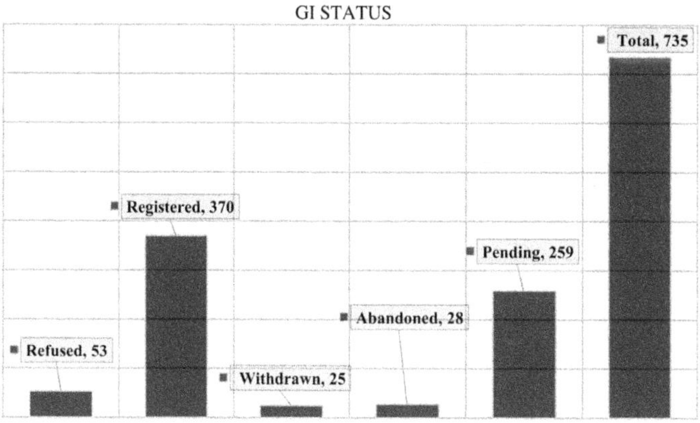

Figure 2.2 GI application status till 4 January 2021. (Source: Compiled from GI Registry database <https://www.ipindia.gov.in/gi.htm>)

the supervening factors present and does not represent conclusive proof of awareness or the efficacy of the GI protection system.

2.3.1 *State/union territory-wise GI registrations*

Table 2.1 the number of GIs that have been registered in each State and Union Territory. Out of the total GIs registered in the country, 42 were registered in the State of Karnataka alone, which is the most for any State in the country. This was followed by the State of Tamil Nadu where the number is 39, followed by Maharashtra with 33 GIs being registered. Kerala stands at fourth position with a total of 31 registrations while Uttar Pradesh has 28 GIs registered. Then comes the State of West Bengal with 21 GIs, followed by Andhra Pradesh and Odisha with 19 and 18 registered GIs, respectively. The States of Gujarat, Odisha and Rajasthan come next with a total of 16 GIs registered. With a marginal difference, Bihar comes in at the next spot with 13 registrations, followed by Madhya Pradesh with 11 and then Assam, Jammu and Kashmir and Himachal Pradesh, each with 9 registered GIs. This is further followed by Chhattisgarh and Mizoram with 6 registered GIs each, followed by Manipur, Nagaland having 5 and 3 GIs registered respectively. In second-last position, with 2 GIs registered each, are Arunachal Pradesh, Haryana, Punjab, Goa, Meghalaya and Pondicherry. The last spot is taken by Dadra and Nagar Haveli, Daman and Diu, Delhi, Sikkim, Tripura and Uttarakhand, with each having just 1 GI registered in their region. Further, there are 11 GIs registered under the broad name of India for multiple States/UTs for e.g. Phulkari, Basmati etc. Furthermore, 15 foreign GIs[26] are also registered.

Table 2.1 State/union territory-wise GI registrations till January 2021

Sr. no.	*State/union territory*	*No. of GIs*
1.	Andhra Pradesh	19
2.	Arunachal Pradesh	2
3.	Assam	9
4.	Bihar	13
5.	Chhattisgarh	6
6.	Dadra & Nagar Haveli and Daman & Diu	1
7.	Delhi	1
8.	Goa	2
9.	Gujarat	16
10.	Haryana	2
11.	Himachal Pradesh	9
12.	Jammu & Kashmir	9
13.	Jharkhand	1
14.	Karnataka	42
15.	Kerala	31
16.	Madhya Pradesh	11
17.	Maharashtra	33
18.	Manipur	5
19.	Meghalaya	2
20.	Mizoram	6
21.	Nagaland	3
22.	Odisha	18
23.	Punjab	2
24.	Pondicherry	2
25.	Rajasthan	16
26.	Sikkim	1
27.	Tamil Nadu	39
28.	Telangana	16
29.	Tripura	1
30.	Uttar Pradesh	28
31.	Uttarakhand	1
32.	West Bengal	21

Source: Compiled from GI Registry database <https://www.ipindia.gov.in/gi.htm>

2.3.2 Trends in annual GI registrations

Figure 2.3 shows the number of GI applications that were filed and registered between April 2004 and March 2020. The bar graph shows the number of applications filed in total, and the line chart shows the percentage growth and decline in registrations approved by the Registry. The peak of applications and acceptance both reached a high in 2010 and in the earlier years; this has declined in recent years, and the percentage of acceptance has also gone down by half in recent years. It is understood that GI registration is a trend among Indian States, which is positive in that there is recognition of the inherent value of traditional knowledge and the unique

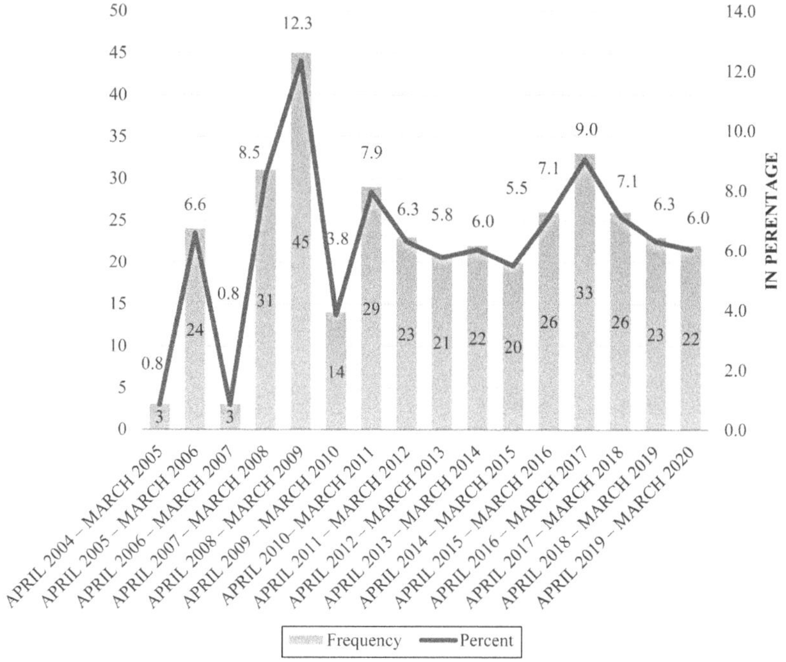

Figure 2.3 Year-wise breakup of GI applications filed as of 31 March 2020. (Source: Compiled from GI Registry database <https://www.ipindia.gov.in/gi.htm>)

attributes of these products; however, the post-recognition phase should be given equal importance.

2.3.3 Category-wise GI registrations

Figure 2.4 and Table 2.2 show the number of GIs registrations according to category of goods filed as of January 2021. Out of the five categories, the number of registered GIs in the handicrafts sector is 214, which is more than for the remaining four categories combined. This is followed by the agricultural sector, which has 112 GIs registered to its name. Thereafter comes a gap, and at third position stands the manufacturing industry with 24 registrations followed by foodstuffs with 18 registered GIs. The last spot is occupied by the natural goods category, with only 2 registered GIs.

2.4 Legal recognition of Indian handlooms: Recounting the experience through select case studies

The handloom industry is one of the oldest and largest cottage industries in India, representing and preserving the vibrant Indian culture.[27] Products

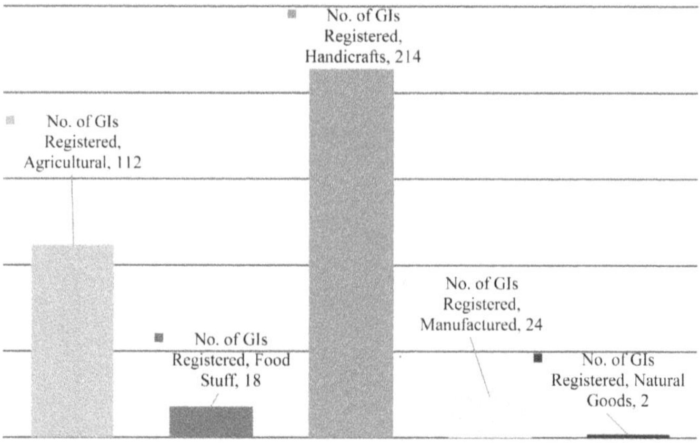

Figure 2.4 Category-wise GI registrations. (Source: Compiled from GI Registry database <https://www.ipindia.gov.in/gi.htm>)

Table 2.2 Category-wise GI registrations

Goods	*No. of GIs registered*
Agricultural	112
Foodstuffs	18
Handicrafts	214
Manufactured goods	24
Natural goods	2

Source: Compiled from GI Registry database <https://www.ipindia.gov.in/gi.htm>

of handlooms are now recognized globally for the elegance of their hand spinning, weaving and printing. The strength of the handloom industry lies in the fact that it is based on human skill, which forms part of traditional knowledge. The existing system of IP is not fully equipped to protect traditional knowledge. Nevertheless, as mentioned earlier, GI has evolved as a legal instrument for the protection and promotion of traditional knowledge. This is true especially in the case of the Indian GI Act, as it extends to a variety of goods from the handloom sector which are exclusively associated with human skill and are not dependent on natural factors such as typical regional climatic conditions.

2.4.1 Selection of the handloom products and their GI registration journey

In order to explore the hypothesis that there exists a gap between the legal right and real right granted under GI, select case studies are discussed here. Taking our cue from previous research studies, we have attempted to provide an explanation on the existing situation of these handlooms and their producers on the ground.

These case studies are divided into two parts; the first part analyses the GI journey of ten handloom products from various States of India, whereas the second part focuses on the handloom products of Gujarat, which have been granted a GI tag. Data regarding registered GIs of handloom products are collected mainly from secondary sources like the Geographical Indications registry website, which gives information on all GI registered products in India from April 2004 to the present. We chose 10 unique handloom products out of 74 registered until January 2021 in India. In order to assess the efficacy of the law, it is essential that the legal rights have been in existence for a reasonable period of time. Considering the GI Act, the reasonable period of time criteria is the completion of one term of protection i.e. 10 years, which is why products registered before 2010 have been chosen. All selected handloom products have completed the first cycle of registration and have been renewed for another term of 10 years. Further, considering the scope of research, only hand-woven fabrics in the form of sarees or shawls as a complete product are studied.

It is pertinent to mention that considering the criteria, i.e. the completion of first cycle of registration (10 years), for selection, out of the 15 States being eligible, 10 were made part of the study, which is 66.6% of the share of total number of States filing GI for handloom products. The details of the case studies are represented in are respresented in Table 2.3.

The *sui generis* protection of GIs in India still under development, and quantitative data on its success is sparse. To build a broad understanding of the current status of handlooms registered as GIs in India, we attempt to assess parameters like their registration journey and registered authorized users as well as to make reference to weavers' stories. The details included here are gathered from various secondary sources. The case studies examine the unique features of these handloom products that justify their suitability as GI. Further, in order to appreciate the granting of GI status to these products, it was found essential to discuss their geographical origin in light of historical evolution. The fact that the GI tag is granted to only those products which are unique in qualitative characteristics that are solely attributable to their geographical origin is well demonstrated through the detailed analysis of these case studies. Additionally, the socio-economic conditions of weavers at a few handlooms have also been highlighted in order to better build the narrative of this work, which in turn supports the argument that the GI law cannot fulfil its desired objectives in the absence of adequate and effective policy support and intervention.

1. Pochampally ikat

A form of ikat that stands out among a host of similar weaves is the Pochampally Ikat. This handloom carries has the reputation of being the

Table 2.3 Registration details of select handlooms

Sr. no.	*Product*	*State*	*Year of registration*	*Registration validity*	*Registered proprietor*
1.	Pochampally ikat	Telangana	2004–2005	14.12.2023	Pochampally Handloom Weavers Co-op Society Ltd.
2.	Chanderi saree	Madhya Pradesh	2005–2006	01.04.2024	Chanderi Development Foundation
3.	Mysore silk	Karnataka	2005–2006	21.07.2024	Karnataka Silk Industries Corporation Limited
4.	Kota Doria	Rajasthan	2005–2006	21.07.2024	Kota Doria Development Hadauti Foundation (KDHF)
5.	Kancheepuram silk	Karnataka	2005–2006	06.10.2024	Department of Handlooms and Textiles
6.	Kullu shawl	Himachal Pradesh	2005–2006	09.12.2024	H.P. Patent Information Centre
7.	Muga silk	Assam	2007–2008	19.07.2026	Patent Information Center
8.	Kashmir pashmina	Jammu & Kashmir	2008–2009	08.12.2025	TAHAFUZ(Registered Under the J & K Societies Act)
9.	Banaras brocades and sarees	Uttar Pradesh	2009–2010	03.07.2027	Banaras Bunkar Samiti, Sharma Katra
10.	Paithani sarees	Maharashtra	2010–2011	04.01.2029	Maharashtra State Handlooms Corporation

Source: Compiled from GI Registry database <https://www.ipindia.gov.in/gi.htm>

first handloom product to be registered on the Indian GI Register. Studying the handloom's history, one is taken to a cluster of at least 40 villages within a 70km radius of Hyderabad, the capital of India's newly formed State Telangana, where the weaving of ikat textiles takes place. Weaving takes place in the capital's adjoining districts of Nalgonda and parts of Warangal including Pochampally, Koyalagudam, Puttapakka, Elanki and Chautupal.[28] Speaking historically, Chirala is considered the oldest weaving centre for Pochampally ikat, from where the craft travelled to the modern centres of Nalgonda and Warangal. However, the term *ikat* stems from the Malay-Indonesian expression *Mangikat*, meaning to bind, knot or wind around.[29]

For families that hand down the talent of crafting a Pochampally ikat, weaving this exquisite fabric is more a way of life, with the eldest to the youngest members all being involved in the process and in weaving and allied activities. The main product is sarees, as well as other products such as dress materials and home furnishings. Many of the traditional looms used for weaving Pochampally ikat are a century old. Pochampally ikat is the single largest handloom of the tie and dye cluster with about 2,000 pit looms and around 5,000 artisans.[30] What distinguishes Pochampally ikat from other ikats woven in Gujarat and Odisha is the uniqueness of its design and weaving process. It is made of cotton, silk or SICO (a combination of silk and cotton) fabric and usually takes one family of four people 10 days to weave. The sarees get their colour from natural elements adorned with geometric motifs.[31] The hard work and manual labour show in the perfect product that you eventually hold in your hands. The weaving cluster for Pochampally ikat features in the UNESCO tentative list of world heritage sites under the "iconic saree weaving clusters of India"[32]

A challenge lined up against this excellent craft was large-scale imitation through powerloom manufacturing, the growth of which took off even further due to reasons that embroiled traditional weaver families. While the cost of an originally handcrafted Pochampally ikat would be high owing to the time and effort invested in weaving it, a powerloom product would be easily available at a much lower price in comparison, thus making it attractive for consumers who are unaware of the reasons behind the affordable prices. A lack of government support and information about schemes for which artisans would be eligible was a crucial factor behind the waning fame of Pochampally ikat. The younger generation, no longer fuelled by mere passion and tradition, were moving out of the trade. Such were the reasons that charted the course for initiating the registration process for acquiring a GI status for the Pochampally Ikat Sari in 2003. The process was taken up by Pochampally Handloom Weavers' Cooperative Society Ltd. and Pochampally Handloom Tie and Dye Silk Sarees Manufacturers' Association. The Cluster Development Programme of the Textile Committee of India facilitated the entire process of GI registration. After the identification of the unique features and reputation that has evolved over generations due to a product's specific historical background, the most important step in the pre-registration phase is to generate awareness among the stakeholders about the legal identity acquired via the GI tag. This herculean task was undertaken by the Andhra Pradesh Technology Development and Promotion Cooperation (APTDC), which is an autonomous body of the Confederation of Indian Industry (CII), the Government of Andhra Pradesh and the Department of Science & Technology, Government of India.[33] The entire process of registration, which took nearly a year, was financially supported by the NABARD.[34] It is registered under three classes i.e., 24, 25 and 27.[35] Considering the uniqueness and its already acquired reputation, Pochampally ikat became the first GI registered handloom product of India.

There are two registered authorized users, Pochampally Handloom Tie & Dye Silk Sarees Manufacturers' Association being one.[36] However, whether this reflects on the awareness and marketing power of individual weavers is a question to be considered. Currently, the handloom has no logo registered with the main application or separately.

2. Kota Doria

Along with being immensely popular among enthusiastic tourists globally, the State of Rajasthan is also well known for a wide range of ethnic handicrafts and textiles, including handlooms. Among the many, Kota Doria is recognized as one of the finest handlooms of Rajasthan. As a weaver cluster, it is one of the most prominent in the State, with more than 1,000 families engaged in the craft. Another notable fact about the craft is that 80% of the weavers engaged are women.[37] The craft is practiced mainly in villages falling in the Kota district and in some villages in the districts of Bundi and Baran.[38]

The craft derives its name from the erstwhile State of Kota and one of the most told tales is that the Doria sarees were originally woven in Mysore, from where a few weaver families were brought to Kota by the then Prince Rao Kishore Singh.[39] Beyond such tales, traces as to the actual beginnings of this handcrafted fabric are a mystery, with no written accounts precisely stating the period of initiation of this craft. However, Bundi State records from as early as the 13th century, supported by other State and British documents, make references to cotton farming and weaving in Kaithun, one of the earliest known centres for Kota Doria.[40]

Kota Doria fabric – famous for its unique square checked pattern, which is also its main distinguishing factor – is woven for sarees as well as other kinds of clothing and products.[41] A distinguishing feature of true Kota Doria fabric is the presence of any of the "Khat" patterns in the fabric.[42] This fabric is produced on very traditional and age-old pit looms using a throw-shuttle technique, and all the processes involved from yarn to fabric are carried out manually. It has been a household activity for generations in this region, with each family having a traditional pit loom for weaving.[43] The uniqueness of this handloom product resides in its fall and sheerness, which is due to the use of cotton as well as silk in predefined proportions in the warp as well as the weft of the fabric.[44]

As described, its unique factors earned Kota Doria the legal status of GI, but as mentioned in the Statement of Case filed as part of the GI application, the socio-economic condition of weavers of this outstanding handloom product was in a sorry State.[45] At one point in time there were at least 10,000 looms functional in the region, which later fell to a drastically low number. In the Haduati region as well, where weaving activity supported around 2500 families, the situation became alarming.[46] The competition from power looms and a lack of consistent income have led the weavers to shift to other professions.[47]

A significant decline in production of this fabric has generated reasonable apprehension that the age-old tradition of weaving Kota Doria may soon disappear in absence of focused efforts to save it. Thus, the United Nations Industrial Development Organization (UNIDO) decided to revive this art through its Cluster Development programme. [48] The process for filing an application for GI registration was initiated by UNIDO in 2003. UNIDO undertook efforts to bring weavers and their associations, such as the Kota Women Weavers' Organization, Master Weavers' Association and other smaller associations in the weavers' villages, under a single umbrella: the Kota Doria Hadauti Federation (KDHF), a registered body for all Kota Doria weavers.[49] Further, the Rajasthan Urban Development Authority assisted UNIDO in the process of acquiring GI status for Kota Doria. In July 2005, the Kota Doria Hadauti Federation received the certificate of registration.

The dismal situation of Kota Doria weavers can be understood from the number of authorized users which are merely 15 in number as opposed to a cluster of approximately 1,000 families as per some studies conducted in the region.[50] The Kota Doria logo is registered separately, registration of which was valid up to 2019, but the same has not been renewed.[51]

3. Chanderi sarees

Home to one of the most popular handlooms of India, Chanderi is situated in the picturesque Vindhyachal Valley in the Ashok Nagar district of Madhya Pradesh.[52] The town also hosts the occasional sightseer since it is dotted with more than 100 monuments, both religious and secular, which stand as testimony to its glorious and eventful past. Chanderi can best be described as a rural town with an urban consciousness.[53] Weaving is the source of livelihood for more than 60% of its population, with around 3,500 looms, while the rest of the population are engaged in agriculture, biri making, stone quarrying and tertiary occupations.[54]

The origin of Chanderi fabric weaving can be traced back to around 1305 AD, when 20,000 weavers from "Lakhnoti"[55] migrated to Chanderi as followers of Maulana Majibuddin Uluf.[56] They started producing fine muslin/malmal which was very soft and transparent,[57] and thus a Chanderi saree is famous for its transparent and sheer fabric. Chanderi fabric is mainly of three types — pure cotton chanderi, silk chanderi and silk–cotton chanderi. Most of these fabrics carry unique motifs on them, such as floral patterns, animals and geometric designs. This unusual fineness of the fabric becomes a symbol of sheer beauty when it is woven in silk with golden threads, known as *zari*. During the Mughal rule, a great variety of garments such as dupattas, lugaras, pagris (turbans) and sarees were produced. The year 1925 marked the beginning of the use of silver and gold threads to produce zari cloth, and in 1940, the use of Indian silk in tana (warp) and cotton in bana (weft) began.[58] However, with the gradual extinction of the royal age, the use of pure gold and silver thread gave way to copper thread polished with golden colours.[59] Despite that, what sets these chanderi fabric sarees apart is the fact that the motifs are still woven by hand, thus lending them a completely different level of sophistication.

In terms of how the weavers do business, between 20% and 25% of the weavers engage in independent production but are dependent on 12 traders and 45 master weavers for marketing. However, the majority (60%–70%) of the weaver community are working as contract-based weavers for traders and master weavers.[60] Until independence, the royal families of Gwalior provided the required patronage for this form of art. After that, State and central government supported the cluster through purchases of the goods as well as subsidies and various promotional activities. But that support has slowly reduced to bare minimum.[61] Apart from this, the continuous threat from the powerloom industry and the exploitative practices of master weavers, small and daily wage-earning weavers continued to remain poor and ill-paid. Additionally, the weavers were unorganized. The absence of any association representing their interests added to the overall vulnerability of the weavers.

In 2003, UNIDO, in active collaboration with the Madhya Pradesh Government, initiated a 3-year long Cluster Development Programme. The Chanderi Development Foundation was established as a representative body. This foundation filed for registration of Chanderi sarees under the GI Act, 1999, in 2004, and this was granted in 2005. It has completed one term of registration and the same has been renewed for another term, which is until 2024. Yet after these efforts to revive the Chanderi weavers' cluster, the count of authorized users unpleasant remains *nil* as per the latest records published by the GI registry.[62] Needless to say, one must question the real State of affairs.

Stories of Chanderi weavers facing severe issues are not just in the past, however. A 2015 article from a national daily carries the story of Chanderi weaver Zaheer Mohammed Tuntani, who claims that when a customer asks for a chanderi saree in the popular saree markets of Chandani Chowk of New Delhi, 15 out of 20 times a fake product is shown to them.[63] Powerloom products have taken over the originally handcrafted fabric and sarees, due to which the weaving community is majorly thrown out of work. Additionally, factors like demonetization and a major overhaul in taxation practices came as an unpleasant surprise for Chanderi weavers, who saw a sharp fall in demand leading to a shrinkage in work orders. [64]

4. Mysore silk

From the land of silk and sandalwood comes a fine textile fit for royalty. The Mysore silk saree is manufactured in Karnataka, which happens to be one of the largest mulberry silk producers in the country.[65]

The silk weaving factory in Mysore is considered to be the oldest and most historically important silk manufacturing unit in India. Presently owned by Karnataka Silk Industries Corporation (KSIC), it was established in 1912 by the Maharaja of Mysore province.[66] Initially the silk fabrics were manufactured and supplied to meet the requirements of the royal family and as ornamental fabrics to their armed forces. Post-independence, the Department of Sericulture[67] took control of the silk weaving industry. In 1980–1981, the management of silk weaving was handed over to the Karnataka Silk Industries Corporation,[68] which claims to be the rightful and only manufacturer of Mysore silk.

A Mysore silk saree, with its extraordinary fabric sheen, the purity of the zari, the distinctive drape, its wonderful non-crush quality, and a butter-soft feel, gives an elegant look to anyone who wears it.[69] These classy sarees are not only washable, but also durable.[70] The zari too rarely fades because the yarn used has more gold and silver content than any other silk saree in the country; the intricate zari work on the borders and pallu set these sarees apart.[71]

Mysore silk is one of the most popular, finest and purest forms of silk, known for its extraordinary quality and permanence of lustre, and it is an integral part of Karnataka's culture.[72] As mentioned before, this silk is famous for its purity, lustre and softness and the richness of its natural colour, which gives it precedence over all other silks. The silk is dyed using natural pigments and woven into intricate but subtle patterns featuring motifs of birds or fruits.[73] The painstaking production process used by the weavers ensures that every aspect of the saree is perfect.[74]

The GI application for Mysore silk was initiated by the Karnataka Silk Industries Corporation in 2005, seeking registration for the handloom under Classes 23, 24 and 25.[75] It was renewed in 2014 and is now valid until 2024. The Mysore silk logo was registered as a GI in 2016, and it is valid up to 2025.[76] An astonishing fact, however, is that there are no registered authorized users as per the latest records from the GI Registry.[77]

5. Kullu shawls

India is known the world over for its woven shawls, available in various regional varieties. As many as six shawls are currently registered as GIs, of which the Kullu shawl was the first to be protected and registered as a GI.[78] Named after the majestic Kullu Valley, also known as the Valley of Gods, in Himachal Pradesh, the Kullu shawl is estimated to have been in existence for around 200 years.[79] Due to the extreme temperatures of Himalayan winters, wool weaving has been undertaken as a tradition and for personal use by the weavers of Kullu shawls.[80]

Due to the perishable nature of the woollen fabrics, old specimens of the same have not survived and there is an acute absence of historical evidence. However, references to these shawls are often found in folk songs. Some written accounts date the origin of the shawl as far back as the 17th century. According to the GI application, in around 1920, the market for Kullu shawls would have come crashing down, making it a forgotten craft, had it not been for the government, which set up an industrial training school in the Kullu district in order to train weavers. Noteworthy contributions from Shri Ved Thakur further aided in reviving this heritage handloom craft by re-introducing various traditional designs; he was also the inspiration behind the foundation of the Bhutti Weavers Cooperative Society in the valley, which is one of the largest Kullu shawl producers.

Kullu shawl designs are geometrical in nature whereas other shawls are embroidery based, and they have unique characteristics which give the same look from both sides due to their weaving, designing and colour combinations.[81] This shawl is woven with certain techniques and processes that must be mastered by hand, which in turn lends certain features to the finished product, and the same effect cannot be expected from a powerloom or a sophisticated loom.[82] Kullu shawls are marked by a harmonious combination of colours and designs that have evolved over time, and they are available in a wide range of types, from extremely fine to extremely coarse.[83] The material traditionally used for shawl weaving is from the fleece of a mountain goat called a pashmina.[84] Shri Thakur, along with four others pioneered the commercial production of Kullu shawls.[85] Further, in 1957 Kullu Shawl Improvement Centre was established, wherein diversification of designs guided the shawl market ahead.

One can generally find two types of Kullu shawls: *Pattu* for women and *Chadru* for men.[86] A distinct feature of the Kullu shawl is the stripes or band portion running horizontally width-wise at the lateral ends; these bands, which vary in size, are decorated with a variety of patterns woven in brilliant colours based on background colours of either black or brown.[87] Additionally, motifs adorning the surface are also woven, popular ones being floral motifs, dolls, birds, stars, waves, dot patterns, interlinked swastikas and more.[88] With time, shawls are now being manufactured in a wide variety of patterns, and the use of vegetable dyes, which augment an exotic array of subdued colours in apricots, ochre, rusts, browns, olives and many more, is in vogue.

The Himachal Pradesh Patent Information Centre under the State Council for Science, Technology and Environment applied for GI protection and registration for Kullu shawls under Class 24 in the year 2004.[89] The shawl was registered as a GI in 2005.[90] The Kullu shawl logo is registered separately.[91]

There are an estimated 28,500 weavers and 22,000 looms in the Kullu Valley and adjoining areas.[92] The weaver, a job worker, receives dyed yarn from traders or the master weaver and does all the activities from pre-weaving to the finished product and then hands it over.[93] The average wage earning as per this 2011 article was ₹ 35–40 per day.[94] However, powerloom shawls are currently available at half the cost and for even less than the original Kullu shawl, the price of which varies from Rs 1,000 to Rs 20,000 depending on its design and labour costs.[95] This is proving a big blow to weavers of the district as a majority of customers prefer buying cheap products.

The base of co-operative societies in Kullu is very strong, comprising around 180 co-operative societies, but most members of these societies are job workers only.[96] The master weaver purchases the raw material from local spinning mills and supplies the yarn to the weaver; later he receives woven product, and sells it through his own outlet. One aspect where the Kullu shawl stands distinct from other handloom case studies till now in this chapter is the number of authorized users according to the latest published record by the GI Registry. The record names 134 users.[97]

The numbers however do not mean that the market for Kullu shawls is not affected by on-ground issues. Although the coveted GI tag is often seen as a saviour for the Kullu shawls, it has still to work effectively and protect the authentically crafted shawls from cheap, powerloom imitations manufactured mainly in Ludhiana.[98]

6. Kancheepuram silk sarees

Nestled in Southern India, this quaint town is the centre of silk weaving in Tamil Nadu. The centuries' old traditional weaving originating in Kancheepuram has put the town on the world map. Of the many kinds of silk sarees that India is home to, Kancheepuram silk has booked itself a top spot, so much so that the originating town is fondly called "Silk City".[99] This silk weaving tradition is estimated to be more than 150 years old. Today, the city's economy is mainly dependant on silk weaving from handloom industries and tourism.

Kancheepuram silk sarees are well known for their interwoven lace (popular throughout the country as zari, which features silver thread coated in a gold colour) work which is made of silver wire, red silk, silver thread and gold.[100] The exclusivity of Kancheepuram silk lies in the hand-weaving of rich gold borders, traditional designs and dense fabric in contrasting colours.[101] The looms mainly used for this weaving are throw-shuttle looms and fly-shuttle looms, although most of the silk fabric used, especially for sarees, is woven on the former type of loom.[102]

The elaborate manufacturing process involves 12 stages: twisting, degumming, dyeing, colour selection, dressing, sizing, piecing, aluppiduthal, fixing the warp to the loom, joining the lace, preparation of adai and weaving.[103] In the silk sarees, the contents of the zari used are gold (0.59%), silver (57%), silk (24%) and copper (18.41%).[104] One of the many unique features of a Kancheepuram silk saree is the finesse with which two pieces are blended together; this blending is unrecognizable to the naked eye because of the artistic use of harmonious colours.[105] Another feature that sets Kancheepuram silk apart is the zari used in the process, which forms one of the main raw materials; the zari is mainly outsourced from Surat, situated in the State of Gujarat, which is a supplier of this raw material to a large base of handloom weavers around the country.[106] Apart from Surat zari, weavers of Kancheepuram silk also depend on the State-owned Tamilnadu Zari Ltd. for the raw material.[107] Lastly, beyond the technical aspects that can usually be beyond a consumer's understanding, the designs woven in Kancheepuram silk are a major attraction and have gained immense fame.[108] One reason behind the popularity of Kancheepuram silk designs is that modern designs are woven using traditional methods, which caters to the latest needs of consumers leading to a steady demand for the product.[109]

The GI application for Kancheepuram silk was filed by the Department of Handlooms and Textiles of the Government of Tamilnadu under Classes 24 and 25 in 2004.[110] The handloom was registered as a GI in 2005.[111] There has been no logo registration to date.

Weavers of Kancheepuram silk can be divided into two broad groups: Co-operative fold and private sector. A large base of weavers have come together to form various co-operative societies, officially called the Weavers' Cooperative Societies.[112] An estimated 30,000 weavers are employed under 23 societies in the town while around 40,000 weavers are engaged privately.[113] Even with these figures, the number of authorized users as per the GI Registry records as of 31 July 2020 stands at a mere 34.[114]

Influxes of counterfeit Kancheepuram silk sarees have disturbed the market for original silk sarees.[115] The fake goods carry all the attributes as detailed by the documents defining the various attributes of Kancheepuram silk sarees, thus making it impossible to differentiate between the original and the lookalike.[116] A great amount of compromise is made in the techniques and raw materials used for producing the silk sarees.[117]

Since its drive for enrolment and issuance of authorized user certificates in 2009, the Department of Textiles and Handlooms has received a number of petitions stating difficulties in adhering to quality parameters standardized under the GI.[118] The representations pertain to the composition of gold in the zari used in the saree, the obligation to weave in the *korvai* or three-shuttle weave and the area of production defined in the GI.[119] These are at variance with those considered feasible, and actually employed, by local producers and hence are the subject of ongoing controversy among various stakeholders at the local level.[120] But many other private producers of silk sarees in Kancheepuram are sceptical about the GI mark and question the viability of adhering to design and technical aspects delineated under it.[121] Apparently it took the president of the IPR Attorneys Association and advocates responsible for the GI registrations for the Kancheepuram saree nearly 4 years to convince producers to become registered users under the GI Act once the government of Tamil Nadu had registered as a proprietor under the first phase of the Act's implementation.[122] As of 2013, a majority of the producers in the town of Kancheepuram were still not authorized to produce the official version or "original" Kancheepuram saree.[123]

7. Muga silk of Assam

A variety of silk which finds mention in *Arthshastra* by Kautilya, dating back to as early as 321 B.C., and in the travelogues in famous historian Edward A. Gait's *A History of Assam*, which has survived through the centuries, is surely worth recognition as a GI.[124] Travelling towards the East of India, the rivers Brahmaputra and Barak run through the State of Assam in the north and south respectively and carve out deep valleys and it is in this strip of the Brahmaputra and Barak valley that the Muga plant cultivation is majorly carried out.[125] This plant yields the Muga silkworms which goes into making of the Muga Silk.

Muga is a purely Assamese word that represents a particular natural colour like golden yellow or brown.[126] The golden-yellow silk produced by the *Anrheraea assama* silkworm is found only in the Brahmaputra Valley.[127] This species of silkworm is semi-domesticated in that the rearers collect the worms, which crawl down at the end of their larval period where they are allowed to spin cocoons.[128] The Muga worm is fed on the leaves of food plants, particularly on *Som* (Machilus odoratissama) and *Soalu* (Teranthera monopetala).[129] The silkworm gives five broods a year corresponding to the different seasons: "katiya" (autumn crop), "jarua" (winter crop), "jethua" (summer crop), "aherua" (early monsoon crop), and "bhadia" (late monsoon crop).[130] The silk goes through five stages in order to finally turn it into a manufactured good: degumming, hand reeling, winding, warping and weaving.[131]

Muga is popular for its natural colour of spun gold, its glossy texture and its durability, which increases with every wash, in sharp contrast to the natural law of the decay of shine in fabrics over time.[132] Muga possesses the highest tensile strength among all the natural textile fibres and is comfortable to wear in both summer and winter.[133]

A GI application for Muga silk was filed by Assam Science, Technology and Environment Council (ACTEC), Department of Science & Technology,

Assam under Classes 23–25, 27 and 31.[134] The handloom was registered as a GI in the year 2007. A logo for Muga silk was registered which is connected to the application number 55 for Muga silk.[135]

The number of authorized users of the Muga silk GI is 286 as per the latest records from the GI Registry.[136] However, this number does not represent the actual number of Muga silk weavers. Muga silk was registered in 2007, and its logo was registered under the GI Register in 2012; however over a period of 8 years, both State agencies and non-government organizations through their combined efforts were able to bring in merely 13 applications, of which the first was accepted only in 2014.[137] This was discovered by Professor Prabuddha Ganguli, the then MHRD IPR chair professor at Tezpur University. To transform this situation, a workshop was jointly organized by Tezpur University IPR Cell, IPR Cell of the Dibrugarh University and faculty members as well as volunteers from Lakhimpur College, where 117 stakeholders from 33 villages were registered.[138]

Highlighting an issue unique to the recognition of Muga silk in the market, Ms. Jupi Gogoi, assistant professor at the Faculty of Law, University of Delhi, through her observations at various textile exhibitions, understood that a silk called "Moonga" is sold on a large scale especially around Delhi NCR (National Capital Region).[139] The sellers mention how this silk is produced in Jharkhand, Chhattisgarh, UP and Bihar. Moreover, certain websites also advertise Muga silk as "Moonga" silk, some with the image of traditional Muga Silk embodying traditional Assamese designs and some with other textile images.[140] Interestingly, most people are not aware of the characteristics of Muga silk and thus end up buying "Moonga", considering it to be synonymous with Muga.[141] The author observes further that despite the Silk Board of India's confirmation that there is no silk variety called "Moonga", the sellers have been brazenly selling this silk.

Likewise, Ms. Nibedita Choudhury conducted a study to understand the status of the Muga silk industry in Assam and the socio-economic issues associated with its weavers.[142] Data was collected from around 165 weavers, these being an active part of co-operative societies, and it revealed some disturbing facts. With the majority of the weavers (37.57%) falling in the age group of 35–44, a minimal percentage of weavers (7.88%) fell in the relatively young age group of 15–24.[143] The author observed a sharp reduction in interest among young weavers in silk weaving, leading to a conclusion that there could be a reduction in the overall number of weavers.[144] Another prominent fact resulting from the study was that due to lack of education, the weavers did not have an alternative profession that could provide a regular income source.[145] It was also observed that there was a lack of organizations working for the betterment of the weavers in the chosen area, due to which policy implementation and work for the overall support of the weavers could not be undertaken in a concerted fashion.[146]

8. Banaras silk and brocades

Akin to other famous silks of India, a type which can be traced back to the Vedic era is the infamous Banaras sarees and brocades.[147] Banaras has been recognized as an important centre for weaving since time immemorial. Of its many crafts, the town's silk sarees and brocades have been much sought after, gathering a massive reputation worldwide.

The weavers of the Banaras generally use old pit looms for weaving sarees, brocades and other products.[148] Among the different varieties of sarees produced in the centres, some exclusive varieties are jangla, tanchoi, vaskat, cutwork, tissue and butidar, which are made of silk warp and silk weft on a plain/satin background, brocaded with extra weft patterns in different layouts, introducing buties, bells, creepers, buttas, borders and anchals to create a glamourous appearance.[149] While motifs are crafted out of zari threads, the rest of the saree is usually made of silk that is dyed in a variety of colours. Traditionally, the weaving was done with naksha draw looms, but now jacquard equipment is used.[150] Before proceeding with weaving, the design is drawn out on paper by a special category of craftspeople called naqshaband.[151] A separate pattern guides each row, and hundreds of such patterns (naksha patras) are created for a single saree. This design is then woven on a small wooden frame. Banarasi sarees are available in a host of colours and are known more for the gold and silver zari work that adorns them.

Apart from Benaras or Varanasi, as it is famously known, this handloom is woven in other places in Uttar Pradesh like the Mirzapur, Chandauli, Bhadohi, Jaunpur and Azamgarh districts.[152] Nine applicants came together to apply for a GI application in the name of Banaras Brocades and Sarees: Banaras Bunkar Samiti, Human Welfare Association, Joint Director Industries (Eastern Zone), Uttar Pradesh Handloom Fabrics Marketing Cooperative Federation Limited, Eastern U.P. Exporters Association, Banarasi Vastra Udhyog Sangh, Director of Handlooms & Textiles, Uttar Pradesh, Banaras Hath Kargah Vikas Samiti and Adarsh Silk Bunkar Sahkari Samiti Limited. The application was made in 2006 under Classes 23–26.[153] The handloom was registered as a GI in 2009. A local NGO, the Human Welfare Association (HWA), played the key role with facilitation from the United Nations Conference on Trade and Development (UNCTAD).[154] It was estimated at the time that registration of the Banaras Brocades and Sarees as a GI would benefit around 12 lakh people working in the Banaras silk industry. As per the data available from the GI Registry, 117 authorized users for Banaras Brocades and Sarees are registered.[155] A logo is separately registered for the handloom.[156]

Issues plaguing the Banaras silk industry have been the focus of study for many researchers. A study conducted by Ms. Sarvjaeta Verma and Ms. Nandita Mishra highlighted some prominent issues surrounding this centuries' old handloom industry, one of which is the viral spread of imitation products due to which the original craft's artisans have suffered heavily.[157] Stiff competition from *Kela Silk* and *Chinese Silk* along with sarees produced on power looms have fast eroded the market share of original handcrafted Banaras Sarees and Brocades.[158] To escape the unpredictability of the trade of original crafts returning to normalcy, some artisans have migrated to cities in search of a way to make a living while some have even quit the trade.

Another factor that has been highlighted prominently was the effect of the work environment on the health of weavers. The intricate designs that adorn the Banarasi handloom require artisans to sit for long hours and work in a dimly-lit atmosphere filled with dust from fabrics, thus leading to harmful effects on their physical condition.[159] An October 2014 draft consultation paper on handlooms released by the erstwhile Planning Commission acknowledges this:

> Body pain, pulmonary problems, chronic bronchitis, decrease in hand-grip strength are observed in weavers. About 94 per cent of weavers with 10–30 years of work experience report pain in the knee, back and neck. Poor eyesight is also a serious problem among them, notes the consultation paper.[160]

In 2012, weavers in Varanasi started receiving insurance benefits for ill health and untimely death or disability but the benefit amounts have reduced over recent years as noted by the weavers' associations.[161] This is evident from the dwindling budgetary allocation for the Health Insurance Scheme and the Mahatma Gandhi Bunkar Bima Yojana (MGBBY) despite a substantial increase in the number of beneficiaries under them.[162] The budget for the Health Insurance Scheme has reduced from Rs 109.64 crore in 2012–2013 to Rs 25.87 crore in 2014–2015, and that for MGBBY from Rs 17.16 crore to Rs 16.39 crore during the same period.[163]

For instance, weavers who work at powerloom factories earn about Rs 125 a day – this is Rs 225 less than the daily wage rate fixed by the Union Ministry of Labour and Employment, but the highest amount a weaver can earn in Varanasi.[164] Likewise, the wages are meagre even for those engaged in the highly specialized handloom weaving.[165] The last Handloom Census released in 2009–2010 shows that an average handloom weaver household of five persons earns Rs 36,498 a year; given that almost all the members of a weaver's family work on a saree, each artisan earns Rs 22 a day, according to a calculation by Rashtra Chenetha Jana Samakhya (RCJS).[166]

The above data sufficiently conveys that certain handlooms, although identified and recognized for their traditional and cultural value through the GI law, remain in a dire condition overall. As discussed in this case, the socio-economic and health-related problems being faced by the weavers are persistent even with GI protection. Thus, the benefits of GI will reach the weavers only when such issues are addressed with appropriate policy interventions.

9. Paithani sarees

It is only from the 6th century BC that more definite historical evidence about the crafts of Paithan is available, and only with the coming of the Satavahanas, however, does some kind of real recorded and detailed history of Paithan become possible.[167] To know the tastes in fabrics of the Western people and to study them, Satavahanas kings dispatched a number of ambassadors to Western countries, due to which trade with Rome and Greece flourished.[168] Pliny, Ptolemy and Periplus wrote of it with admiration, giving a truly kaleidoscopic view of its State of abundance and prosperity.[169] Thus, Paithan was truly on the world map.[170]

The art of Paithan is more than 2,000 years old, developed in the then splendid city of Pratishthan ruled by the legendary Satavahanas ruler Shalivahana, curently some 50 km away from Aurangabad.[171] It was the capital of the Satavahanas dynasty (200 B.C.) and once exported cotton and silks to the great Roman Empire.[172] Historically, Paithan has always been centred around the weaving industry; every household in Paithan was linked with weaving and ancillary activities such as dyeing the silk, winding the zari or even selling the silk sarees.[173]

The Paithani saree is a handwoven silk saree which is known the world over for its uniqueness. A special feature of Paithani is that it is woven without the assistance of a mechanical contrivance like a jacquard or *jala*.[174] One of the unique features of the Paithani saree is the design which is woven on its border; this design is woven to be exactly alike on both sides (borders) of the Paithani saree,[175] and this distinguishing skill and artistic knowledge of the manufacturers sets the majestic Paithani saree apart from other sarees available across India.

The GI application for Paithani Sarees and Fabrics was made in 2009 under Classes 24 and 25 by the following applicants: Maharashtra State Handlooms Corporation, Maharashtra Small Scale Industries Development Corporation Limited, Shri Rajasva Bahu-Uddeshiya Sanstha, Oudhyogik Sahakari Mandal Limited, Bhagwan Birsa Winkar Oudhyogik Utpadak Sahakari Sanstha Maryadit, Poonam Paithani Hastakala Winker Oudhyogik Sahakari Sanstha Maryadit, Asavali Mahila Hatmag Winkar Sahakari Sanstha Maryadit, Godavari Paithan Taluka Handloom Weavers Co-operative Society Limited and Pratisthan Paithani Weavers Association.[176] Paithani Saree was registered as a GI in 2010. It has no registered logo.

A fact of concern evident from the latest records available is that there are no authorized users for this registered GI, a State similar to or far worse than the previous handlooms studied in this chapter.[177] An issue surfacing around Paithani sarees and fabrics is that only a few families remain involved in the traditional occupation of weaving. This, accompanied with products from power looms flooding the market and overtaking originally crafted Paithani sarees, led to a major reduction in weavers' interest in continuing with the craft. A powerloom can replicate designs fed into a computer, after which the manufacturing process for each saree will take merely 5–6 hours. Due to such ease in manufacturing, these Paithani sarees are priced competitively ranging from ₹ 2000 to ₹ 10,000.[178] Another cheaper Paithani is the Yeola Paithani, which is made on a Kadhiyal loom and is also faster to weave.[179] However, due to a lack of awareness of the defining points of a Paithani saree, customers are easily duped by shops.[180] A quick customer survey showed that in traditional saree shops that have been patronised by families for generations, a powerloom Paithani is often sold at the cost of a handloom Paithani as the customers are not aware of the original product and trust the shop owner.[181] Even in Paithan, several shops can be found which promise a Paithani at prices as low as ₹ 500 to ₹ 2000.[182] This data is evidence of the fact that consumer awareness plays an equally crucial role in building a successful GI model.

Issues similar to those faced by other handlooms plague the Paithani handloom industry. The time and effort invested in creating an original and authentic Paithani saree demands a befitting compensation for the weavers. However, higher prices also mean a decreased demand from consumers who can buy a so-called authentic Paithani saree made with powerloom. The scarce demand has brought doom to the weavers' community, which has continued to shrink even after the craft's protection as a GI. It is harder to find traditional weavers or weavers who have complete knowledge of the original techniques. Further, as the process of weaving is slow and tedious, young members of the weavers' community tend to prefer a city life and job in comparison to traditional weaving, which may not earn them rightful rewards.[183]

10. Kashmir pashmina

Apart from its picturesque landscapes and snow-clad mountains, Kashmir is globally well known for its handicrafts and handlooms. The State has a history of rich crafts being practised for centuries. Known for their intricacy and exclusivity, these crafts contribute an estimated ₹ 3,000 crore to the State's economy.[184]

Among a rich list of crafts produced in Kashmir, pashmina is hugely renowned and has attracted attention of consumers from all over the world since time immemorial. Despite several upheavals in the State, pashmina stays at the forefront of international textile crafts. In fact, shops in far-off locations often use the term "pashmina" for the woollen items they sell. The use of this aesthetically crafted apparel has been the pride of oriental royalty and European lords.

Pashmina is the fabric woven from Pashm, the delicate fibre which gives the Kashmir fabric its special properties and is produced by Himalayan mountain goats reared on high-altitude pastures in Ladakh and Tibet, miles away from Kashmir.[185] Pashmina is a down fibre or undercoat derived from a domestic goat known as Capra Hiracus which is native to India; the fabric has a special lustre due to its long, fine fibres, which are as thin as 12–16 microns.[186]

In order to safeguard the interests of the stakeholders of the regional handicraft industry, Craft Development Institute (CDI) Srinagar facilitated the formation of "Tahafuz", a society of handicraft artisans and practitioners, to register six local crafts as Geographical Indications, Kashmir pashmina being one.[187] Though around 16 crafts are practised in the region, it was observed that GI is more relevant for some crafts like pashmina due to the fact that these are important in terms of their historical background, contribution to the economy and employment generation as well as their potential to be marketed globally.[188] Over 100,000 workers, including women, are directly engaged in the production of Pashmina, and about 10,000 more are benefited by the industry indirectly.[189] Further, among the other registered crafts, pashmina is most important in terms of its high export potential and also due to the fact that cheap imitations of Pashmina are being produced almost everywhere in the world.

The GI application for Kashmir pashmina was made by Tahafuz under Classes 23–25 in 2005, and the handloom was registered in 2008.[190] Presently there are 251 authorized users of the Kashmir pashmina as per the records published by the GI registry.[191]

Competition from imitations and lookalikes from other countries has marginalized the share of Kashmir handicrafts, which significantly increases the need to safeguard regional handicrafts inherited through generations with the help of a mechanism that will not only ensure the protection of Kashmir handicrafts but also develop a distinct brand identity.[192] The growth of cashmere, an industrially produced pashmina, globally known by this name has received a tremendous push from demands from the international market.[193] While Kashmir is producing around 40–50 tons of genuine, handmade pashmina annually, countries like China, Mongolia, Nepal, Scotland and the USA are annually producing 14,000–16,000 tons of cashmere, of which China alone produces 7,500–12,000 tons annually.[194] This has been a troubling issue for the Kashmir pashmina.

2.4.2 Case studies from Gujarat

The State has secured GI registration for 16 products.[195] The first registration was acquired for Sankheda furniture in the year 2008. Currently, of the 16 registered GIs as shown in Table 2.4, 2 are granted for agricultural products,

3 are for logos and the remaining 11 are for handicraft products. Further, out of the 11 handicraft products, 4 are handloom products, namely Tangaliya shawls, Kachchh shawls,[196] Patan patola and Rajkot patola. Patan patola and Rajkot patola were granted GI tags in 2013 and 2018, respectively.[197]

Table 2.4 GIs of Gujarat

Sr. no.	*Product*	*Category*	*Year of registration*	*Registered proprietor*
01.	Sankheda furniture	Handicraft	2r07	Development Commissioner (Handicrafts)
02.	Agates of Cambay	Handicraft	2007	Development Commissioner (Handicrafts)
03.	Kutch embroidery	Handicraft	2007	Development Commissioner (Handicrafts)
04.	Tangaliya shawl	Handicraft (Handlooms)	2008	Tangaliya Hastkala Association
05.	Surat zari craft	Handicraft	2009	The Surat Jari Manufacturers Association
06.	Gir Kesar mango	Agriculture	2009	Gujarat Agro Industries Corporation Limited
07.	Bhalia wheat	Agriculture	2009	Gujarat Agro Industries Corporation Limited
08.	Kachchh shawls	Handicraft (Handlooms)	2009	Kutch Weavers Association
09.	Patan patola	Handicraft (Handlooms)	2011	Patan Double Ikat Patola Weavers Association
10.	Warli painting	Handicraft	2014	Adivasi Yuva Seva Sangh
11.	Sankheda furniture (logo)	Handicraft	2015	Development Commissioner (Handicrafts)
12.	Kutch embroidery (Logo)	Handicraft	2015	Development Commissioner (Handicrafts)
13.	Agates of Cambay (logo)	Handicraft	2015	Development Commissioner (Handicrafts)
14.	Jamnagari Bandhani	Handicraft	2010	Jamnagar Chamber of Commerce and Industry
15.	Rajkot patola	Handicraft (Handlooms)	2012	Rajkot District Weavers Association
16.	Pethapur printing blocks	Handicraft	2017	Gujarat Council on Science and Technology

Source: Compiled from GI Registry database <https://www.ipindia.gov.in/gi.htm>

1. Patan patola

This town is a seamless confluence of art and architecture. Home to the UNESCO World Heritage Site called Rani ni Vav, Patan dates back to 745 AD, when it was founded as a fortified town by the first ruler of the Chavda dynasty.[198] The influence of Patan's rich legacy has traversed time, sustaining its relevance and popularity through the years. Besides its architectural marvels, Patan has also earned a name for itself in handloom weaving of the legendary patola saris. Often called the most complex Indian textile, the complexity and time-intensiveness involved in weaving a patola saree give it an enhanced value.

The timelessness of the weaving of patola is evident from the fact that it receives mention in a 2,000-year-old book titled *Kalpsutra*, a religious text under Jainism; it is the subject of carving at the infamous Ajanta caves and is found in folk tales across various languages.[199] Must this proof of its unique craftsmanship fall short, patola weaving is accompanied with a 900-year-old kingly story of Kumarpala, whose passion for donning a patola went as far as bringing 700 weaver families to his capital Patan from the then States of India.[200] From the accounts of European travellers, patola was known from the year 1516 AD. Correa (1523 AD) speaks of patola which were offered for sale at Malecca at high prices.[201] A letter dated 1616 AD from the East India Company mentions patola bought by the English merchants.[202] After the discovery of the sea route to India, it is probable that other European nations trading in Indian commodities carried the patola across the distant seas.[203] In Gujarat it is said that patola has been around since the tenth century.[204]

The complexity and time-intensiveness is what makes patola so valuable.[205] Patola sarees make use of natural dyes like catechu, cochineal, indigo, turmeric, natural lakh, harde, madder roots, manjistha, ratnajyot, katha, kesudo, pomegranate skin, henna, marigold flower, etc. in the colouring process. Alum, copper sulphate, ferrous sulphate, tin chloride, potassium dichromate and other mordents are also used, the result of which is vibrant colours dominated by patterns of bright red, dark green and yellow.[206]

There are some ten basic patterns, mainly of plant, zoomorphic and geometrical motifs; the most common motifs in Patan patola are parrots, elephants, plants, ladies, flowers, trellis, baskets, leaves, etc., which are used in many different permutations and combinations for the body, border and the pallav, making different designs.[207] The distinctive motifs on patola remain the same on the front and reverse sides, permitting the saree to be reversible with no change in the appearance of the entire attire.[208] Geometric designs on patola are such that the appearance of the entire saree is the same regardless of which of the four corners it is worn from.[209]

A single Patan patola carries many unique features. Patolas are manufactured by the resist-dyeing process using the warp and weft technique and it normally takes three people about 4–7 months to weave a patola, making it expensive and time-consuming.[210] The first step involves the tying of the yarn with cotton threads according to the pattern.[211] Measurements can be as small as 1/100th of an inch.[212] The yarn undergoes multiple cycles of tying and dyeing following a specific order of colours, and the displacement of even a single yarn can disturb the design arrangement and make the entire set redundant.[213]

The patola art which is about 300 years old is a classic handloom disntinguished by features like durability despite the base fabric's tenderness.[214] Patan patola is such a fine piece of handwork that it requires a special measurement tape that can measure even a 100th part of an inch.[215] Over and above this, these silk sarees adorned with gorgeous colours and striking patterns are products of exquisite workmanship, setting them apart and eligible to be registered as a GI.

Even though the artists are snowed under with orders for the next couple of years, issues of investment, time and the disinterest of the younger generation makes the survival of the craft very difficult.[216] Coupled with cheaper, single ikat patola imitations flooding the market and jarring chemical dyes that are replacing natural dyes, genuine patola is dying out.[217]

The Patan patola is registered as a GI in the name of Patan Double Ikat Patola Weavers Association.[218] The association applied for GI under Classes 24 and 25 in 2011 and registration was granted in the year 2013.[219] As per the latest records of the GI registry, there are 14 authorized users of the Patan patola GI.[220]

2. Rajkot patola

A younger version of the majestic double ikat Patan patola, single ikat patola is found in the State of Gujarat. The single ikat saree weaving is a relatively new form, only about 60 years old.[221] The pioneering status for Rajkot Patola is attributed to Shri Karamchand Godhamdas, who established an Ikat weaving workshop in Rajkot in 1951, after acquiring knowledge from the Salvi family of Patan.[222] Further, with the help of the All India Handloom Board, Shri Karamchand modernized the weaving process to such an extent that the Rajkot patolas made rapid progress and gave fierce competition to the Patan patolas.[223]

The single ikat version of patola has found a market among middle-class and lower-middle-class sections of consumers who cannot afford the Patan patola.[224] According to the GI application, private traders also support this variant of patola.[225] The popularity of the single ikat patola has soared even with the presence of the double ikat patola due to the reduced cost of production and a perceived liking due to the affordability factor.[226] The application further claims that these characteristics of the single ikat Rajkot patola have brought a very welcome change to the lives of many weaver families who were finding it difficult to engage in their original profession for a variety of reasons.[227]

The GI application for Rajkot patola was filed by Rajkot District Weavers Association in 2012, and the handloom was registered as a GI in 2018.[228] According to the authorized users' record published by the GI registry, there are no authorized users registered for this GI protected handloom.[229]

2.5 Concluding observations

The case studies discussed here make it very clear how these products are apt illustrations of regional diversity and traditional heritage. Local communities, mostly socially, economically and educationally backward, are involved in the production of these handloom products. Handloom being an unorganized sector, it is very difficult to draw quantitative conclusions on the impact that GI has created on such products, especially when statistical data is almost unavailable. The secondary data that is available mainly through the GI journal and authoritative studies provides for a history of such art and the process of registration that has been followed. Analysing this secondary data, we are convinced that the success of GI is dependent on its ability to unlock the commercial benefits. As mentioned earlier as well, Geographical Indications are not just about the strong link between the place and the product. Its overall contribution to economy is equally an essential part of it. With the quality and merits associated with the GI tag, it must result in the adequate generation of income and a sustainable livelihood. However, that does not seem to be the case with most of the GI registered products in India. This is further evident from the sparse number of infringement cases and the lack of a system for a post-grant benefit sharing mechanism. These issues occupy a significant place in the GI protection system of India. The following conclusions are made based on the evidence offered by the case studies explored in this chapter.

- The handloom products that have been studied here are already well recognized and established. This suggests that such recognition is not solely attributable to their GI status. However, a few of them were on the verge of extinction, and have been revived through GI registration, e.g., chanderi silk, Kota Doria, Tangaliya shawl etc. with GI registration considered to have been the first step towards their revival.
- The government through its agencies has taken key initiatives in applying for registration in most of the case studies discussed here. However,

it is evident from these case studies that small-scale producers struggle to understand the benefits of GI registration. It is observed that GI registration does not have an impact on awareness and marketing power in terms of individual weavers. Hence, generating awareness before registration becomes a crucial step to accrue the benefits of a *sui generis* protection system.

- While reviewing the GI journey of these handloom products, it has been observed that it involved active assistance and support from external actors, such as governmental agencies, NGOs and educational institutes, as is evident from official documents submitted to the GI registry. Considering the lengthy and complex registration process, this assistance, ranging from creating awareness to obtaining registration, becomes indispensable. The process of an uncontested GI registration normally takes a year or two, and it involves visiting the GI office repeatedly and also replying to the queries of the Registrar, for which small-scale producers are not well equipped. The required knowledge and competence for GI registration is generally missing among weavers and producers. It is observed that weavers are unable to assess and enhance the market value for their registered products, especially in case of the abovementioned handlooms.
- The number of authorized users for the protected GIs as discussed through the case studies and highlighted in Table 2.5 comes as a fact that cannot be overlooked.

  The law of GI as mentioned earlier, identifies two distinct categories i.e., Registered Proprietor and Authorised User. The right conferred on registration does not give the Registered Proprietor the right to use the GI tag as well. To acquire the same, registration as an Authorized User is mandatory under Section 17 of the GI Act.

Table 2.5 Number of Authorized Users of select handlooms

Sr. no.	*Handloom*	*No. of registered authorized users*
01.	Chanderi	0
02.	Paithani saree	0
03.	Mysore silk	0
04.	Rakjot patola	0
05.	Pochampally ikat	2
06.	Patan patola	14
07.	Kota Doria	15
08.	Kancheepuram silk	34
09.	Banaras brocade and sarees	117
10.	Kullu shawl	134
11.	Kashmir pashmina	251
12.	Muga silk	286

Source: Compiled from GI Registry database <https://www.ipindia.gov.in/gi.htm>

The numbers discussed here prove that the legal innovation of extending protection to weavers, producers, manufacturers, traders, dealers and exporters outside the fold of the registered proprietor is underutilized. Registration as an Authorized User enables a producer to use the Geographical Indication in relation to the goods produced by him. If used in the correct sense, such registration can curb the entry of infringing goods, but without the awareness that such a right is available to him and the benefits thereof, a weaver is sadly left with nothing but a legal right on paper. An insufficient number of registered Authorized Users is certainly one of the main reasons for the non-realization of the benefits of GI.

- The mere granting of a GI tag does not guarantee that it will contribute to the socio-economic well-being of the producers. The sale of such handloom products is generally undertaken by the master weaver. Thus, the weavers are dependent on the middlemen or the master weavers not only for raw materials but also for sales. In the absence of a successful business model which promotes and market the GI products, tangible benefits do not reach the actual producer.
- In the absence of an appropriate system of marketing and brand promotion for these handloom products, the desired benefits have failed to materialize even after a decade of registration.
- Powerloom products have taken over the originally handcrafted fabric and sarees, due to which the weaving community is majorly thrown out of work.
- The focus of the system must shift from merely granting GI status to actual enforcement of the same through the creation of an efficient system of brand promotion, marketing and benefit sharing.

Notes

1 Thomas Erskine Holland, *The Elements of Jurisprudence* 83 (13th edn, Indian Economy Reprint, Universal Law Publishing 2006).
2 P.J. Fitzergerald, *Salmond on Jurisprudence* 222 (12th edn, Indian Economy Reprint, Universal Law Publishing 2004).
3 Delphine Marie-Vivien, *The Protection of Geographical Indications in India: A New Perspective on the French and European Experience* (SAGE Publications 2015).
4 Kasturi Das, "Prospects and Challenges in India" (2010) 13(2) Journal of World Intellectual Property 148–201, 149 <https://onlinelibrary.wiley.com/doi/abs/10.1111/j.1747-1796.2009.00363.x> accessed 02 September 2020.
5 The Geographical Indications of Goods (Registration & Protection) Act, 1999, s 23.
6 Ibid s18 (1).
7 Ibid s18 (3).
8 Ibid s 29(e) ["'Geographical Indication' in relation to goods, means an indication which identifies such goods as agricultural goods, natural goods or

manufactured goods as originating, or manufactured in the territory of country, or a region or locality in that territory, where a given quality, reputation or other characteristic of such goods is essentially attributable to its geographical origin and in case where such goods are manufactured goods one of the activities of either the production or of processing or preparation of the goods concerned takes place in such territory, region or locality, as the case may be'].

9 The treatment of GI under international instruments is discussed in Chapter 1, 1.3.

10 "Trade-Related Aspects of Intellectual Property Rights", Article 22.1, see Chapter 1, 1.3 for further discussion.

11 The GIs Act, 1999 (n 6) s 11 (1).

12 Ibid s 2 (1) (k).

13 Ibid s 9.

14 Ibid s 10.

15 Ibid.

16 "Geographical Indications Journal No. 40, Application Number 174" (*Geographical Indications Registry*, 2011) <http://ipindiaservices.gov.in/GIRPublic/Application/ViewDocument> accessed 1 March 2021; "Geographical Indications Journal No. 29, Application Number 127" (*Geographical Indications Registry*, 2009). <http://ipindiaservices.gov.in/GIRPublic/Application/ViewDocument> accessed 01 March 2021.

17 "Geographical Indications Journal No. 1, Application Numbers 1 & 2" (*Geographical Indications* Registry, 2004) <http://ipindiaservices.gov.in/GIRPublic/Application/ViewDocument> accessed 01 March 2021.

18 The GIs Act, 1999 (n 6) s. 11(1).

19 "Geographical Indications Journal No. 7, Application Number 19" (*Geographical Indications Registry*, 2005) <http://ipindiaservices.gov.in/GIRPublic/Application/ViewDocument> accessed 1 March 2021; "Geographical Indications Journal No. 16, Application Number 55" (*Geographical Indications Registry*, 2007) <http://ipindiaservices.gov.in/GIRPublic/Application/ViewDocument> accessed 1 March 202.

20 This documentation requirement is prescribed under The Geographical Indications of Goods (Registration and Protection) Act, 1999 s 11(2) and The Geographical Indications of Goods (Registration and Protection) Rules, 2002 r 32(1).

21 "Manual of Geographical Indications Practice and Procedure" (*Office of the Controller General of Patents, Designs and Trademarks & Registrar of Geographical Indications*, 2011). <https://ipindia.gov.in/writereaddata/Portal/IPOGuidelinesManuals/1_31_1_manual-of-geographical-indications-practice-and-procedure.pdf> accessed 01 July 2020.

22 The GIs Act, 1999, s 21.

23 Achim Spiller and Bernhard Tschofen, "Taste – Power – Tradition. Placing Geographical Indications on an Interdisciplinary Agenda" in Sarah May, Katia Laura Sidali, Achim Spiller and Bernhard Tschofen (eds), *Göttingen Studies in Cultural Property* (Vol. 10, Universitätsverlag Göttingen 2017) 4.

24 Daniele Giovannucci, Timothy E. Josling, William A. Kerr, Bernard O'Connor and May T. Yeung, *Guide to Geographical Indications: Linking Products and Their Origins* (International Trade Centre 2009) 3. <https://www.origin-gi.com/images/stories/PDFs/English/E-Library/geographical_indications.pdf> accessed 20 July 2020.

25 The GIs Act, 1999, s 2(1) f.

26 Currently there are 15 foreign GIs registered in India: Porto and Douro from Portugal; Champagne and Cognac from France; Napa Valley from USA; Peruvian Pisco from Peru; Scotch Whiskey from United Kingdom; Prosciutto di Parma, Parmigiano Reggiano, Prosecco and Asiago from Italy; Tequila from Mexico; Lamphun Brocade Thai Silk from Thailand and Irish Whiskey from Ireland. <https://www.ipindia.gov.in/writereaddata/Portal/Images/pdf/GI_Application_Register_10-09-2019.pdf> accessed 6 March 2021.

27 Export Import Bank of India, "Indian Handloom Industry: Potential and Prospects" (September 2018) Export Import Bank of India Working Paper No. 80, 9 <https://www.eximbankindia.in/Assets/Dynamic/PDF/Publication-Resources/ResearchPapers/102file.pdf> accessed 10 December 2020.

28 "Geographical Indications Journal No. 95" (*Geographical Indications Registry*, 1 September 2004) <http://ipindiaservices.gov.in/GIRPublic/Application/ViewDocument> accessed 1 March 2021.

29 Ibid.

30 Digital Empowerment Foundation, "Digital Cluster of People, Skills & Empowerment: Baseline Survey of Pochampally, Nalgonda District, Telangana" 5 <http://dcdpindia.org/wp-content/uploads/2017/09/Pochampally-Report_Ed.pdf#:~:text=Baseline%20Survey%20of%20Pochampally%2C%20Nalgonda%20District%2C%20Telangana%20The,Vinoba%20Bhave%20visited%20Pochampally%20mandal%20in%20Nalgonda%20district.> accessed 10 December 2020.

31 A motif is a single or repeated design or colour <https://www.merriam-webster.com/dictionary/motif> accessed 10 December 2020.

32 United Nations Educational, Scientific and Cultural Organization, "Iconic Saree Weaving Clusters of India" (Ref No. 5890 April 15, 2014) <https://whc.unesco.org/en/tentativelists/5890/> accessed 12 August 2020.

33 Subhajit Saha, "Non Agricultural GI's: A Strategic Issue" (International Conference on GI in The XXI Century at Bordeaux, organized by oriGIn & AREPO, 21 May 2013) <https://www.origin-gi.com/images/stories/PDFs/English/Event/International_Conference_Bordeaux/21-41_Saha_IG_non_agricoles_en_Inde.pdf> accessed 25 September 2020.

34 Fibre2Fashion, "The Fine Art of Pochampalli Weavers" (August 2015) [The National Bank for Agriculture and Rural Development (NABARD) supported Pochampalli ikat weavers and manufacturers to get protection for the Pochampalli art form. NABARD launched its cluster development programme in Pochampalli village under its National Programme for Rural Industrialization, in association with the Textiles Committee of the Central Government for the benefit of handloom silk weavers. Establishment of Pochampalli Handloom Park is an initiative in this direction] <https://www.fibre2fashion.com/industry-article/7610/the-fine-art-of-pochampalli-weavers> accessed 25 September 2020.

35 The GIs Rules, 2002 (n 20) r 20, sch 4.

36 "Application Details" (*Geographical Indications Registry*, 2021) <http://ipindiaservices.gov.in/GIRPublic/Application/Details/4> accessed 01 March 2020.

37 Ruppal Sharma and Shraddha Kulhari, "Marketing of GI Products: Unlocking Their Commercial Potential" (2015) WTO Research Study, Centre for WTO Studies 71 <https://wtocentre.iift.ac.in/Papers/Marketing%20of%20GI%20Products%20Unlocking%20their%20Commercial%20Potential.pdf > accessed 25 September 2020.

38 "Geographical Indications Journal No. 5, G.I. Application Number 12" (*Geographical Indications Registry*, 1 March 2005) <http://ipindiaservices.gov.in/GIRPublic/Application/ViewDocument> accessed 25 September 2020.

39 Ibid.
40 Ibid.
41 Ibid.
42 Ibid.
43 Ibid.
44 "Statement of Case for Kota Doria for Class 24 and 25 of the Fourth Schedule (Classification of Goods – Names of the Classes) of the Geographical Indications of Goods (Registration & Protection) Act, 1999" (*Geographical Indication Registry*, 22 July 2004), 9. <http://ipindiaservices.gov.in/GIRPublic/Application/ViewDocument> accessed 20 February 2021.
45 Ibid.
46 Ibid, 10.
47 Anutosh Biswas and Kritika Kapil, "Geographical Indications in India: A Case Study of Kota Doria" CUTS Centre for International Trade, Economics and Environment Briefing Paper, GRANITE II-1/2010, 1. <http://demo.net-commlabs.net/citee/pdf/Briefing_Paper10-Geographical_Indications_in_India-A_Case_Study_of_Kota_Doria.pdf > accessed 20 February 2021.
48 Ruchi Pant, "Protecting and Promoting Traditional Knowledge in India: What Role for Geographical Indications?" (2015) International Institute for Environment and Development Working Paper, 27. <https://pubs.iied.org/1657 6IIED/> accessed 10 December 2020.
49 Ibid.
50 "Details of Registered Authorised Users as on July 31, 2020" (*Geographical Indications Registry*, 2020) <https://ipindia.gov.in/writereaddata/Portal/Images/pdf/Registered_GI_Authorised_User_Details_-_Till_Dates.pdf> accessed 1 March 2020.
51 "Certificate of Registration, 2009" (*Geographical Indications Registry*, 2021) <http://ipindiaservices.gov.in/GIRPublic/Application/ViewDocument> accessed 1 March 2021.
52 "Our Story, Chanderiyaan" (Digital Empowerment Foundation, 2009) <https://dcdpindia.org/chanderiyaan/> accessed 20 December 2020.
53 Ibid.
54 Suresh C. Sharma, "Impact Assessment and Mid-Term Evaluation of the Handloom Cluster of Chanderi" (United Nations Industrial Development Organization, August–September 2005), 2 <https://ilrtindia.org/downloads/Chanderi-Report-Final_28.pdf> accessed 20 December 2020.
55 Lakhnoti is now in Bangladesh.
56 "Geographical Indications Journal No. 2, Application Number" (*Geographical Indications Registry,* 2004) <http://ipindiaservices.gov.in/GIRPublic/Application/ViewDocument> accessed 01 March 2021.
57 Ibid.
58 "Statement of Case for Chanderi Sari" (*Geographical Indications Registry*, 2 April 2004) at 2. <http://ipindiaservices.gov.in/GIRPublic/Application/ViewDocument> accessed 20 December 2020.
59 Ibid.
60 Suresh C. Sharma (n 53) 1.
61 Ibid, 2.
62 "Details of Registered Authorised Users as on July 31, 2020" (*Geographical Indications Registry*, 2020) <https://ipindia.gov.in/writereaddata/Portal/Images/pdf/Registered_GI_Authorised_User_Details_-_Till_Dates.pdf> accessed 1 March 2020.

63 Malini Nair, "Cloning the Chanderi" (*Times of India*, 21 June 2015). <https://timesofindia.indiatimes.com/home/sunday-times/deep-focus/Cloning-the-Chanderi/articleshow/47750085.cms> accessed 15 December 2020.

64 Khushboo Joshi, "Cash-Crunch Hit Weavers in MP Find it Tough to Run Households" (*Hindustan Times*, 14 December 2016) <https://www.hindustantimes.com/bhopal/cash-crunch-hit-weavers-in-mp-find-it-tough-to-run-households/story-dReamXZELtiit1WhzRUnpL.html> accessed 15 December 2020; Hemender Sharma, "Economic Slowdown: Madhya Pradesh Weavers Suffer due to Low Sale of Chanderi Sarees" (*India Today*, 31 August 2019) <https://www.indiatoday.in/india/story/economic-slowdown-madhya-pradesh-weavers-suffer-due-to-low-sale-of-chanderi-sarees-1593743-2019-08-31> accessed 15 December 2020; Mohit M. Rao, "MP Weavers Hanging by a Chanderi Thread" (*People's Archive of Rural India*, 7 May 2020) <https://ruralindiaonline.org/en/articles/mp-weavers-hanging-by-a-chanderi-thread/> accessed 15 December 2020.

65 "Functioning of Central Silk Board & Performance of Indian Silk Industry" (*Ministry of Textiles, Government of India*, 1 January 2018) at 23 <http://ministryoftextiles.gov.in/sites/default/files/note-on-sericulture2017-18-ThirdQtr.pdf> accessed 20 December 2020.

66 "Statement of Case for Mysore Silk" (*Geographical Indications Registry*, 22 July 2004) 1 <http://ipindiaservices.gov.in/GIRPublic/Application/ViewDocument> accessed 20 December 2020.

67 "Department of Sericulture" (*Mysuru District Website*) [Karnataka sericulture has a history of more than 215 years. In 1785, Tipu Sultan established sericulture in Channapatana. Since its inception, the Channapatana silk farm has been working on silk seed breeding and breeding experiments. The sericulture department is one of the oldest independent departments to be established during British rule in 1914] <https://mysore.nic.in/en/department-of-sericulture/> accessed 20 December 2020.

68 Ibid [The Management of Silk Weaving Factory was handed over to KSIC Ltd., Till date KSIC, a wholly owned undertaking of the Govt. of Karnataka, is managing the activities of the Silk Factory and is the rightful and only manufacturer of Mysore silk fabrics within the geographical area of Mysore].

69 "Geographical Indications Journal No. 3 for Application Number 11" (*Geographical Indications Registry*, 1 November 2004) <http://ipindiaservices.gov.in/GIRPublic/Application/ViewDocument> accessed 20 December 2020.

70 Ibid.

71 Ibid.

72 "Geographical Indications Journal No. 86 for Application Number 532" (*Geographical Indications Registry*, 30 June 2016) <https://ipindia.gov.in/writereaddata/Portal/IPOJournal/1_317_1/Journal_86.pdf> 20 December 2020.

73 Ibid.

74 Ibid.

75 "Geographical Indications Journal No. 3" (n 68) 9.

76 "Geographical Indications Journal No. 86" (n 71).

77 "Details of Registered Authorised Users as on July 31, 2020" (*Geographical Indications Registry*, 2020) <https://ipindia.gov.in/writereaddata/Portal/Images/pdf/Registered_GI_Authorised_User_Details_-_Till_Dates.pdf> accessed 1 March 2021.

78 "State Wise Registration Details of G.I. Applications" (*Geographical Indications Registry*) <https://www.ipindia.gov.in/writereaddata/Portal/Images/pdf/GI_Application_Register_10-09-2019.pdf> accessed 1 March 2021.

79 "Geographical Indications Journal No. 7, Application Number 19" (*Geographical Indications Registry*, 1 July 2005) <http://ipindiaservices.gov.in/GIRPublic/Application/ViewDocument> accessed 20 December 2020.
80 Ibid.
81 Ibid.
82 Ibid.
83 Ibid.
84 Ibid.
85 Ibid.
86 Ibid.
87 Ibid.
88 Ibid.
89 "Geographical Indications Journal No. 7, Application Number 19" (n 78).
90 "State-Wise Registration Details of G.I. Applications" (n 77).
91 "Certificate of Registration" (*Geographical Indications Registry*, 2021) <http://ipindiaservices.gov.in/GIRPublic/Application/ViewDocument> accessed 1 March 2021.
92 "Kullu Cluster: Synonym of Handwoven Shawl" (*Fibre2Fashion*, May 2011). <https://www.fibre2fashion.com/industry-article/5592/kullu-cluster-synonym-of-handwoven-shawl> accessed 25 December 2020.
93 Ibid.
94 Ibid.
95 Dipender Manta, "Weavers Finding it Hard to Deal with the Sale of Fake Kullu Shawls" (*The Tribune*, 1 December 2018) <https://www.tribuneindia.com/news/archive/himachaltribune/weavers-finding-it-hard-to-deal-with-sale-of-fake-kullu-shawls-691631> accessed 25 December 2020.
96 "Kullu Cluster: Synonym of Handwoven Shawl" (n 90).
97 "Application Details" (*Geographical Indications Registry*, 2021) <http://ipindiaservices.gov.in/GIRPublic/Application/Details/19> accessed 01 March 2021.
98 Anand Bodh, "Kullu Shawl, Made in Ludhiana" *Times of India* (Chandigarh, 15 February 2015) <https://timesofindia.indiatimes.com/city/chandigarh/kullu-shawl-made-in-ludhiana/articleshow/46248839.cms> accessed 25 December 2020.
99 "Geographical Indications Journal No. 4, Application Number 15" (*Geographical Indications Registry*, 1 January 2005) <http://ipindiaservices.gov.in/GIRPublic/Application/ViewDocument> accessed 10 October 2020.
100 Ibid.
101 Ibid.
102 Ibid.
103 "Statement of Case" (*Geographical Indications Registry*, 7 October 2004) <http://ipindiaservices.gov.in/GIRPublic/Application/ViewDocument> accessed 10 October 2020.
104 Ibid.
105 Ibid.
106 Ibid.
107 Ibid.
108 Ibid.
109 Ibid.
110 Ibid.
111 "State-Wise Registration Details of G.I. Applications" (n 77).
112 Mandeep Kaur, "An Overview of Kanjivaram Silk Sarees of Tamil Nadu" (2016) 29 (5) *Journal of Farm Sciences* 836–838 <http://14.139.155.167/test5/index.php/kjas/article/viewFile/8344/8595> accessed 14 October 2020.

113 Ibid.

114 "Details of Registered Authorised Users as on July 31, 2020" (*Geographical Indications Registry*, 2020) <https://ipindia.gov.in/writereaddata/Portal/Images/pdf/Registered_GI_Authorised_User_Details_-_Till_Dates.pdf> accessed 1 March 2021.

115 Roshni Muthukumar, "The Weavers of Kanchipuram: A Detailed Report about the Issues Faced by Weavers in Kanchipuram" (*National School of Journalism and Public Discourse*, 25 February 2020) <https://www.nsoj.in/stories/the-weavers-of-kanchipuram> accessed 14 October 2020.

116 Ibid.

117 Ibid.

118 Arti Kawlra, "Duplicating the Local: GI and the Politics of 'Place' in Kanchipuram" (2014) NMML Occasional Paper, *Perspectives in Indian Development*, New Series 29 <http://125.22.40.134:8080/jspui/bitstream/123456789/888/1/29_Aarti_Kawlra.pdf> accessed 10 October 2020; Aanchal Agarwal, "Geographical Indication – A Study of Kanchipuram Silk" (*Ex Gratia Law Journal*, 5 July 2020) <https://exgratialawjournal.in/journal/volume-1/vol1-issue1-aug2020/geographical-indication-a-study-of-kanchipuram-silk/> accessed 10 October 2020.

119 Arti Kawlra (n 116).

120 Ibid.

121 Ibid.

122 Ibid.

123 Ibid.

124 "Geographical Indications Journal No. 52, Application Number 384" (*Geographical Indications Registry*, 30 October 2013) <http://ipindiaservices.gov.in/GIRPublic/Application/ViewDocument> accessed 12 October 2020; Edward Gait, *A History of Assam* (1st edn., Thacker Spink & Co.) <http://ipindiaservices.gov.in/GIRPublic/Application/ViewDocument> accessed 12 October 2020.

125 Ibid.

126 Ibid.

127 Ibid.

128 Ibid.

129 Ibid.

130 Ibid.

131 Ibid.

132 Ibid.

133 Ibid.

134 Ibid.

135 "Application Details" (*Geographical Indications Registry*, 2020) <http://ipindiaservices.gov.in/GIRPublic/Application/Details/384>accessed 1 March 2021.

136 "Application Details" (*Geographical Indications Registry*, 2020) <http://ipindiaservices.gov.in/GIRPublic/Application/Details/55> accessed 1 March 2021.

137 Kiran George, "When the Tezpur University Came to GI Tagged Muga Silk of Assam's Rescue" (*SpicyIP*, 29 April 2015). <https://spicyip.com/2015/04/when-the-tezpur-university-came-to-gi-tagged-muga-silk-of-assams-rescue.html> accessed 12 October 2020.

138 Ibid.

139 Jupi Gogoi, "The Need to Look beyond Wines and Spirits: GI Law in India and the Woes of Muga Silk" (*SpicyIP*, 11 May 2019) <https://spicyip.com/2019/05/

the-need-to-look-beyond-wines-and-spirits-gi-law-in-india-and-the-woes-of-muga-silk.html> accessed 12 October 2020.

140 Ibid.

141 Ibid.

142 Nibedita Choudhury, "Socio-Economic Problems of Muga Silk Weavers of Sualkuchi Silk Industry" (2019) 8 (9) *International Journal of Scientific and Technology Research* <http://www.ijstr.org/final-print/sep2019/Socio-economic-Problems-Of-Muga-Silk-Weavers-Of-Sualkuchi-Silk-Industry.pdf> accessed 12 October 2020.

143 Ibid.

144 Ibid.

145 Ibid.

146 Ibid.

147 "Geographical Indications No. 29, Application Number 99" (*Geographical Indications Registry*, 19 March 2009) <http://ipindiaservices.gov.in/GIRPublic/Application/ViewDocument> accessed 10 October 2020.

148 Ibid.

149 Ibid. These are types of motifs woven for the finished product.

150 Ibid.

151 Ibid.

152 Ibid.

153 Ibid.

154 Servjaeta Verma and Nandita Mishra, "Recognition and Marketing Opportunities of a 'GI' Tag in Handloom Product: A Study of Banaras Brocades and Sarees" (2018) 23 *Journal of Intellectual Property Righ*ts 101–110. <http://nopr.niscair.res.in/bitstream/123456789/45333/1/JIPR%2023%282-3%29%20101-110.pdf> accessed 10 October 2020.

155 "Application Details" (*Geographical Indications Registry*, 2021) <http://ipindiaservices.gov.in/GIRPublic/Application/Details/99> accessed 01 March 2021.

156 "Geographical Indications Journal No. 49, Application Number 237" (*Geographical Indications Registry*, 30 November 2012) <http://ipindiaservices.gov.in/GIRPublic/Application/Details/237> accessed 1 March 2021.

157 Ibid.

158 Ibid.

159 Anupam Chakravartty, "Golden Thread of Misery" (*Down To Earth*, 15 November 2016) <https://www.downtoearth.org.in/news/economy/golden-thread-of-misery-56195> accessed 12 October 2020.

160 Planning Commission, Government of India, "Draft Consultation Paper on Handlooms" 2014, 19 <http://niti.gov.in/planningcommission.gov.in/docs/reports/genrep/drft_cosulpapr_1410.pdf> accessed 12 October 2020.

161 Ibid.

162 Ibid.

163 Ibid. Chapter 4 deals in detail with such programmatic interventions.

164 Ibid.

165 Ibid.

166 Ibid.

167 "Geographical Indications Journal No. 33, Application Number 150" (*Geographical Indications Registry*, 30 April 2010) <http://ipindiaservices.gov.in/GIRPublic/Application/ViewDocument> accessed 20 October 2020.

168 Ibid.

169 Ibid.

170 Ibid.

171 Ibid.
172 Ibid.
173 Ibid.
174 Ibid.
175 Ibid.
176 Ibid.
177 "Details of Registered Authorised Users as on July 31, 2020" (*Geographical Indications Registry*, 2020) <https://ipindia.gov.in/writereaddata/Portal/Images/pdf/Registered_GI_Authorised_User_Details_-_Till_Dates.pdf> accessed 01 March 2021.
178 Ruchita Belapurkar, "Paithani Saree: Woven Histories of Maharashtra" (*Sahapedia*, 16 July 2018) <https://www.sahapedia.org/paithani-saree-woven-histories-of-maharashtra> accessed 10 October 2020.
179 Ibid.
180 Ibid.
181 Ibid.
182 Ibid.
183 Ibid.
184 Yaseer Ahmad Mir and Mushtaq Ahmad Darzi, "Kashmir Pashmina – A Journey of Standardization through Geographical Indication" (2017) 3 (5) IJAR <https://www.allresearchjournal.com/archives/2017/vol3issue5/PartA/3-4-149-517.pdf> accessed 20 October 2020.
185 "Geographical Indications Journal No. 13, Application Number 46" (*Geographical Indications Registry*, 1 August 2006) <http://ipindiaservices.gov.in/GIRPublic/Application/ViewDocument> accessed 20 October 2020.
186 Ibid.
187 Yaseer Ahmad Mir and Mushtaq Ahmad Darzi (n 180).
188 Ibid.
189 Ibid.
190 "Geographical Indications Journal No. 13, Application Number 46" (n 181).
191 "Application Details" (*Geographical Indications Registry*, 2021) <http://ipindiaservices.gov.in/GIRPublic/Application/Details/46> accessed 1 March 2021.
192 Ibid.
193 Ibid.
194 Ibid.
195 "State-Wise Registration Details of G.I. Applications" (n 77).
196 Both *Kutch* and *Kachchh* refer to the same geographical region as well as the handloom investigated here and are used interchangeably. However, the we have made maximum use of the word *Kachchh* which is also the official title for the handloom which is granted GI registration.
197 "State-Wise Registration Details of G.I. Applications" (n 77).
198 "Geographical Indications Journal No. 50, Application Number 232" (*Geographical Indications Registry*, 7 May 2013) <http://ipindiaservices.gov.in/GIRPublic/Application/ViewDocument> accessed 26 December 2020.
199 M. V. Sindhu, "The Story of Patan Patola: A Fabric that Never Fades and One Family's Tryst with Keeping it Alive" (*Your Story*, 24 October 2016) <https://yourstory.com/2016/10/patan-patola-fabric> accessed 28 December 2021.
200 Alex Reynolds, "Patan Patola, the Cloth of Kings" (*Lost with Purpose*, 5 January 2021) <https://www.lostwithpurpose.com/patan-patola/> accessed 26 December 2021.
201 Ibid.
202 Ibid.
203 Ibid.

204 Ibid.
205 Alex Reynolds (n 196).
206 Ibid.
207 Ibid.
208 Ibid.
209 Ibid.
210 Praachi Raniwala, "What Makes the Gujarati Patola Sari a Priceless Heirloom?" (*Vogue India*, 22 March 2019) <https://www.vogue.in/content/gujarati-patola-sarees-history-significance-weaving-process> accessed 30 December 2020.
211 Ibid.
212 Ibid.
213 Ibid.
214 "Geographical Indications Journal No. 50, Application Number 232" (n 194).
215 Ibid.
216 Sindhu MV (n 195).
217 Ibid.
218 "Geographical Indications Journal No. 50, Application Number 232" (n 194).
219 Ibid.
220 "Application Details" (*Geographical Indications Registry*, 2021) <http://ipindiaservices.gov.in/GIRPublic/Application/Details/232> accessed 01 March 2021.
221 "Geographical Indications Journal No. 77, Application Number 380" (*Geographical Indications Registry*, 30 November 2015) <http://ipindiaservices.gov.in/GIRPublic/Application/ViewDocument> accessed 28 December 2020.
222 Ibid.
223 Ibid.
224 Ibid.
225 Ibid.
226 Ibid.
227 Ibid.
228 Ibid.
229 "Application Details" (*Geographical Indications Registry*, 2021) <http://ipindiaservices.gov.in/GIRPublic/Application/Details/380> accessed 28 December 2020.

3

EVALUATING THE SUCCESS OF GI STATUS

Tangaliya and Kutch shawls of Gujarat

3.1 Background for the investigative study

India is widely acknowledged as a textile-rich country. Its handlooms have carved out a special status since time immemorial. Each State in India boasts of communities working wonders through the art of weaving, which gradually became a part of their cultural heritage, passed on through the generations. Rooted in ancient times, the handlooms of India represent an ancient cottage industry, and handloom weaving constitutes one of the richest and most vibrant aspects of Indian cultural heritage. Historically, these roots stretch back to Vedic literature, where Indian weaving styles are mentioned. The first fragments of Indian handlooms were excavated from parts of Egypt, after which traces of finely woven and dyed cotton fabrics were found in the Mohenjo Daro (Indus Valley Civilization).[1] Archives from the travel accounts of Fa-hsien, Hiuan Tsang, Warthima, Bernier, Garriri, Tavernier, General Ormi and Marcopolo are proof of the times when India was also known as the "Land of the Golden Bird".[2] Among the many praises that these travellers heaped upon India, the handloom and handicraft culture found a special mention. Further, specific instances show that Indian handloom products were patronized by many in faraway lands of the East and West. Similar travel accounts of Herodotus of Greece and scholars like Megasthenes and Pliny speak extensively about Indian cloth.[3] It can be safely said that the handloom and handicraft sectors embody the rich traditional, historical and cultural diversity that distinguishes India from the rest of the world.[4]

The handloom weaving industry, besides offering full-time employment to many weavers, is also a subsidiary means of income for agriculturists. Mr. Arthur Blennerhassett, in his monograph on the cotton fabrics of the Central Provinces, has Stated that spinning is still practiced as a part-time activity among the well-to-do, or as a household duty.[5] A large number of people belonging to weavers' families are also employed either directly or indirectly. Further, at least an equally large number of citizens including yarn merchants, cloth wholesalers, retailers, cotton cultivators, loom

DOI: 10.4324/9781003002147-4

manufacturers, dyers, twisters, warpers, sizers etc., earn their livelihood from this industry.[6]

In modern times, the handloom sector is the second largest unorganized economic activity after agriculture, providing direct and indirect employment to more than 43 lakh weavers, [7] and constitutes an integral part of the Indian rural and semi-rural livelihood, thus contributing tremendously to the economy. The sector has sustained itself over the centuries by transferring skills from one generation to another. The strength of this sector lies in its uniqueness, flexibility of production, openness to innovations, adaptability to the supplier's requirements and the wealth of its tradition.

The handloom industry acts as a backbone for Indian culture and tradition with a large variety of designs, printing techniques, weaving art and materials used inter-generationally, which have gained popularity globally. Phulkari from Punjab, chanderi from Madhya Pradesh, ikats from Andhra Pradesh, tie and dye from Rajasthan and Gujarat, daccai from West Bengal, brocade from Banaras and jacquard from Uttar Pradesh are some of the jewels adorning the crown of our domestic heritage. Thus, the handloom industry is truly the torchbearer of Indian traditional heritage and a representative of its cultural brilliance.

To better appreciate the significance of the handloom industry's contribution towards a number of factors in the Indian economy, some important statistical figures are highlighted here:

i. Of the total textile production in India during 2016–2017, production through handlooms contributed 17.44%.[8]
ii. As per the Third Handloom Census carried out in 2009—2010, 43.3 lakhs workers were engaged in weaving and allied activities.[9]
iii. In the Sixth Economic Census, which collected data on handicraft and handloom establishments for the first time, the total number of handicraft and handloom establishments was 1.87 million.[10]
iv. In terms of export, 95% of the world's handwoven fabric comes from India.[11] The export of handloom items during 2018–2019 was ₹ 2392.39 crore and during the year 2019–2020 (up to October 2019) is ₹ 1405.41 crore.[12]

Looking at these figures, it is clear that handlooms have a mammoth share in employment, establishments, exports and economic growth of India. However, time and again, researchers across various disciplines have studied the health of the sector and emphasized the increasing intensity of problems plaguing the handloom industry. Taking cue from the existing literature, made up of research studies carried out in India and other similar nations that have enforced a systemic protection for Geographical Indications, we chose to investigate the efficacy of the domestic system.

3.2 Rationale for the investigative study

The position of India's handlooms is inversely proportional to the sector's annual contribution to the economy, and neither the pitiable position nor the contribution of the sector can be ignored. Indian handicrafts and handloom industries have flourished through the generations, thus marking out an important territory in terms of employability. However, in the years post 1970s, a decline in the magnanimity of this sector began with the penetration of cheaper yarns and power looms. The arrival of these modern tools and techniques strongly questioned the existence and usage of raw materials and simple handlooms. Ultimately, doubt was cast on the productivity and efficiency of handloom workers. However, in this tussle of traditional versus modern, the knowledge and skills of a huge sector dating back 500–700 years were largely disregarded. Employing more than 70% of people in the Indian textiles industry, i.e. around 4.4. million people and contributing 57% to the total cloth production, the present day powerloom industry is growing by leaps and bounds.[13] However, its existence is also a threat to the ingenuity involved in the craft of weaving due to the near-perfect imitations that are created on power looms.

An answer to this mass destruction of the second largest unorganized sector after agriculture is the Law on Geographical Indications (GIs), which has rigorously recognized, registered and protected these crafts across India. However, despite the availability of the characteristics of GI registration, which include collective monopoly, non-transferability, non-excludability, non-rivalry and perpetuity of rights as long as good place-quality link is maintained, key challenges are involved in the implementation of GIs in traditional livelihood sectors such as handloom weaving in India. One of the key challenges lies in the post-registration phase of its implementation. an objective of the GI system is to keep all stakeholders cohesive by way of creating a long-term beneficial system rather than eyeing immediate and temporary commercial gains through registration. In light of a remarkable and consistent rise in the number of applications filed by various States for GI registration, inquiry into the tangible benefits of such registration becomes essential. Such inquiry can be undertaken through investigative field study. Though 74 handloom products have been granted a GI tag to date,[14] not many studies have been undertaken to probe into the parameters of its success. It is essential to study whether the registration actually provided the benefits that it envisaged. The success of GI registration, as mentioned earlier, largely depends on its effective implementation. Has the enforcement of the right taken place to the extent it should have? In the absence of effective enforcement, the efforts in registering the handloom product turn out to be futile and the right under the GI Act remains only on paper. In the previous chapter, we examined the GI registration procedure and highlighted a few debatable issues such as complexities in the registration process, the status of authorized users, the lack of functional inspection bodies, etc., through 10 case studies of handloom products. In this chapter, an attempt is made to examine the impact of GI registration as evidenced from the investigative study we conducted on two handloom products from Gujarat during the period from November 2017 to October 2018. Gujarat is immensely vibrant and has a unique forte in handloom products and handicrafts, which is truly reflected in the lifestyle, culture and spirit of the State, especially the Kutch-Saurashtra region. These are accorded unique recognition and protection through registration under the domestically adopted *sui generis* GI law. It is expected that GI registration ensures an enhanced level of safeguarding of traditional and cultural ethos from piracy and must also open up a wider, international market for the artisan communities.

The we' interest in the status of Tangaliya shawls was especially heightened with a chance glance at a newspaper article about a visit by the then Union Textiles Minister Smriti Irani to Surendranagar.[15] There, upon listening to the grievances of Tangaliya weavers, Minister Irani announced government support for purchasing looms and other redemptive measures.[16] Further, a literature survey presented insights into the art, history, near-extinction and revival of the Tangaliya handloom industry. Taking inspiration from the sensational life-cycle of Tangaliya weaving art, we expanded our research into Kutch shawls while trying to determine how the market standing of both shawls was affected by their GI tags. Interesting doctrinal results came to surface which gave a base for further inquiry in the form of an empirical study. Meanwhile, a short write-up (abstract) from the preliminary doctrinal observations was submitted for the 3rd Work-In-Progress Conference "IP Scholars Asia",[17] which made it to the presentation phase. This selection acted as a thrust to initiate a pilot study and conduct a final study later on in order to collect, analyze and bring to a global platform a comprehensive study of Tangaliya and Kutch shawl weavers from the point of view of Indian GI law and policy initiatives.

Further, for the purpose of conducting this investigative study probing the efficacy of GI registration, as mentioned in Chapter 2, it was considered essential that the registered product must have completed one cycle, i.e. 10 years of protection. In light of this, Tangaliya shawls and Kachchh shawls were the only two products that had completed the first term of protection.

Two districts in the Kutch-Saurashtra region of Gujarat specialize in weaving shawls, which go by the names "Tangaliya shawls" and "Kachchh shawls". The weaving of Tangaliya shawls has its origination in the Surendranagar district, and its history goes back about 700 years. The weaving was carried out in 26 villages by a particular community, Dangasia, a shepherd community. It was this community that evolved the exquisite art of Tangaliya weaving. Tangaliya was woven using yarns made from the wool of the sheep. The Tangaliya product that evolved was a rough product, but the unique "Dana" work created to pattern the shawl is not reported to be practiced anywhere else in the world.[18] The "Danas" created this special product and it continues to represent the identity of the Tangaliya. Originating in Kutch district, meanwhile, is a traditional shawl largely woven with *Kutchi* motifs in villages of this region. These woollen hand-woven shawls have long represented the cultural identity of different communities at Kutch. The art of weaving shawls woven with motifs has been passed down through generations of artisan communities. They were originally made from local wool. The intricate woven patterns and compact weaving are the USP (unique selling point) of these shawls.

The Tangaliya and Kachchh shawls are exquisite examples of the handloom legacy that is handed down from one generation to another across India; their exemplary designs and unique weaving techniques are practiced by and known only to weavers hailing from the geographical areas where these crafts originated. Such characteristics, along with a rich history of belongingness to a specific place that can be traced back hundreds of years, made Tangaliya and Kachchh shawls worthy of GI recognition. After crucial interventions from the National Institute of Fashion Technology (NIFT), Gandhinagar,[19] Tangaliya Shawls was registered in the proprietary name Tangaliya Hastkala Association in 2009 under Classes 24, 25 and 27.[20] The Kachchh shawls' handloom was registered as a GI under the proprietary name Kutch Weavers Association in the year 2011 under Class 24.[21] On behalf of the association, this application was filed by KHAMIR, an organization working towards the development of creative industries in the Kachcch area.[22] Both handlooms have completed one cycle of registration and were sent renewal notices as per the GI Registry official digital record.[23] Upon completion of the first registration period, the Kutch Weavers Association made a renewal application, against which the Kutch Shawls GI registration has been renewed until 2029.[24] However, an alarming fact in the case of the Tangaliya Shawls can be seen in the digital record of the GI Registry, wherein upon issuance of the renewal notice, there has been no action from the weavers' association, due to which the period of GI registration for the handloom is shown as valid only up to 2018.[25]

Despite their Geographical Indications status for a decade and a half, these handlooms lack the desired strength. With the present law on GI and welfare schemes in place, doubts arise as to why the legal right coupled with the sectoral initiatives have not brought the anticipated recognition and growth for the handlooms. The investigative study undertaken here, which also forms the central part of this work, attempts to understand the status of these handlooms post GI registration and to scrutinize the adequacy of government support through schemes introduced to bring a sustainable extension to these crafts.

3.3 Historical evolution of Tangaliya Shawls and Kachchh Shawls

As discussed in the earlier chapter, GI protection is granted to those products which have unique characteristics attributable to their geographical origin, which is an essential part of their historical evolution. Thus, we found it necessary to discuss the histories along with the unique characteristics of both the handlooms in order to better appreciate their eligibility for Geographical Indications.

3.3.1 Tangaliya Shawls

A 700-year-old handloom art under the name Tangaliya is prevalent in the villages of the district of Surendranagar in the Saurashtra region of Gujarat. The district is divided into ten talukas, namely Wadhwan, Chotila, Dhrangadhra, Dasada, Limbdi, Halvad, Sayla, Muli, Chuda and Lakhtar.[26] As per the application made for registering the handloom under Geographical Indications, Tangaliya art is present in eight talukas out of ten in the district.[27]

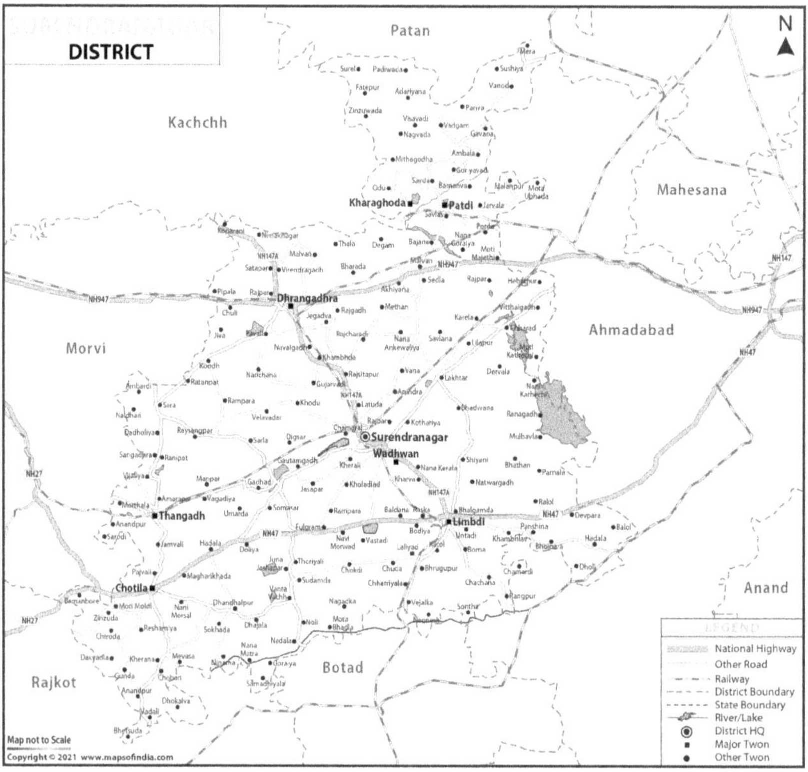

Map 3.1 Geographical territory of Surendranagar District. Source: https://www.mapsofindia.com/maps/gujarat/districts/surendranagar.htm. Used with permission of Mapping Digiworld Pvt. Ltd. *Note:* The international boundaries, coastlines, denominations and other information shown in any map in this work do not necessarily imply any judgement concerning the legal status of any territory or the endorsement or acceptance of such information. For current boundaries, readers may refer to the Survey of India maps

History

The distinctiveness of the Tangaliya art form is in its dotted designs that are given various shapes, for example, temples, birds and geometrical shapes, as well as a combination of these designs. This 700-year-old art was born as a response to necessities created by the climatic, social and cultural conditions.[28] The origination of Tangaliya art dates back to early settlement life in the Saurashtra region; however, among the locals, there are two stories attached to the origination of the art.

The popular version of the story says that a young boy from the *Bharwad* (shepherd) community fell in love and married a girl from the weaver community; however, the couple was ostracized from both communities.[29] Further, the couple's offspring formed a separate community named *Dangasia* and started residing with other weavers, and they started weaving with raw material from sheep.[30] This mixture of talents – the sheep keeping practice of the *Bharwad* community and weaving skills from weavers – gave birth to a unique art form named Tangaliya. Another version of the story says that the young boy from the *Bharwad* community who got married to the girl from weaver's community had a tough time earning a livelihood after being ostracized from his community; seeing this, the parents were saddened and made him an offer whereby the boy was Provided with wool and grain, and in turn he had to weave shawls and other garments for the *Bharwad* community.[31] The shawl weaving was taken to another level by introducing thread beads, thus developing *Daana* weaving, from which the Tangaliya art was born.

The *Dangasia* community inhabiting this region is the sole group that has knowledge of the Tangaliya weaving technique. The art has proliferated into different communities as well, where women of the *Bharwad* community are also seen wearing dotted wraparound skirts in black with contrasting embellishments created by woven dotted forms; these are known as Tangaliya, a name derived from the *tang* or leg.

After a thorough study of the area and craft prevalent therein, a total of 498 families were enlisted as practicing the craft in the application No. 127, and the registration of Tangaliya shawls was done under Class 24 (textile and textile goods), 25 (clothing, including shawls, sarees and stoles, including rumals) and 27 (home furnishings, rugs and mats).[32]

Tangaliya – a touch of distinctiveness

The uniqueness of Tangaliya lies in its *daana* work. Motifs made by arranging the *daanas* have a very geometric and graphic texture.[33] The selection of the motifs has been largely based upon the daily practices and natural surroundings of the craftsmen. Cited in Ms. Devanshi Mehta's extensive work on Tangaliya craft, traditionally the basic motif of Tangaliya is *Laadwa*, termed after the popular Indian sweet in the shape of a circle; apart from the *Laadwa*, motifs of peacocks, temples, trees and aeroplanes as well as geometric forms like circles, squares and triangles were traditional basic motifs used for Tangaliya.[34] Other motifs like *phandi*, *pag* (feet of the peacock), *aambo* (mango tree), *bajariya ni jaadavi*, *chakalo*, *karoliyo*, *piyali zhaad*, *kangasi zhaad*, *navdhari zhaad*, *sitamadhi*, tower, *mor zhaad*, *haveli* etc. are made by combining these basic elements.

The different types of Tangaliya designs are Ramraj, Dhunslu, Charmalia and Lobadi.

Ramraj: This type of Tangaliya has heavy *daana* work, and bright colours like vermillion, fuchsia and green are used along with white; the base fabric is black over which horizontal running lines in maroon wool are embroidered throughout the garment, and the borders are hemmed with woven zari.[35]

Dhunslu: This involves less *daana* work and is made using two colours – white and maroon. It is worn by older women.[36]

Charmalia: Charmalia has maroon and black warp and black weft which gives an alternate effect, with the *daanas* being mainly made white in colour and including some maroon.[37]

Lobadi: This is a long woollen shawl with simple *daana* work, which serves to cover a woman's head and veil her face; lobadi is generally made in off-white wool which is later dyed red to convey religious significance.[38]

Over the years, the *Dangasia* community have experimented with many different types of yarn, ranging from wool to cotton to acrylic.[39] Cotton, silk and acrylic yarns are the most important raw materials used to make contemporary *daana* woven garments.[40] What yarn or combination of yarns are used depends upon the orders and market requirements.

Presently, the scenario has undergone a tremendous albeit negative transformation whereby fewer families and individuals are weaving by handloom in a fewer number of villages, thus reducing the scope of the handloom in various talukas as identified before. A large portion of weavers who have walked away from handloom weaving now work on farms or construction sites.

Revival of Tangaliya

Traditionally, daana weaving was used only to weave garments like the *tangalia*, *galmehndi*, *dhabalo*, *dhunslu* and *charmalia* for the *Bharwad* community. With modernization and the availability of less expensive printed textiles in the market, the *Bharwad* slowly stopped wearing *tangalia*. The *Dangasia* weavers started losing their only clientele. Seeing this, organizations like SAATH[41] and design colleges like NIFT[42] collaborated and conducted design workshops for weavers. The outcome was a product range in cotton, silk and acrylic which was suitable for the contemporary market. The main challenge in coming up with new products is value addition. The product should complement the composition of dots, bring out the texture of the plain weaved fabric and raised dots and produce a design on both sides of the fabric. Only if a product demonstrates these three qualities of the *Daana* weave is it a successful product.

3.3.2 *Kutch*

Kutch is an erstwhile princely State of India and presently the largest district in the State of Gujarat. It is divided into five distinct regions and ten talukas, namely Bhuj, Anjar, Mandvi, Mundra, Abdasa-Nalia, Lakhpat, Rapar, Bhachau-Nakhtrana and Gandhidham.[43] After an extensive study made by Ahmedabad Textile Industry's Research Association (ATIRA), it was found that the weaving community is spread across the ten talukas of the district, and for the registration of this craft as a Geographical Indication (GI), Application No. 174 was filed in the name of the organization KHAMIR under Class 24 (Textile and Textile Goods).[44] As per the GI application made for Kutch Dhabda, Shawl and Stole, there were a total of 1,200 weavers working in 210 villages, out of which 800–900 weavers practiced the craft full-time.[45]

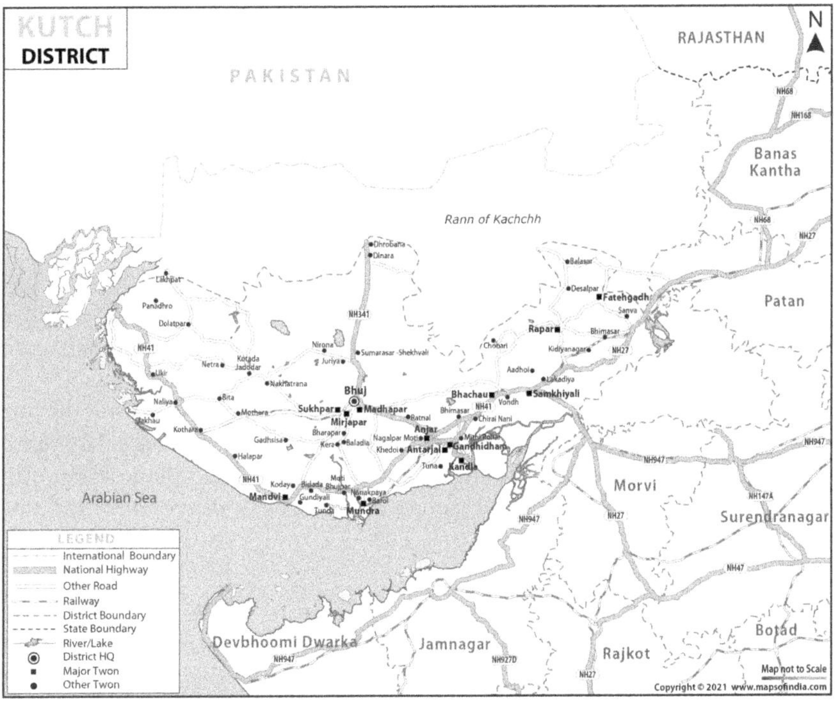

Map 3.2 Geographical territory of Kutch. Source: https://www.mapsofindia.com/maps/gujarat/districts/kachchh.htm. Used with permission of Mapping Digiworld Pvt. Ltd

History

Kutch craft has a history dating back 500 years, its weavers identifying themselves as having originated from Rajasthan.[46] Stories of this craft relate to the migration of the weaving community from Rajasthan to Gujarat; again, there are two stories that lay claim to the craft. One story goes that when a girl from a very rich *Rabari* family was given in marriage and came to Kutch, a weaver was included as part of her dowry so that he could weave the clothes that she would need.[47] This family of weavers gradually grew into a larger community and spread to different settlements in Kutch.

According to a second story, Shri Ramdev Peer[48] came to Narayan Sarovar in Kutch on a pilgrimage from Rajasthan. At the time some followers, who were goldsmiths of Faradi in Mandvi, built a temple for him and requested him to bring his kin from Marwar in Rajasthan for the upkeep of the temple.[49] With this, the Meghwal community from Marwar began settling in Kutch; the community was further divided into four sub-castes – Maheshwari, Marwada, Chaaran and Gurjara – out of which the Maheshwari and Marwari sub-castes practiced weaving and leather work.[50] This is how the Meghwal community from Rajasthan migrated to Kutch, bringing with them the art of handloom weaving. Traditionally, weavers used hand-spun yarn provided by *Rabaris*, a nomadic community of sheep and goat herders.[51]

When looking at the craft of weaving that originated and developed in Kutch, the climatic conditions of the area must be considered. Kutch is virtually an island, bounded by the Arabian Sea to the west, the Gulf of Kutch to the south and southeast and the Great Rann (Desert) of Kutch to the north and northeast, out of which the Great Rann of Kutch makes up the majority of the district. Due to the extreme conditions in the desert, weaving by the local communities majorly included woollen products like dhabda (blankets), shawls and the likes, but the craft has developed into many more products, using raw materials apart from wool and also a combination of materials as and when required.

Kutch weaving is unique in the sense that distinct traditional motifs and bright colours are used to weave medium to heavy-weight textiles. However, the value of the Kutch handloom is not merely in the aesthetic appeal; its value is created by the hands of skilled artisans who weave their tradition and way of life into each piece.

Kutch – A colourful legacy

The rich and diverse creative traditions of Kutch live at the intersection of cultures and communities.[52] Handloom products woven under the Kutchi style are different from a straight weave. In a weaver's language, the highlight of this handloom work is an extra weft, woven using a technique typical of this place.[53]

The usage of raw material for weaving has undergone tremendous change. Earlier, raw wool from white sheep was hand spun and wound onto bobbins, and this was used to weave the warp and weft portions, while black wool was obtained from black sheep; however as they were found in limited numbers, the use of such wool was restricted to forming the border designs. Thereafter, natural dyes were used in shades like black, red, green and indigo. In 1976, a weaver on a trip to Pragati Maidan for an exhibition noticed that some shawls in the exhibit were woven from acrylic. On inquiring further, he was informed that acrylic yarn is cheap, involves less labour and had more colour options to choose from; thus, acrylic yarn was introduced in Kutch in 1980–1981 and has been widely used since.[54]

There are various specialties and sub-specialties of Kutch craft such as blankets, shawls and stoles, among many others.

Dhabda (Kutch blanket)

A dhabda is a traditional Kutchi blanket made from hand-woven local wool, and it is a regional specialty. The people of the Rabari and Meghwal communities wear these blankets during the harsh winter months in the desert. On the dhabdas, traditional motifs and designs that were brought to Kutch by weaving communities upon their migration are used. These traditional patterns are intricate and complex, and each dhabda is woven in two narrow pieces and later hand stitched together. While weaving continues to be a predominantly male craft, women are responsible for hand stitching. This traditional blanket was recognized on a national platform in 1974 when Shri Vishram Valji Vankar, a weaver from Bhujodi, received a national award as "Best Craftsman of the Year".[55] An evidently proud son of the award winner, Shamji Vishram, fondly recalls recognition earned by his father after which blankets from Kutch travelled places.[56]

Apart from blankets, Kutch is well-known for its colourful shawls woven with motifs which have been passed down through generations of artisan communities. They were originally made from local desi wools and were traditionally worn as veils. Artisans continue to design and produce shawls for the local market as their shawls are widely worn throughout Kutch in the winter months. As in the case of dhabdas, artisans introduced a variety of yarns including cottons, wools and acrylics to the craft in order to make it sustainable and marketable. These shawls are widely worn throughout Kutch in the winter months.

3.4 Investigative study on efficacy of GI registration of Tangaliya and Kutch Shawls

The chapter now looks into the extensive survey undertaken in Surendranagar and Kutch districts in two phases. From the preamble of the GI Act, we took away key functions of Geographical Indication, in that it is not limited to recognition of goods originating from a specific geographical area with characteristics that can be traced to the area but also must provide post-registration protection leading to commercial benefits. These post-registration protective measures are mainly policy initiatives from both the Central and State authorities concerned, with the help of which a wholesome safeguarding of handlooms can be expected. However, these measures can be implemented in the true sense only when the producers and weavers are aware of their legal rights. Thus, without empirical evidence of the situation on the ground, mere discussion and debate on the significance of GI remain a futile academic exercise. What is required is data that can lead to meaningful and feasible policy recommendations. Hence, the present study is conducted not only to make a mere addition to the existing knowledge bank on GI but also to significantly contribute towards adequate policy framing by way of answering the following questions.

- What are the reasons behind insufficient realization of the legal rights granted under the GI Act to these handlooms?
- What is the level of awareness among Tangaliya shawl and Kutch shawl weavers/producers about GI registration and the rights granted under the Act?
- What is the status of governmental support in terms of mobilizing local human resources to take up handicrafts on professional lines for self-employment for adequate enforcement of GI?
- What would be an appropriate set of recommendations that the existing system of Geographical Indications in India could adopt in order to bridge the gap between the legal right and the actual right?

In order to answer these questions, a two-phase structured investigative study, i.e., a preliminary stage and a final stage, was conducted in the districts of respective crafts.

3.4.1 Preliminary phase: Pilot study

Ample stories of various crafts facing problems of ineffective GI implementation exist, out of which two were located in the State of Gujarat, namely Tangaliya Shawls in the district of Surendranagar and Kutch shawls in the district of Kutch. After an initial study on the crafts and their geographical presence, it was found in both districts that handloom weaving is concentrated in specific centres: Dedadara village from Wadhwan Taluka in Surendranagar and Bhujodi from Bhuj Taluka in Kutch. Thereafter, a plan for conducting a pilot study at these villages was framed. The study was conducted with help of a questionnaire. The questionnaire aimed at assessing knowledge and awareness of weavers about their rights under the Geographical Indications Act, 1999 and understanding the present condition of both handlooms. At this level, through a simple random sampling, 50 weavers from two villages were surveyed, out of which all responses were complete and fit for further usage and analysis.

Findings of pilot study

From the pilot study, the following findings were derived:

A considerable lack of awareness was identified among Tangaliya as well as Kutch weavers regarding GI protection granted to their craft due to which there was no knowledge about the legal right and related benefits. Further, there was similar lack of awareness on the part of weavers of their participation in the association/collective that has been granted the GI certification. Due to lack of awareness *prima facie* it was observed that the producers haven't been able to develop premium market for themselves.

Further, it was observed that the Tangaliya weavers were uninformed about the government schemes for marketing, distribution and promotion for handlooms. The focus of awareness campaigns run through Cluster Development Schemes is to get GI registration for various handicrafts and handlooms, which is considered to be a conclusion while the post-registration regulatory and promotion mechanism is not in place. Extensive gaps were located in operationalizing of GIs. The data suggests that GI registration has not benefitted Tangaliya and Kachchh handlooms due to a lack of awareness on part of the weavers regarding the benefits of GI registration as well as government schemes. Kutch handloom products are more popular than Tangaliya. However, the data indicates that the popularity is not due to GI registration but is on account of the region's development as a tourist spot over the past decade.

3.4.2 Final phase

Based on the findings from the pilot survey, an extensive final phase survey in the districts of Surendranagar and Kutch was conducted. In this phase, as shown through Table 3.1, coverage of the survey in terms of Talukas and weavers was broadened. For this phase, responses were collected via a questionnaire from ten villages of six talukas in the district of Surendranagar and from twenty villages of six talukas in the district of Kutch. Three hundred questionnaires were distributed among the weavers of both the districts, and 289 responses, were received out of which 254 responses were duly filled. From these responses, 80 were from Surendranagar and 174 were from Kutch.

Table 3.1 Details of data collection from Kutch and Surendranagar districts

District	*Talukas/blocks*	*Villages/clusters*	*Total responses*
Kutch	Bhuj	Chunadi – 12 Nagor – 1 Jambudi – 2 Sarli – 45 Mota Varnora – 35	95
	Mandvi	Don – 1 Bidada – 1 Godhra – 9 Faradi – 10 Gangon – 17	28
	Nakhatrana	Ramdevnagar – 11 Sangnara – 5 Devpar – 1	17
	Bhachau	Adhoi – 17	17
	Abdasa	Varadiya – 2 Naredi – 5 Ningal – 2	9
	Anjar	Bhimasar – 2 Khambhra – 3 Mathak – 3	8
			Responses: 174
Surendranagar	Dasada	Kanthada – 2 Bajana – 8 Dervala – 23	33
	Sayla	Sudamda – 15	15
	Limbdi	Jobala – 9	9
	Muli	Liya – 4	9
		Godavari – 5	
	Wadhwan	Wadhwan – 5	
		Vastadi – 2	7
	Lakhtar	Devaliya – 7	7
			Responses – 80
Total districts – 2	**Total talukas – 11**	**Total villages – 30**	**Total responses – 254**

Source: Authors' field survey

The questionnaire was prepared in line of the research objectives of the study, which aimed at the following:

i. To assess weavers' awareness about the GI status and knowledge about their rights under GI certification;
ii. To understand weavers' awareness about promotional schemes devised by the government and their readiness to avail of the benefits of such schemes;
iii. To comprehend weavers' willingness to continue with the profession and adopt the latest marketing and promotion methods;
iv. To evaluate the role of the association through which the handlooms have been granted GI protection, of which the weavers are a part;
v. To appraise the current status of handlooms;
vi. To examine the common needs and grievances of weavers.

3.4.3 Data analysis of investigative study

The data collected from the investigative study is analyzed to answer the research questions. The empirical result is presented graphically along with a detailed description.

Question 1

What are the reasons behind insufficient realization of the legal rights granted under the GI Act to these handlooms?

It is widely understood that the aim of the formulation of a *sui generis* GI law is twofold: to recognize products the characteristics of which are traceable to a specific geographical origin and to bring benefits, as a result of the registration, to the primary right-holder. Thus, the law is not limited to mere registration of products that can be linked with a geographical area but also extends to post-recognition protection. This is distinctly reflected in the preamble to the GI Act. However, in probing the situation on ground for the selected handlooms recognized as GIs, We learnt that the law does not yield the envisaged benefits and rather lacks the strength of protective enforcement. It is pertinent to note that the noble objectives of the law in question must be coupled with a variety of policy solutions in order to achieve a holistic support to the homegrown products. From the collected data, we noted the following causes behind insufficient realization of the legal rights granted under the GI Act to these handlooms.

1. Weavers face difficulty in marketing and selling their products despite GI registration.
2. The GI tag could not generate a sufficient market, leading to difficulty in creating demand and sale for such genuine products.
3. Owing to various challenges, weavers are leaving the craft to work as full-time labourers on farms or construction sites.
4. Young members of weaving families are reluctant to continue weaving despite GI registration.
5. Weavers were not part of the National Handloom Census carried out in 2009–2010.

6. Weavers invest a considerable amount of time and energy in weaving one genuine shawl in contrast to a powerloom shawl, but this goes unnoticed due to a lack of general awareness about the value of GI products.
7. There exists a noticeable disconnect between weavers and the associations/organizations/NGOs responsible for acquiring the GI registration of the selected handlooms.

1. **Weavers face difficulty in marketing and selling their products.**

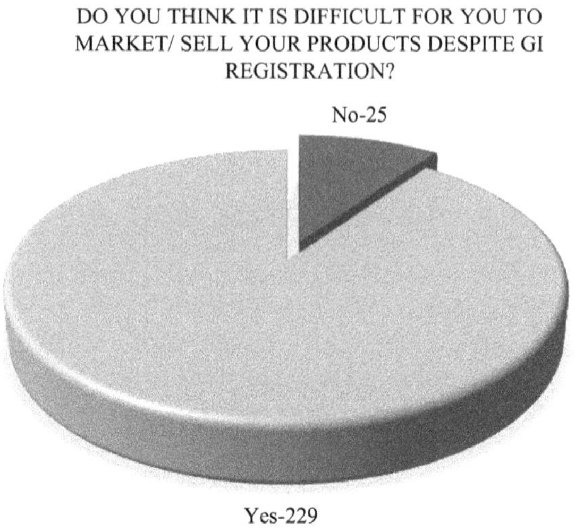

Figure 3.1 Marketing and selling of product. Source: All figures are by the authors unless otherwise specified.

Empirical result: To the question of whether weavers face difficulty in selling and marketing the product despite the GI registration, 254 responses were received. While 229 weavers answered this question, affirmatively confirming the difficulty, 25 weavers conveyed that they are able to market and sell their products. The second reason mentioned below for the poor protection of GI post registration also serves as one of the most equated reasons for the difficulty in marketing and selling the products.

2. **The GI tag could not generate a sufficient market, leading to difficulty in creating demand for and selling such genuine products.**

Empirical result: In order to know whether the grant of a GI tag has brought about a positive change in the conventional methods of selling and marketing these products, the research team framed a question on awareness among

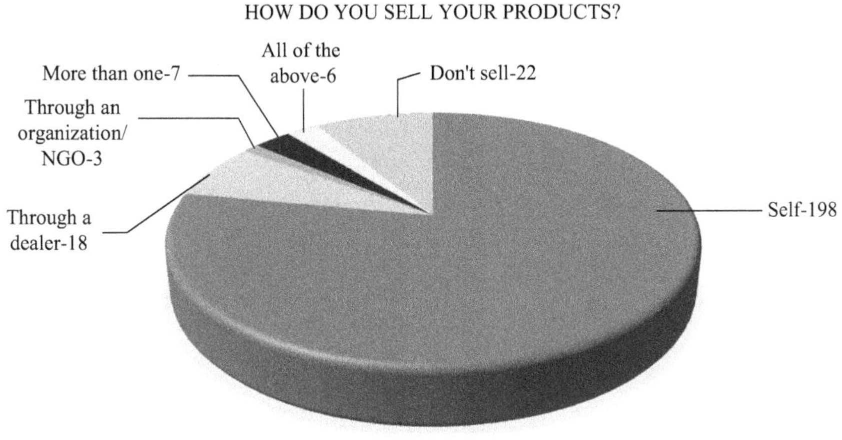

Figure 3.2 Methods of sales

weavers regarding other platforms available for sales such as e-commerce. Data revealed that there are conventional methods such as self-selling, sale through a dealer or through an NGO which are generally used by the weavers. Out of 254 responses, 198 use the self-selling method, 18 attempt to sell their handloom products through a dealer, and 3 sell work through an NGO. Seven weavers attempt selling through more than one such method, while six use all these methods. Interestingly, there are 22 weavers who do not sell these products at all as they work for a master weaver on a contractual basis. It is evident from the data that the awareness about the modern e-commerce platform for sale has not reached the weavers, which adds to their dependence on the conventional methods of sale and marketing.

3. **Owing to various challenges, weavers are leaving the craft to work as full-time labourers on farms or construction sites.**

Empirical result: During the investigative study, a disturbing reality concerning weavers not continuing with full-time weaving was brought to light. Investigating this reality, it was learnt that the weavers are faced with multiple challenges that in turn lead them to explore other sources of income. Due to a lack of market opportunities, weavers are left with unsold products, which consequently creates difficulty in generating capital that can be employed for future weaving. Lack of awareness about GI registration as well as capital-intensive schemes offered by the government further contribute to their decision to look beyond the inter-generational profession of weaving, which to date has been their primary source of income. The data is indicative that weavers are leaving the craft to work as full-time labourers on farms or construction sites etc. According to the responses received from

Figure 3.3 Weavers' preference to continue with their occupation

254 weavers, 239 are involved in part-time weaving and only 15 are carrying on full-time weaving.

4. **Young members of the family are reluctant to continue weaving.**

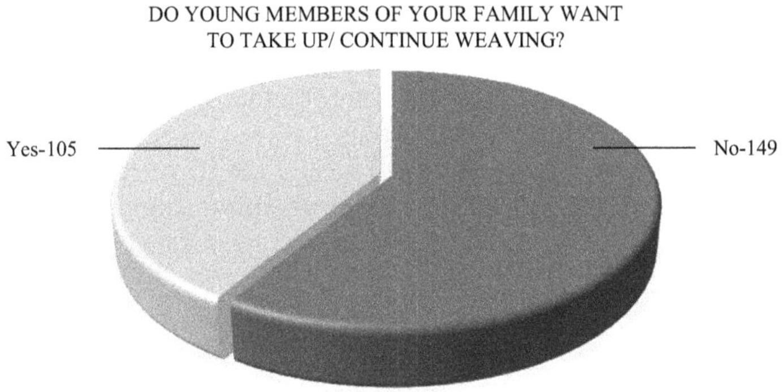

Figure 3.4 Preference of young weavers

Empirical result: Out of 254 responses, 149 agreed concerning the unwillingness of young family members to continue weaving, while 105 responded positively about the willingness of young weavers to continue. Although more middle-aged weavers display reluctance to continue to weave, the same cannot be said about young weavers. The data for young weavers suggests some positivity and the glass can be seen as half-full. If attempts are made at reviving interest in weaving among young members, this sector will be positively benefitted.

5. **Fewer weavers were part of the Third National Handloom Census conducted in 2009–2010.**

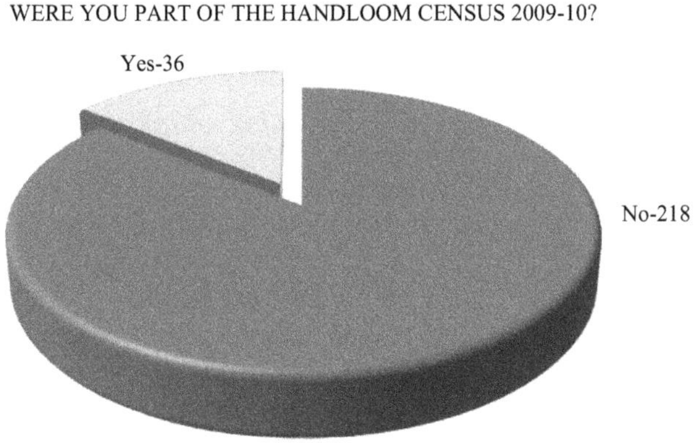

Figure 3.5 Participation in Handloom Census (2009–2010)

Empirical result: A question on weavers' participation in the National Handloom Census – India's unique initiative to collect data on the number of people employed within the handloom sector across all States – was considered an essential inclusion in this study. During the period of this study, the Third Handloom Census of 2009–2010 was the relevant document. Out of 254 responses, 36 weavers agreed to submit their details for the census while 218 weavers responded in the negative.

6. **Weavers invest a considerable amount of time and energy in weaving one genuine shawl, as opposed to a powerloom shawl, which goes unnoticed due to lack of general awareness about the value of GI products.**

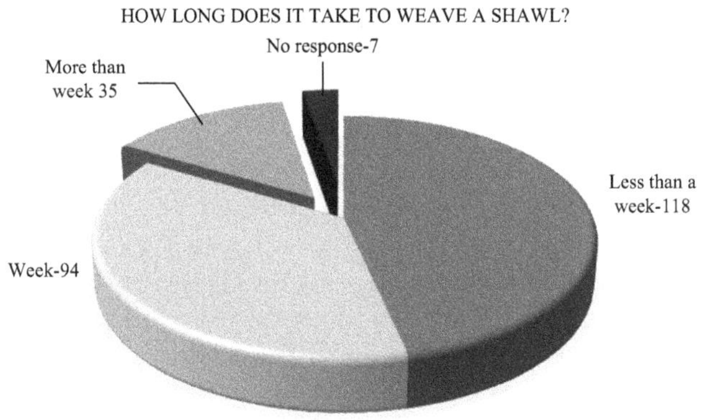

Figure 3.6 Weaving duration for one shawl

Empirical result: Weaving is a lengthy and tedious process carried out from start to finish by skilled weavers, contrary to the product made mechanically on a powerloom. Naturally, the time taken in bringing the finished product to life is more than is involved in creating the same product on a powerloom; however, uniqueness of the skills and techniques involved give the selected handloom products an edge over powerloom goods. These factors of time investment and skills involved result in a high labour cost, which is then reflected in the final price for the product. However, when the two products – handloom and powerloom or machine-made – reach the market, customers tend to appreciate a cheaper price more than better quality, leading to disparity in the market for these different products. So, during the study, the data collected reveals a mixed result, where the majority (46%) of weavers take less than a week to weave one shawl, while 37% take a week to prepare a finished product. This aspect was studied to establish how a lengthy weaving process involving hard work on the part of the weavers goes unnoticed due to a lack of general awareness about the value of GI products.

7. **There exists a noticeable disconnect between weavers and the associations/ organizations/NGOs responsible for acquiring GI registration for the selected handlooms.**

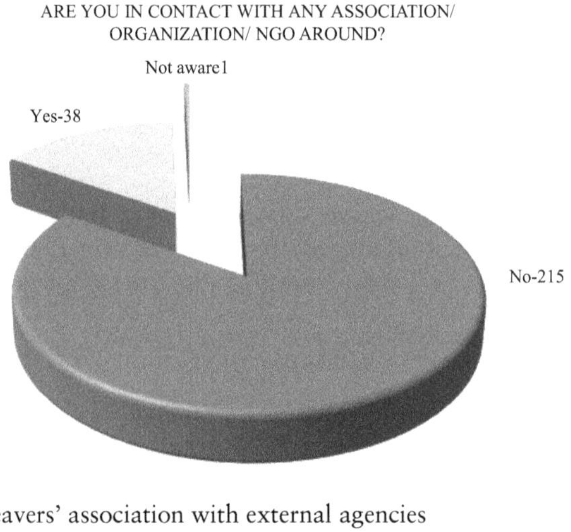

Figure 3.7 Weavers' association with external agencies

Empirical result: The registration process for GI is complex and technical. One of the most important preconditions for it is the establishment of an association. The experience across India for GI registration in the case of various products suggests that continuous support in terms of financial and administrative requirements should be provided by external agencies such as government departments, educational institutes and NGOs. Further, handholding with them in the post registration phase can lead to success stories. Thus, a strong link between the weaver communities and such agencies is a sine qua non for the effective enforcement of the legal rights granted by GI registration. However, the data has a different story to tell. It reveals that out of 254 respondents, only 38 are associated or in contact with any NGO or organization, while 215 respondents are not associated.

Question 2

What is the level of awareness among the Tangaliya shawl and Kutch shawl weavers/producers about GI registration and the rights granted under the Act? The journey of any right from being a legal right on paper to being realized as a real right involves both recognition and enforcement, which cannot take place in the absence of the required awareness about the same. The second question is set to determine the gap between legal right and real right in this context. We found it imperative as part of the investigative study to assess the level of awareness about the GI tag among the weavers of Tangaliya and Kutch shawls. This has been tested generally in terms of GI rights and specifically in terms of legal recognition of the product they are weaving. Analysis of the collected data answered the research question in the following manner.

1. **There is a partial awareness among weavers about GI. There are weavers who have heard the term "GI" but are unaware of what it means.**

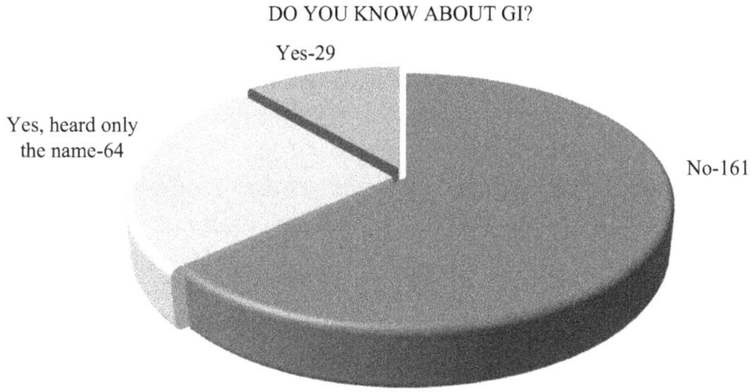

Figure 3.8 Status of general GI awareness

Empirical result: Out of 254 weavers, 161 are uninformed about the term GI while 64 have only heard of the term. Of the respondents, 29 weavers are aware of the term GI and also are informed about its meaning. In a major finding, the study reveals that around 63% weavers are not aware of the term GI, indicating a lack of awareness among them.

2. **Weavers are not aware that their handloom product is legally recognized and protected as GI.**

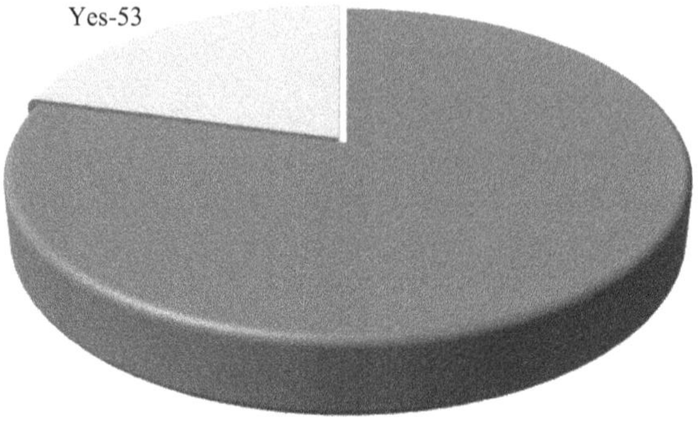

Figure 3.9 Status of specific awareness about GI registration

Empirical Result: Out of 254 weavers, 79% are unaware that thier handloom is a recognized GI.

Question 3

What is the status of governmental support in contributing towards adequate enforcement of GI?

With the second question in the context of locating a gap between protection on paper and its realization, it was necessary to look into the status of governmental support. Hence, the third question was set up in order to investigate the adequacy of governmental support to mobilize local human resources to develop handloom production on professional lines for self-employment.

It is understood that artisans engaged in the handloom and handicraft sectors require financial assistance for the development of their businesses. Often, financial support from private money lenders or financial institutions comes at a high interest rate which is unaffordable for the weavers and makes their survival in the market a challenge. Therefore, various schemes have been formulated by central as well as State governments, some of which as promulgated by the Government of Gujarat are outlined. Schemes relevant and in force during the period of the study have been enunciated here.

Besides investigating the general schemes, two schemes that required specific attention in the study were the Yarn Supply Scheme and the Cluster Development Scheme.[57] Handlooms are dependent in large part on the availability of yarn, which is a basic raw material for weaving; however, over the years there has been an escalation in yarn costs along with a shortage in supply of the same due to the excessive control of traders. This led to the Government of India making an effective intervention in the yarn market. An apex body – the National Handloom Development Corporation (NHDC) – was established in 1983, and in 1992, the Yarn Supply Scheme was introduced to supply yarn at the price at which it is available at the Mill Gate. Under the scheme, the transportation expenses involved in the supply of yarn are reimbursed by the central government. Further, handloom clusters were sanctioned under IHCDS/IHDS/CHCDS/CHDS/NHDP/NERTPS during 2006–2007 and 2015–2016, whereby both Bhuj and Limbadi talukas in the Kachchh and Surendranagar districts respectively were allotted ₹ 16.25 lakh and 15.85 lakh to undertake cluster development in the designated geographical areas.[58] So, to understand whether and to what extent weavers of Tangaliya and Kachchh shawls are aided by the Yarn Supply Scheme as well as the Cluster Development Scheme, this study posed particular questions.

I. **Shri Vajpayee Bankable Yojana, 2011**[59]
   This is a State government scheme to facilitate self-employment opportunities for the literate unemployed youth in the State and craftsmen of cottage industries, providing financial assistance through nationalized banks, co-operative banks, public sector banks or private Banks. The maximum amount of financial assistance for the industrial and service sectors is ₹ 2 lakh and for trade and business sectors is ₹ 1 lakh. The scheme enlists 395 project profiles that can gain benefits from the same, under which hand-woven shawls is a category. Apart from financial assistance, the scheme envisages support to the weavers for marketing and selling their products through commercial dealers, the Gujarat State Handloom & Handicrafts Development Corporation Limited, the Gujarat Sheep & Wool Development Corporation Limited and by aiding weavers' participation at State and national-level exhibitions.

   Persons in the age range from 18 to 65 years are eligible to benefit from this scheme. There is no income criteria for availing of the said benefits; however, the beneficiary must have undergone training for a specified period or should have at least one year of experience in the activity or should be a hereditary craftsperson.

II. **Jyoti Gramodyog Vikas Yojana (Scheme), 2015**[60]
   This is a State government scheme for establishment of village industries in rural areas and is applicable to all new village industry projects that cost from ₹1 lakh to 25 lakh. Any extensions or renovations of existing units are not eligible for this facility.

   Beneficiaries who are eligible under this scheme are i) individual artisans or entrepreneurs within the age range of 25 to 50 years, who have a mandatory educational qualification up to Class 10 and who work with the proposed project and ii) Grade II Self-Help Groups (SHGs) engaged in the production of goods on a small level.

III. **Dattopant Thengadi Artisan Interest Subsidy Scheme, 2014**[61]
This scheme was launched after it was identified that handloom and handicrafts artisans need to make fixed investments in order to continue or develop their businesses. It provides financial assistance to registered artisans for the purchase of raw materials or tools and machinery or both. Often, artisans have to depend on financial institutions or private money lenders to get regular funding to keep the business running, whereby they are exploited through high interest rates. So, to make sure artisans can sustain, develop and maintain their businesses, this scheme has been introduced. Various financial institutions like nationalized banks, all regional rural banks, co-operative banks, public sector banks and private banks are a part of this scheme.

To avail of the benefits of this scheme, an artisan must be above 18 years of age and must possess an identity card issued by the Handloom Development Commissioner or under iNDEXT-c (Industrial Extension Cottage – a State government organization). Beneficiaries can avail of up to ₹ 1 lakh for the purchase of raw materials or machinery or both. Additionally, margin money and interest subsidies are provided under this scheme.

IV. **Gramodyog Vikas Kendra, 2000**[62]
Previously implemented in different forms, this scheme is now in place after the merger of two schemes for providing infrastructure facilities at village level to artisans. Financial assistance is provided of up to ₹ 13 lakh.

NGOs, co-operative societies or trusts with a working experience of 2 to 3 years, that own 1,000–1,200 square feet of land and can provide employment to at least 25 artisans under activities in the village industries sector are eligible for benefits under this scheme.

V. **Cluster Development Scheme, 2006–2007 to 2015–2016**[63]
Supporting several categories of people in rural India was one of the objectives for which the Swarnajayanti Gram Swarozgar Yojana (SGSY) was introduced in 1999 as a rural development programme under which rural artisans were also featured. Through this scheme, it was envisaged that all aspects of self-employment would be covered, such as the creation of self-help groups, training, credit issuance, technology updating, infrastructure and marketing. As part of this scheme, the Ministry of Textiles identified clusters of geographical areas, popular in arts and crafts, across India to implement the Cluster Development Scheme. Drafted for the development of artisans from the handloom and handicraft sectors, this scheme offered a variety of assistance like diagnostic surveys, skill upgrades, design and product development, marketing support, modernization of tools and equipment, publicity etc. in order to achieve the larger objectives of rural alleviation from poverty. The Tangaliya handloom was one of the five clusters identified for the implementation of this scheme in Gujarat.

Further, Block Level Clusters were sanctioned under the National Handloom Development Programme (NHDP) and Comprehensive Handloom Cluster Development Scheme (CHCDS) from 2015–2016 and 2016–2017 where both handlooms, especially those producing shawls, are enlisted under the respective cluster.[64]

VI. **Intensive Handloom Development Programme**[65]
The Gujarat State Handloom & Handicraft Development Corporation was established to provide employment to those weavers outside the co-operative fold. The Corporation establishes various programs for the support of handloom weavers, such as the modernization of looms, training, providing yarn, design input and the marketing of goods produced by the weavers associated with the corporation. Assistance is also included for setting up emporia and sales depots within and outside the State, and also organizing exhibitions and participating in expos. All handloom weavers registered with the Gujarat State Handloom & Handicraft Development Corporation were eligible to benefit from the programme.

In light of the schemes elaborated here, the data collected shows the following results.

1. **Lack of awareness about government schemes for weavers.**

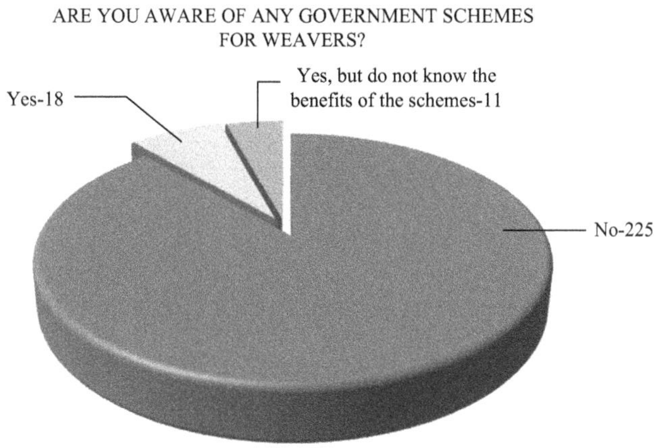

Figure 3.10 Status of awareness on government schemes

Empirical result: The data shows that there exists a general lack of awareness about the governmental support schemes available to weavers. Out of the total of 254 weavers, 225 are unaware of the available governmental schemes, while 11 are aware but lack knowledge on the benefits of the schemes. Only 18 weavers are aware of the schemes in place and the benefits under them.

2. Non-acquaintance with the India Handloom Brand

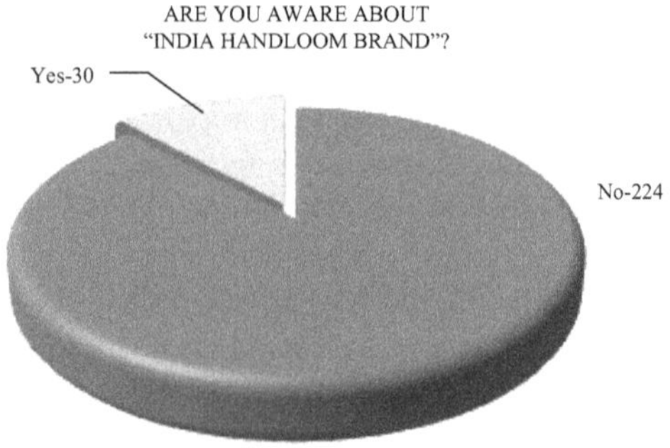

Figure 3.11 General awareness of India Handloom Brand

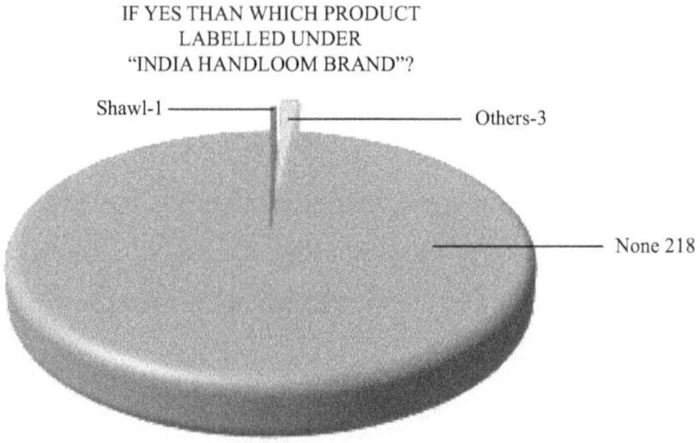

Figure 3.12 Specific awareness about IHB

Figure 3.13 Labelling preference for IHB

Empirical result: The India Handloom brand (IHB) is a marketing initiative for branding high-quality handloom products by the Ministry of Textiles of the Government of India.[66] Both handlooms studied here are eligible to make use of IHB. [67] As the IHB is advertized as an initiative to add further value to products registered as GI, the study probed the 254 weavers to assess their awareness of IHB and their usage of the same. The data indicates that the branding of handloom products is not in trend as the weavers are generally unaware of the India Handloom Brand; only 30 weavers are aware while 224 are unaware about the brand. This is supported by evidence from the IHB website enlisting users to register to the brand. A single weaver is registered to use the brand for his Tangaliya shawls.[68] This shows the dismal State of IHB. Due to this lack of awareness, handloom products are not labelled with the IHB mark. On the basis of the responses received, only 36 weavers admitted that their products are labelled with the IHB mark. There is only one response with regard to the branding of the shawls. The data collected is surprising as out of the sample size of 254 weavers, 168 weavers responded that they do not want their product to be labelled "IHB".

The India Handloom Brand has been designed to create a suitable platform for handloom weavers and customers. In order to gain consumer trust by endorsing the quality of handloom products in terms of raw materials, processing, embellishments, weaving design and other quality parameters, the brand lists certain social and environmental compliances for the handloom products. A high quality handloom product will ensure the creation of a market catering to the demands of a younger generation and that of the export markets, resulting in an increase in the earnings of the weavers.

This initiative is intended to differentiate premium Indian handloom products from other products in terms of quality, which will in turn generate customers at not only the domestic but also the global level, thus assuring handloom weavers of a steady source of income with provisions for bulk buying and export present under the brand.

3. **Lack of awareness about the ongoing Cluster Development Scheme for Tangaliya Handloom.**

Empirical result: We observed that a specific initiative for revival of the Tangaliya Handloom under the Block Level Clusters (BLCs) under the National Handloom Development Programme (NHDP) has been introduced. Out of 80 weavers from Surendranagar district, 42 are taking part in the scheme and 10 are aware of the scheme. There are 28 weavers who are not aware of the scheme.

Figure 3.14 Awareness about Cluster Development Scheme

4. **Lack of awareness about the Yarn Supply Scheme adds to the difficulties being faced by the weavers in procurement of raw material under the said scheme.**

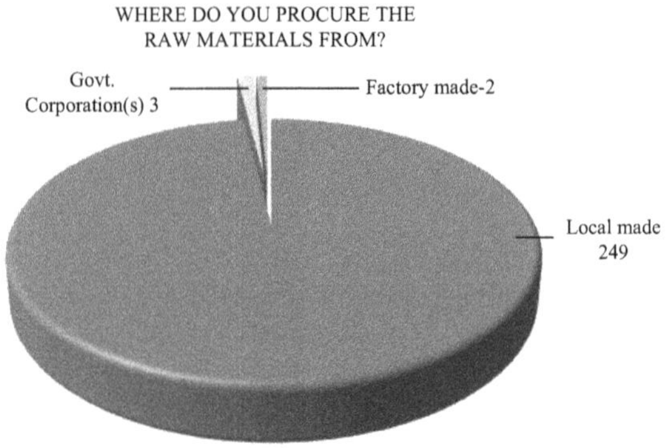

Figure 3.15 Source of raw materials' procurement

Empirical result: Procuring raw material is a fixed investment incurred by weavers. Only 3 out of the 254 weavers purchase yarn from a government corporation, while 2 procure factory-made yarn and 249 weavers procure locally made yarn. Next, the awareness of the Yarn Supply Scheme and related benefits is found only among 2 respondents, while 25 are unaware of the benefits and 227 are unaware of the scheme itself.

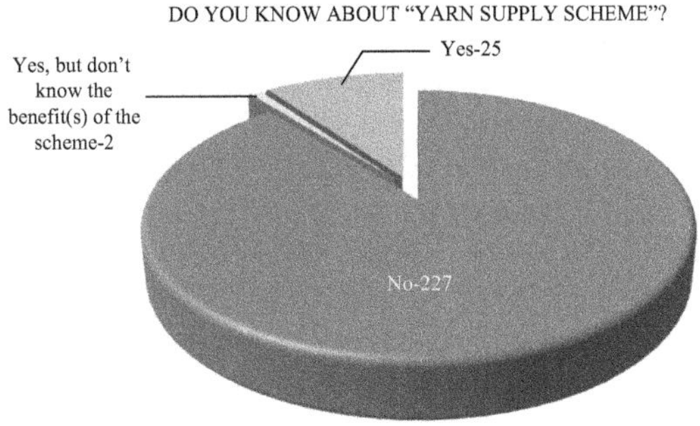

Figure 3.16 Awareness about Yarn Supply Scheme

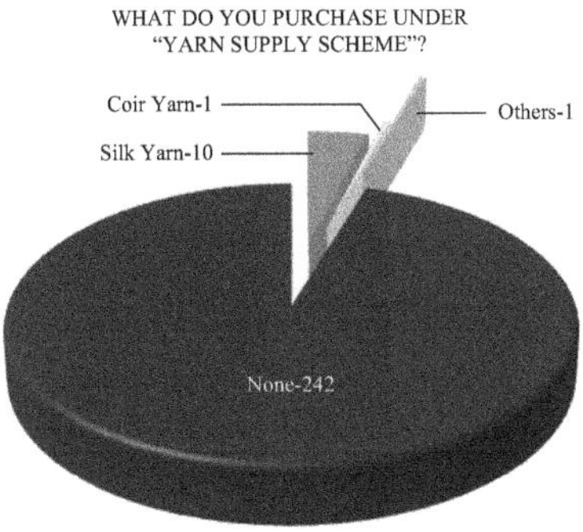

Figure 3.17 Particulars of purchase under Yarn Supply Scheme

3.4.4 Market survey

As part of the final phase, a market survey for both handlooms was also undertaken in order to understand the market reach and placement of the handlooms. The city of Ahmedabad was selected as the principal place for this survey. This selection was made post-assessment about the presence of a variety of handloom shops in the city. Responses were collected through interview method from seven shops: FabIndia, Garvi Gurjari, Sanskruti, Kairi, Bhujodi, Craft Roots and Handloom House.

The focus of questions was twofold, involving 1) a survey of shops for the availability of both handlooms and an understanding of the type of customers that the shops deal with; and 2) a survey of staff members in terms of their awareness of Tangaliya and Kutch handlooms, primarily shawls, as well as awareness about the fact that the shawls are recognized as Geographical Indications. The outcome of this survey is summarized below:

1. Looking into the availability of both the handlooms, we observed that Kutch shawls are widely available and also popular, whereas this is not the case with Tangaliya shawls. A lack of market and marketing abilities on the part of the producers is a primary reason for this. Further, the disconnect between the producers of Tangaliya shawls and various organizations/NGOs becomes more evident here. With the onset of the winter season, all the shops have stocked up on Kutch shawls; however, Tangaliya shawls are difficult to find even during the peak season.
2. The customers arriving at the shops have prior knowledge about Kutch shawls but the majority are not aware of Tangaliya shawls.
3. Staff members at shops are aware about Tangaliya and Kutch handloom products, especially shawls; however, there is inadequate knowledge about their recognition as GIs. Staff members specifically pointed out that the Kutch shawls and other handloom products are widely available and popular among buyers but due to the non-availability of Tangaliya shawls, its market reach and popularity are very poor.

3.4.5 Analysis of empirical result

The following observations provide for an analytical framework of the data collected from 254 weavers as part of this study.

- Weavers are unaware of the term GI, and even if they have heard the term, they are only vaguely aware of their legal rights and the protection of their craft under the law. Their participation in the collective, i.e. the weavers' association which has been granted the GI certification, as a right-holder is negligible to the extent that many are unaware of their membership, which led to the conclusion that the weavers are unaware of the benefits that can be availed under this community right.
- Weavers are unable to create a proper market despite GI registration of their products, leading to a decline in business and sales. Due to this inadequate market outreach, weavers are unequipped to appreciate the modern-day buyer's needs.
- More weavers of the relevant GIs have renounced the craft to adopt newer ways of earning a living; for example, they prefer to work as full-time labourers on farms or construction sites, at local grocery stores etc., while the young generations in weaver families opt for higher education instead of carrying on the traditional craft due to a palpable lack of recognition and economic advantage. They say weaving is their passion, but passion alone cannot earn them a living, leading to the search for different ways of surviving.
- A point of concern highlighted during the study was the absence of Tangaliya and Kutch handloom weavers from the National Handloom Census, taken in 2009–2010, which means they are not officially a part

of the handloom sector. It is worth mentioning that the census referred to while conducting this study was the All India Third Handloom Census of Weavers and Allied Workers, 2009–2010.

- Power looms and their products have gained an edge over authentic handloom products. If a handloom weaver takes 7 days to complete an authentic shawl, the same can be woven on a powerloom in a comparatively lesser time. Such reasons give imitation products made on powerloom a sales advantage over authentic handloom products. Considering the present study, on the basis of the data collected, in case of Tangaliya shawls, it takes more than a week to weave a genuine shawl while Kutch shawl weaving takes approximately 3–4 days.
- The associations/organizations/ NGOs responsible for acquiring GI registration for the selected handlooms are unable to play a specific role in supporting the weavers' community in the socio-economic sense due to a noticeable disconnect with the weavers in particular and other stakeholders in general.
- Kutch handloom products are more popular than Tangaliya products. However, the data indicates that the popularity of Kutch products is not due to the GI registration but is on account of the region's development as a tourist spot over the past decade.
- Only a few weavers are aware of the various central and State government schemes established in order to promote and support the handloom sector. These schemes address issues like health and insurance, loan dispersal, yarn supply and business development, which play a vital role in the overall improvement of the socio-economic status of the weavers. It also has a significant role in the effective enforcement of the rights granted through GI registration, as in the absence of adequate policy support, this law cannot produce the desired result. Due to this gap in the chain of communication between the government and weavers, vital information is left uncommunicated, which consequently results in poor protection of these handlooms.
- Apart from the promotional schemes, the government has designed a Cluster Development Scheme to strengthen the Tangaliya handloom market. However, the majority of weavers are unaware of this developmental programme and its many benefits.
- The government has also designed and promoted the "India Handloom Brand" in order to recognize quality Indian handlooms at the national and international levels. A large number of weavers are unaware of this brand and its benefits due to which their products are not labelled as part of this brand campaign, thus limiting their outreach to a large extent.
- Authentic raw materials used for handloom weaving are procured at a high cost in comparison to the acrylic yarns used in a powerloom. Financial schemes for easing the cost of the procurement of yarns are in

place, but weavers are unaware of availability of such schemes or their benefits. They use locally made raw materials which may not be quality tested, serving as a reason for their products' ineligibility to be labelled under the India Handloom Brand.

- During the study, it was discouraging to note that the first term of protection for Tangaliya shawls, which began in 2008, came to an end in 2018. A notice for renewal from the GI office was served to the association. However, the same has been ignored by the association or the related authorities who played a major role in acquiring this status in 2008.

3.5 Concluding observations

As this study reached its conclusion, the Geographical Indications register continues to expand. The total number of registered GIs has reached 370, as many more products try their luck. In this regard, the Indian law on Geographical Indications has managed a noteworthy achievement; after all, identifying the genuineness of products across States and recognizing them as GIs, post a lengthy verification procedure, is an enormous endeavour given the length and breadth of the country. However, the task does not end with recognition and registration. Effective enforcement along with a post-registration mechanism is essential in order to harness all the benefits of this noble legislation, which attempts to revive forgotten marvels of Indian culture and traditions. In the absence of effective enforcement strategies, the situation is alarming as the survival of many registered GI products is called into question.

Coming to this study, both Tangaliya shawls and Kutch shawls were registered as GIs in the years 2009–2010 and 2011–2012 respectively. Although their popularity and presence have improved, their GI registration cannot be ascribed as the prime reason. Thus, benefits of GI registration as envisaged under this law are not fully realized.

The crafts of Tangaliya and Kutch, especially shawls, have managed to survive and flourish for more than 500 years and have passed down through generations. In the past, these hand-crafted shawls were merely a seasonal necessity for the communities that produced them; however, with time, some artisans realized the economic potential of the crafts and attempted to direct these hereditary handlooms differently. In fact, even as the government laid out elaborate reports and schemes for revival of the handloom sector, it was left to die. The law of Geographical Indications was yet another elaborate attempt to revive these crafts through their recognition and protection under the Act, thus not only identifying the intellectual property in these crafts but also aligning traditions with their unleashed economic potential. However, though there has been recognition of these crafts, their revival is still to take place, especially in the case of Tangaliya shawls.

Notes

1 Annapurna Mamidipudi, "Towards a Theory of Innovation in Handloom Weaving in India" (Doctoral thesis, Maastricht University 2016) <https://cris.maastrichtuniversity.nl/portal/files/4083287/c5295.pdf> accessed 1 August 2020.

2 Devdutt Pattanaik, "14 Things Historians Taught Me" (Devdutt, 1 November 2015) <https://devdutt.com/articles/14-things-historians-taught-me/> accessed 1 August 2020.

3 Ibid.

4 VSE Division, Planning Commission Government of India, *Report on the Steering Committee on Handloom and Handicrafts* (2012) <http://handicrafts.nic.in/CmsUpload/22342016043422str_handloom0305.pdf>accessed 1 August 2020.

5 George Watt, *Indian Art at Delhi 1903: Being the Official Catalogue of the Delhi Exhibition 1902–03* (Motilal Banarsidass Publications 1987).

6 A. P. S. Sawhney, J. B. Price and T. A. Calamari, "A Successful Weaving Trial with a Size-Free Cotton Warp" (2004) 29 *Indian Journal of Fibre and Textile Research* 117–121 <http://www.niscair.res.in/sciencecommunication/researchjournals/rejour/ijftr/Fulltextsearch/2004/June%202004/IJFTR-Vol%2029-June%202004-pp%20117-121.htm> accessed 10 August 2020.

7 National Council of Applied Economic Research, Development Commission (Handlooms) Ministry of Textiles, Government of India, *Handloom Census of India 2009–10*, 22 <http://handlooms.nic.in/Writereaddata/Handloom%20report.pdf > accessed 1 March 2021.

8 Gunti Amaravathi and K. Bhavana Raj, "Indian Handloom Sector – A Glimpse" (2019) 8 *International Journal of Innovative Technology and Exploring Engineering* (IJITEE) 645–654, 650 <https://www.ijitee.org/wp-content/uploads/papers/v8i6s4/F11330486S419.pdf > accessed 20 February 2021.

9 Third Handloom Census (n 6) 5.

10 Ministry of Statistics and Programme Implementation, *Sixth Economic Census 2013–14, 5* <http://www.icssrdataservice.in/datarepository/index.php/catalog/146/study-description> accessed 20 February 2021.

11 Ministry of Textiles, *Annual Report 2019–20*, 4 <http://texmin.nic.in/documents/annual-report> accessed 10 August 2020.

12 Ibid.

13 "Powerloom Industry and Exports in India" (*India Brand Equity Foundation*, January 2021) <https://www.ibef.org/exports/powerloom-industry-in-india.aspx> accessed 10 August 2020.

14 "State-Wise Registration Details of G.I. Applications" (*Geographical Indications Registry*, 2021) <https://www.ipindia.gov.in/registered-gls.htm>accessed 1 March 2021.

15 "Smriti Irani Visits Tangalia Weavers of Surendranagar, Announces Society, Subsidy for them" *DeshGujarat* (Surendranagar, 19 January 2017) <https://www.deshgujarat.com/2017/01/19/smriti-irani-visits-tangalia-weavers-of-surendranagar-announces-society-subsidy-for-them/> accessed 1 February 2021.

16 "Govt. to Support Tangaliya Weavers: Smriti Irani", *Times of India* (Ahmedabad, 20 January 2017) <https://timesofindia.indiatimes.com/gujarat/govet-to-support-tangaliya-weavers-smriti-irani/articleshow/56684251.cms> accessed 1 February 2021.

17 The Conference was conducted by Applied Research Centre for Intellectual Assets and the Law in Asia, Singapore Management University in March 2018.

18 "Statement of Case for Tangaliya Shawl" (*Geographical Indications Registry*, 2021) <http://ipindiaservices.gov.in/GIRPublic/Application/ViewDocument> accessed 1 February 2021.

19 "Meeting of Consultative Group for Registration of Tangaliya Craft under Geographical Indication". This document created by the NIFT is part of the GI Application for Tangaliya shawls (*Geographical Indications Registry*, 2021) <http://ipindiaservices.gov.in/GIRPublic/Application/Details/127> accessed 2 February 2021.
20 "Certificate of Registration" (*Geographical Indications Registry*, 2021) <http://ipindiaservices.gov.in/GIRPublic/Application/Details/127> accessed 2 February 2021.
21 "Certificate of Registration" (*Geographical Indications Registry*, 2021) <http://ipindiaservices.gov.in/GIRPublic/Application/Details/174> accessed 2 February 2021.
22 As per the Application for Registration, a study was organized by Ahmedabad Textile Industry's Research Association (ATIRA) under the project *Strategies & Preparedness for Trade & Globalization in India*, by the Ministry of Commerce and Industry, UNCTAD and DFID. This study was undertaken by KHAMIR and is part of the GI Application for Kutch shawls <http://ipindiaservices.gov.in/GIRPublic/Application/Details/174> accessed 2 February 2021.
23 "Renewal Notices Sent by the Registrar of Geographical Indications" (*Geographical Indications Registry*, 2021) <http://ipindiaservices.gov.in/GIRPublic/Application/Details/127> and <http://ipindiaservices.gov.in/GIRPublic/Application/Details/174> accessed 2 February 2021.
24 "Certificate of Registration" (n 20).
25 "Certificate of Registration" (n 19).
26 "Gujarat Census" <https://www.census2011.co.in/data/district/189-surendranagar-gujarat.html> accessed 01 March 2021.
27 "Certificate of Registration" (n 19).
28 "Statement of Case" (n 17).
29 "Statement of Case" (n 17).
30 Ibid.
31 Ibid.
32 "Geographical Indications Journal No. 29, Application Number 127" (*Geographical Indications Registry*, 19 March 2009) <http://ipindiaservices.gov.in/GIRPublic/Application/ViewDocument> accessed 1 February 2021
33 Devanshi Mehta, "The Uniqueness of Tangaliya Weaving of Gujarat" 10 (M.A. Thesis, National Institute of Fashion Technology, 2017).
34 Ibid.
35 Ibid.
36 Ibid.
37 Ibid.
38 Ibid.
39 Ibid.
40 Ibid.
41 SAATH has been working with Patola, Tangaliya and cotton-weaving artisans from the district of Surendranagar since 2006 through the Snehal project, supported by CARE India.
42 "Meeting of Consultative Group" (n 18).
43 "Geographical Indications Journal No. 40, Application Number 174" (*Geographical Indications Registry*, 3 May 2011) <http://ipindiaservices.gov.in/GIRPublic/Application/Details/174> accessed 2 February 2021.
44 (n 21).
45 "Geographical Indications Journal No.40, Application Number 174" (n 42).
46 Ibid, 9.
47 Ibid.

48 Ibid.
49 Ibid.
50 Ibid.
51 Ibid.
52 "Crafts of Kachcch", (*KHAMIR*, 2021) <http://www.khamir.org/crafts/weaving> accessed 20 August 2020.
53 "Vankar Shamji Vishram" (*Border & Fall*, 2021) <http://www.borderandfall.com/vankar-shamji-vishram/> accessed 20 August 2020.
54 Ibid.
55 "Craft of Gujarat" <https://craftofgujarat.gujarat.gov.in/AwardWinners> accessed 20 August 2020.
56 *Border & Fall* (n 47).
57 "Yarn Supply Scheme, 2018", (*Government of India, Ministry of Textiles*, 2021<https://www.nhdc.org.in/UPLOAD/TopMenuFile/Yarn-Supply-Scheme.pdf > accessed 18 January 2021; Cluster Development Scheme, 2016<http://cottage.gujarat.gov.in/Home-242566262A74-214079-2824725E2572-3F2E72> accessed 18 January 2021.
58 "State-Wise Details of Handloom Clusters Sanction under IHCDS/ IHDS/ CHCDS/ CHDS/ NHDP/ NERTPS during 2006–07 to 2015–16 as on 31.03.2016" (*Office of the Development Commissioner (Handlooms) Ministry of Textiles*, 2021) <handlooms.nic.in> accessed 18 January 2021.
59 "Shri Vajpayee Bankable Yojana, 2011" (*Commissioner of Cottage and Rural Industries*, 2021) <http://www.cottage.gujarat.gov.in/Home-5E25726C3B65-214079-2824725E2572-5E2572> accessed 18 January 2021.
60 "Jyoti Gramodyog Vikas Yojana, 2015" (*Industries & Mines Department, Government of Gujarat*, 2021) <http://www.imd-gujarat.gov.in/jyoti-gramodyog-vikas-yojana>accessed 18 January 2021.
61 "Dattopant Thengadi Artisan Interest Subsidy Scheme, 2014" (*Commissioner of Cottage and Rural Industries*, 2021) <http://www.cottage.gujarat.gov.in/Home-28247221713D-214079-2824725E2572-282472> accessed 18 January 2021.
62 "Gramodyog Vikas Kendra, 2000" (*Industries & Mines Department, Government of Gujarat*, 2021) <http://www.imd-gujarat.gov.in/gramodyog-vikas-kendra> accessed 18 January 2021.
63 "Cluster Development Scheme, 2016" (*Commissioner of Cottage and Rural Industries*, 2021) <http://cottage.gujarat.gov.in/Home-242566262A74-214079-2824725E2572-3F2E72> accessed 18 January 2021.
64 "State-wise Handloom Cluster Sanction" (n 52).
65 "Intensive Handloom Development Programme" (*Commissioner of Cottage and Rural Industries*, 2021) <http://cottage.gujarat.gov.in/Home-2425665B5D2D-214079-2824725E2572-28247221713D> accessed 18 January 2021.
66 The India Handloom Brand is an initiative of branding high-quality handloom products with zero defects and zero effect on the environment. It differentiates high-quality handloom products and helps to earn the trust of customers by endorsing their quality in terms of raw materials, processing, embellishments, weaving designs and other quality parameters and by ensuring social and environmental compliances in their production. The India Handloom Brand is aimed at generating a special market space and increased earnings for the weavers. Thus, the concept of India Handloom Brand is to brand the handloom products, which are exclusively catering to the quality needs of the socio-environmentally conscious consumers.

67 "Frequently Asked Questions, India Handloom Brand" (*Ministry of Textiles, Government of India*, 2021). This document enlists all products eligible for registration under the IHB, <http://www.indiahandloombrand.gov.in/downloads/FAQ_India_Handloom_Brand_English.pdf> accessed 18 January 2021.

68 "Registered Users List" (*Ministry of Textiles, Government of India*, 2021) <https://www.indiahandloombrand.gov.in/Members/user_list/> accessed 18 January 2021.

4

POLICIES FOR REVIVAL OF HANDLOOM SECTOR IN INDIA

Tapping the lost potential

4.1 Preliminary note

The domestic textile industry set in motion an unprecedented revolution of modernization and industrialization, gradually thrusting India towards its own story of development amid a turmoil-filled British era. The importance and relevance of the textile sector thus cannot be denied or undermined. However, while studying this sector for its contribution to the thriving Indian economy, an inevitable factor came to light: that the vast textile sector can be divided into several fragments such as the mill segment, the powerloom segment and the handloom segment. These segments differ in terms of volume of output, technology, the organization of production and so on and are often placed in competing positions with one another, competing for raw materials, markets, etc., thus rendering futile any attempt to generalize the textile sector as a whole.[1]

India has been handed down a rich legacy constituting the centuries-long sustained tradition of weaving. Akin to the linguistic diversity that India is home to, the handloom industry also involves a diverse range of crafts practiced across the length and breadth of this nation. These handloom products generally produce different fabrics based on their end use, either as a kind of clothing or as a home-based product. Through centuries of practice, India has earned a global reputation for its great handloom culture which depends on the splendid artistry of its weavers, its exclusive designs and its overall finesse. Not only the prime employment-generating sector after the agriculture sector, the handloom industry is also one of the oldest and largest cottage industries in India. The Indian handloom industry thus provides more than a single reason to preserve, and further cultivate this unforgettable, valuable heritage by way of generating a rigorous legal and policy regime.

Located mainly across rural India (88.7% as per the latest Handloom Census[2]), the handloom industry is largely decentralized. Its operations are set up completely within a weaver's household, where members across age groups come together in order for a basic yarn to be turned into a finished

DOI: 10.4324/9781003002147-5

product. Most handloom crafts are inter-generational in nature. A laudable aspect of this industry lies in gender proportionality, as we get to see an equal ratio of men and women working according to their creative strengths and specialities on various parts of the craft. Based on the raw materials used, the handloom industry relies heavily on the agriculture sector. Thus, handloom weaving in rural India is as much for household needs as much for contributing to the overall textile industry production.[3] While a fully mechanized power loom is capable of producing and re-producing any design, the level of artistry and intricacy achieved on a handloom fabric is unparalleled and beyond the scope of modern machines.[4] In fact, it is this factor of the unmatchable genius of our handloom weavers that makes the sector resilient in the face of existing modern machineries. This legacy of exquisite traditional and cultural knowledge expressed through handlooms is recognized and protected through GI registration, thus making the two inseparable. However, this recognition and protection of handlooms under the domestic GI law would be incomplete without the policies, schemes and other programmatic interventions by the government. Having dealt with the legislative framework and procedural aspects of the law along with case studies as well as empirical evidence, we now move to discuss the policy aspects so as to complete the circle of enquiry into the efficacy of the GI Act.

4.2 Institutional structure of the handloom sector

To comprehend the functional aspects of any entity – formal or informal, organized or unorganized – it is essential to understand its structural setup. This is true even as we speak of the handloom sector, the challenges pertaining to which can be better appreciated by knowing the participating stakeholders. Domestic GI law, as discussed in the earlier chapters, is concerned mainly with the primary stakeholder, i.e. a weaver in case of handlooms; however, as this chapter moves forward to highlight the policy initiatives taken for this sector, additional stakeholders come to the fore, whose role in handloom development is indisputably important and who are responsible for bridging the gap between the benefits and the beneficiaries.

Certain factors distinguish the handloom sector from the other components of India's massive textile industry. Firstly, the entire process of weaving demands significant financial and infrastructural investment, increasing a weaver's dependence on various external agencies. Secondly, weaving being an activity spread mainly throughout rural India, the socio-economic conditions of families that are in the trade force them to not engage in it entirely but rather to blend weaving with other sources of income. Thirdly, a lack of education and general awareness put weavers in a vulnerable spot when it comes to their understanding of the complexities involved in

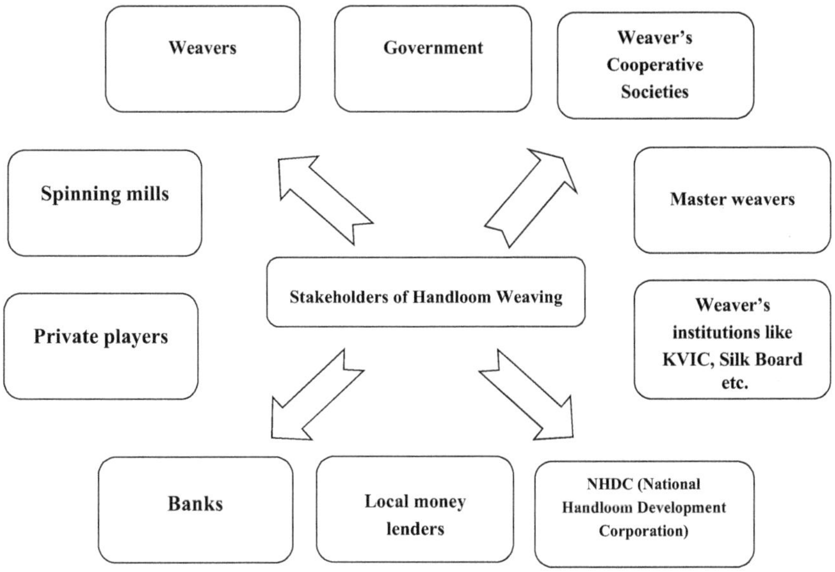

Figure 4.1 Stakeholders in the handloom sector. (Source: Bankers Institute of Rural Development (BIRD), Lucknow *Study Report on Problems and Prospects of Handloom Sector in Employment Generation in the Globally Competitive Environment* (2016) at 37 <http://www.birdlucknow.in/wp-content/uploads/2016/04/Study-Report-on-Probelms-Prospects-of-handloom-Sector-by-BIRD-Lucknow1.pdf> last accessed 3 March 2021)

the benefit-claiming mechanism. And lastly, weaving comes as an inheritance, and at times it is also necessary for household use, and therefore making trade gains out of this activity may not be a skill possessed by each weaver. These factors building the core of the handloom sector are apparent and need to be taken into consideration in policy framing and enforcement.

4.3 Government actions to preserve the handloom sector of India – a factual insight

In a preface succinctly describing India's agricultural and weaving prowess by Shri Romesh Chandra Dutt – a learned economic historian of the pre-independence era – we learn that products of the Indian loom were supplied in the markets of Asia and Europe.[5] However history is replete with divided scholarly interpretations of the times and leadership under which the flourishing handloom sector entered a major declining phase. The debate, to put it simply, has centred on whether colonial contact destroyed traditional Indian industry, or whether it created conditions for a creative

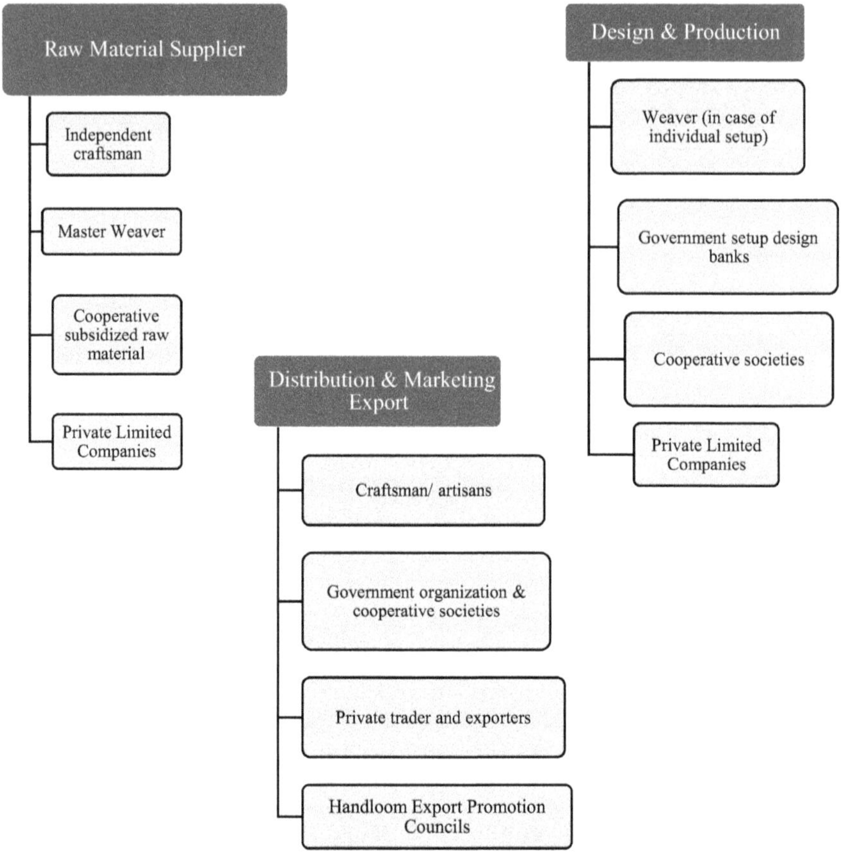

Figure 4.2 Value chain of the handloom sector. (Source: National Skill Development Corporation *Human Resources and Skill Requirements in the Handlooms and Handicrafts Sector* [2013–2017, 2017–2022] <https://nsdcindia.org/sites/default/files/Handlooms-Handicrafts.pdf> at 23 last accessed 3 March 2021)

re-organization of the institutional structures and the adaptation of the handloom industry.[6] The Marxist school of thought has argued that colonial contact destroyed pre-existing industrial systems and brought about economic retardation.[7] By contrast, historians and other scholars working for a little over a decade have documented the dynamism of the indigenous artisanal economy, which, during the last century of British rule, responded with changes in the conditions under which cloth was produced and sold.[8] While this is an endless debate, there is little doubt about the fact that colonial contact brought about a disruption in hitherto integrated processes like the spinning of yarn and weaving of cloth.[9]

Scholars of the view that the British reigned over a dark era for Indian looms have provided reasons along with data to further cement this belief. The imposition of restrictive measures upon the Indian weaving industry resulted in a major collapse which gradually led the country from being a net exporter of textile goods to being a net importer of the same. Further, with the introduction of the spinning jenny[10] in England, a large number of people were suddenly out of work, as hand spinning, which was their primary occupation was mainly replaced by machine-produced yarn. Locally, with the establishment of the first textile mill in Bombay in 1851, the handloom industry started facing competition from indigenous textile mills too.[11] Plagued with such challenges, the despairing handloom sector sought urgent support and the then Government's attention was drawn towards it. The Royal Commission on Agriculture took up the cause in 1928, expressing the view that the development of cottage village industries based on a co-operative structure was crucial for their survival.[12] Later, to review the position of the Indian handloom industry, a handloom conference was organized in 1940, on the recommendations of which a fact-finding committee was established under the aegis of Dr. P.G. Thomas; the committee submitted its report in 1942.[13] This report, we consider, is worth a mention as it was the first authoritative report detailing various aspects of the handloom sector like production, employment potential and the sector's standing in the national economy.

Independence from colonial rule brought an opportunity to understand priority sectors that fuelled the Indian economy and implement policies that were long called for, the handloom sector being one. Approximately 30 lakh handlooms were present in India at the time; however the majority of the looms were in a dismal condition and of poor quality due to inferior raw materials and an inefficient marketing infrastructure. This dire situation called for an urgent measure which the Government of India undertook by setting up a Handloom Standing Committee just one year into independence.[14] The Committee was allotted ₹ 10 lakhs under a Handloom Development Fund. However, the situation deteriorated further in 1952, resulting in the establishment of an All India Handloom Board.[15] Largely, the functions of the Board pertained to examining the overall health of the handloom sector as well as different schemes implemented for its improvement.[16] Since then, with suggestions from the Board and other Committees formed through the years, incoming Governments have attempted a rejuvenation of the handloom sector with the help of policies in order to sustain what is the second-largest unorganized sector in India. Some notable steps taken in the early years were the following:

1. The Khadi and Other Handloom Industries Development Act, 1953, was passed with the objective of raising funds and creating weavers'

co-operative organizations for the handloom industry.[17] Interestingly, in the same year, The Khadi and Other Handloom Industries Development (Additional Excise Duty on Cloth) was passed with the objective to create a "cess" fund out of profits from the mill sector with the purpose of promoting handloom products.[18]

2. The Institutionalization of All India Handloom Fabrics Marketing Cooperative Society was a national apex body established to facilitate the marketing of fabrics in handloom co-operatives in 1955.[19]
3. In order to provide vital support under research, service and training, four Weavers' Service Centres (WSC) were established in 1956 in accordance with the decision of the then Planning Commission.[20] Initially set up as design centres, the objectives of WSCs now span across product development, technological development, skill upgrading for weavers, extending documentation support, revival of languishing crafts and implementing Central Government schemes for weavers, dyers and printers.[21] There are more than 20 centres at present.[22]
4. An institution in the name of the Handloom Board was set up as early as 1945 and it functioned until 1947.[23] A revised set up with separate boards for handicrafts and handlooms was introduced in 1957 with its latest version established in 1992.[24] This board was considered among the most important steps for the betterment of the handloom sector as it provided policy inputs for promotion, development, marketing of crafts and co-ordination of actions from other government agencies, in consultation with weavers and artisans – the primary stakeholders of the sector – who constituted part of the advisory setup.[25]
5. On the advice of All India Handloom Board, the decision was taken to create national institutions that cater for upgrades in technology and training technical personnel who can further guide the widely rural-based handloom industry.[26] With this motive, two institutes of Handloom Technology were set up in Salem and Varanasi respectively.
6. The Handloom and Handicrafts Export Council (HHEC) was set up in 1958 for the promotion of handloom exports.[27] In its current version, this council is now the Handloom Export Promotion Council, constituted in the year 1965 with 96 members, and its present membership is around 1,500, spread all over the country.[28]
7. The Office of the Development Commissioner (Handlooms), an apex level nodal agency, was set up in 1975 with a vision to develop a strong, vibrant handloom sector to provide sustainable employment to weavers.[29]
8. The National Handloom Development Corporation (NHDC) was established in 1983 for ensuring the regular provision of raw materials such as yarn, dyes and chemicals to the State Handloom Organisations.[30]

Along with the above listed and similar interventions that have been implemented from time to time, the handloom industry has received attention and assistance from the Government of India, allowing it to survive amidst competition from the powerloom and mill sectors; however, its situation is still not as had been envisaged, and to ensure long-term sustainability, more efforts are required to power this homegrown industry. Certain challenges in the development of the sector continue to remain long after gaining independence. In fact, this is noted by scholars, expert committees and the like who have studied the sector's growth, problems and prospects.

In a fast-growing mechanized world, it was hard to resist the economic leverage provided by power looms. Therefore, besides the enlisted programmatic interventions, there were also major policy shifts undertaken to make these segments – handlooms and power looms – complimentary rather than competitive. One such move, considered a major blow to the handloom industry, was the recommendation by the Textile Enquiry Committee of a phased programme for the conversion of handlooms into power looms, except for 50,000 handlooms producing special fabrics.[31] It was expected from the move that steady employment would be maintained for the short term while efficiency would be secured for the long term. So, based on this recommendation, during the second Five Year Plan (1956–1961), the installation of 35,000 power looms within the co-operative fold was allowed.[32] However, this scheme was discontinued in 1961 as it was found that the main beneficiaries were not handloom weavers due to the opportunity being largely seized by the mill owners, resulting in a significant increase in the number of unauthorized power looms in the country.[33]

One way to keep business within the handloom sector up and running was through reservations. Vide a notification in 1950, the then Textile Commissioner promulgated a prohibition on the production of certain items, e.g. dhoties, coarse cloths of plain weave, table cloths and napkins, sarees with a border exceeding 2.5 inches, etc.; this prohibition extended to cotton textile mills and powerloom units with five or more units.[34] Further, the Textile Policy of 1985 and the following Handloom Reservation Act 1985 are considered to represent the most comprehensive textile policy and a formal, legislative push towards conservation of the handloom sector through reservation. Prior to these, the Textile Policy Statement of 1985 recognized, post analysis of various difficulties faced by the industry, that the crisis in the textile industry was neither cyclical nor temporary but suggested deeper structural weaknesses.[35] Although made for the textile industry as a whole, this Statement fit perfectly for the similar (or worse) problems facing the handloom sector at that time. So, after careful consideration, a new textile policy for restructuring the industry was formulated. This policy was a major departure from earlier policies while removing the constraints and restrictive policies of the earlier years and bringing into sharper focus its objectives in terms of the consumer, labour, employment, exports and so on, laying greater emphasis on cost efficiency and the free play of market forces.[36]

With an understanding that challenges such as technical and technological constraints, an unorganized system and inadequate availability of inputs inhibit the potential of a very promising handloom sector, the Handloom (Reservation of Articles for production) Act, 1985, was introduced.[37] The Act aimed to protect the livelihoods of handloom weavers and protect the cultural heritage of the handloom industry from encroachment by the powerloom.[38] The Act initially reserved 22 articles for exclusive production through handlooms which was subsequently reduced to 11 via an amendment in 1996. As handlooms were the focus of this Act, power looms were targeted to be firmly kept outside the production territory reserved for the former. However, these handloom-friendly objectives of the Act were challenged in the Supreme Court of India as being violative of fundamental rights under Article 14 and 19(1) (g) of the Indian Constitution, which ordered a stay on the enforcement of the Act.[39] The stay was vacated in 1993 with an observation that "the reservation of articles for handlooms does not pose threat to power looms".[40] However, in between the stay and its vacation, the Act remained dormant, and during this period the share of power looms increased at a rapid pace. Thus, the handloom sector may have paid a heavy price for a doing which was not its own. In the coming years, a mixed variety of measures have been introduced to restructure, reform and revive the handloom sector; however, the situation remains unchanged to a large extent. Even today, this Act remains largely unused and inadequately enforced.

Also, after the judgment, the Act wasn't implemented in real earnest as is evident from the fact that only 656 First Information Reports (FIR) were lodged out of 72,553 power looms inspected up to January 1995, demonstrating the strength that the powerloom lobby had come to acquire.[41] Before any significant steps to improve the implementation could be taken, the Act faced attack from various quarters.[42] Just after the Supreme Court judgment, the Advisory Committee under the Act was freshly constituted in October 1993 "to review the reserved items in terms of provisions of Section 4(2) of the Act".[43]

The Advisory Committee conducted field studies through five zone-wise sub-groups and, after reviewing 22 items reserved for handlooms, made recommendations for reducing them to 11 items.[44] In 1994, a Rajya Sabha committee was formed under the chairmanship of Mrs. Sushma Swaraj to review the 1985 Act, which recommended a reduction in the number of reserved articles, and in 1995, the Meera Seth Committee on Handloom Industry was appointed to review the impact of the Government of India's policy on handlooms.[45] The major thrust of the report was on re-orienting the handloom sector towards the globalization process as a principal strategy for its survival, and it recommended the articles in the reserved category to be reduced by half.[46] The committee also recommended modernization and mechanization of handlooms as it was felt that handlooms were not capable of competing in the global market.[47] Based on all these recommendations, the number of reserved articles were reduced to the point where items like Kota Doria sarees, shirting, crepe fabrics, table cloths, dusters, basta, bukram cloth and low reed pick cloth were deleted.[48]

Understanding the massive share of both the handloom and handicrafts sectors in India's development as well as their employment-generating capacity, the Government of India along with State governments have time and again made programmatic interventions. The policy initiatives have majorly aimed at generating sustained, productive and gainful employment with decent working conditions for the entire weavers' population. Although certain programmes have yielded positive results, the work is far from complete even at present. Over and above factors like demographic, social, technical and cultural aspects, the immense popularity of low-cost, eye-catching synthetic materials over the products of traditional handlooms has led to a partial turnaround in the sector. The handloom sector being spread across all regions of the country – albeit not equally, but mainly in rural India – brings a unique challenge for policy and programme interventions to be implemented effectively. Adding to this, the fact that the sector is decentralized only adds to the enforcement and implementation challenges. Consequently, the creation of sustainable livelihoods in the sector remains a major concern, making the situation only slightly better than in post-independence days. Statistically, according to the first Handloom Census carried out in 1987–1988, the total number of weavers across the country was 67.39 lakh, and as per the second handloom census conducted in 1995–1996, this had remained almost stable at 65.5 lakh. However, in the third and fourth census exercises the number had reduced significantly to 43.31 lakh and 35.2 lakh respectively. The cause of this reduction in handloom weavers' numbers cannot be attributed to a single factor but rather to a combination of factors that have equally contributed to the decline. Some factors negatively affect the handloom industry, and these have been addressed by a variety of interventions with the aim of rescuing the sector from its age-old woes. Recognition and protection through GI registration represents one such effort to make handloom weaving practices more attractive, sustainable and economically viable. However, the sector is plagued with several challenges coupled with a mix of characteristics that vary State-wise, making its revival even more challenging.

4.4 Handloom census

During the course of this research, we came across several novel initiatives put into practice for the growth and sustainability of the handloom sector. Among these initiatives, the law of Geographical Indications adapted as a *sui generis* legislation is one. In an earlier chapter, we discussed exclusive features of the law that give it a unique flavour – or rather, the law has been given a unique edge keeping in view the traditional domestic sectors it caters to. However, it is widely understood that the law by itself is not effective if not backed up by policy measures. So in this chapter, we bring forth a discussion on relevant past and current policy measures enforced for the betterment of handlooms. Although this may seem a repetitive narration, it becomes essential to build an understanding as to why, out of the many central and State initiatives, only some are selected for further discussion. After going through various texts, we realized there are certain remarkable policy measures in practice but due to a general unfamiliarity, the majority of the population (that also forms our reader base) remain oblivious of the stellar importance held by handlooms within the government's policy framework. Chances are, if the end user, i.e. the consumer, is ignorant of certain facts, the real value of what he/she is purchasing goes unnoticed. Thus, we felt it was absolutely essential (almost obligatory) to make the readers aware of some very distinct measures that have been in place to boost the Indian handloom sector so that the next time they come across a handloom, they feel instantly connected with it.

Among the various initiatives we showcase here, one stands out more distinctly and speaks louder than the others in the invaluable handloom industry, which is the handloom census. This novel exercise was envisioned to provide comprehensive statistical information on handlooms across the country. In a world increasingly inclined to mechanization and standardization, the handloom sector provides a refreshing change with its unique richness of manual skill and diversity.[49] This exercise undertaken at an interval of ten years, albeit not at regular intervals, is an important tool for gauging the handloom sector's health[50] and aids in mapping the required policy and systemic shuffles.

The first handloom census of 1987–1988 was conducted entirely by the Central Government, with the objective being to build a reliable database for the handloom sector in recognition of the need to understand the differential impact of policies formulated by planners and policymakers.[51] The second census of 1995–1996 was also conducted by the Central Government with National Council of Applied Economic Research (NCAER) as the nodal consultant.[52]

The first census included only handloom weavers, while the second was a joint census of handloom and powerloom sectors.[53] The purpose behind the conduction of a census exercise was to enforce better-planned handloom development programmes across the country for the weavers engaged therein by providing a multilevel database. As the handloom industry remains mainly a household rural activity, the qualifying criterion for inclusion in the census was the involvement of any household member in handloom weaving for at least 7 days during the past year.[54] As a handloom weaver may not own a loom and yet can be part of the industry by working for a master weaver or within the formation of a co-operative or other weaving establishment, these are also featured under the category of a non-household unit in the handloom census. Inclusion of a cooperative society or a weaving establishment is based on ownership and operation of a loom at least for seven days. Thus, after careful consideration of major characteristics of this sector, the handloom census is an exercise in collecting data by identifying different types of looms; the status of weavers; the division of weavers according to gender, religion, education etc.; the number of working and non-working days; average earnings; and other relevant factors.

4.4.1 First handloom census (1987–1988)

The first census covered 27 States and Union Territories. The broad findings of the first handloom census were the following:

1. There were 30.6 lakh weaver households in the country, of which 26.3 lakh were resident in rural areas; the total population of these households was 156.1 lakh.[55]
2. There were 43.7 lakh handloom weavers, out of which 22.4 lakh were full-time weavers and the rest were part-time weavers.[56]
3. 12.1 lakh weavers were working independently while 4.5 lakh weavers were working under co-operative societies and 3.4 lakh under master weavers.[57]
4. There were 21.6 lakh persons engaged in preparatory works, of which 10.9 lakh were working on a full-time basis.[58]
5. There were 38.9 lakh looms, of which 36.9 lakh were owned by the households and 2.0 lakh by non-households. Out of the total looms, 36.1 lakh looms were in working order while 2.8 lakh were lying idle.[59]

4.4.2 Second handloom census (1995–1996)

Owing to various structural changes since 1987–1988 as well as the major economic policy reforms that were launched in India as a result of which the economy was liberalized and "opened up", a considerable impact was created on distributional aspects in the economy while also impacting each sizeable sector in a different manner. It was during this massive structural shift that studying critical sectors like handlooms gained more attention, as the workings of such sectors and workers therein needed to adjust with this shift. Therefore, to analyse the impact and effects of economic liberalization, a joint census for handlooms and power looms was launched in 1995–1996. The aim was to bring into motion appropriate policy changes for the betterment of the sector.

Findings from the 1995–1996 census were the following:

1. A total of 25.2 lakh households were engaged in handloom-related activities, of which 21.9 lakh households were in rural areas while 3.3 lakh were in urban areas, and the total population of these households was 128.0 lakh.[60]
2. There were 34.7 lakh handloom weavers in the country, out of which 16.5 lakh were full-time weavers and the rest were part-time weavers.[61]
3. The majority of full-time weavers, i.e., 9.9 lakh, worked independently, while 2.4 lakh weavers worked under co-operative societies and 2.9 lakh under master weavers.[62]
4. Household units owned a total of 32.9 lakh looms, of which 29.9 lakh were in working order while 3.0 lakh were idle.[63] Non-household units owned a total of 2.0 lakh looms, of which 1.5 lakh were working looms while the rest were lying idle.[64]

The 1995–1996 census indicates the same conclusion as the first census, which is a decline in handloom weaving activity.

1. At the All India level, there has been a decline in 1995–1996 compared to 1987–1988 in the number of household[65] and non-household units[66] engaged in handloom-related activities of over 15%.[67]
2. Changes in the number of workers are minor (from 6.74 million in 1987–1988 to 6.55 million in 1995–1996, i.e., a decline of 2.81%).[68]
3. The number of looms has declined by nearly 8% in 1995–1996 over 1987–1988.[69]

4.4.3 Third handloom census (2009–2010)

Objectives, geographical coverage, limitations

In order to obtain the total number of units, both household and non-household, engaged in handloom activities, the number of weavers and allied workers, weavers' photographs and individual details of weavers aged 18 and above for the issuance of photo ID cards and the looms available (both working and idle), an extensive survey (covering 29 States and Union Territories) was carried out through the third census.[70] Another objective of the census was to assess the number of workers involved in pre-loom and post-loom activities and understand the employment structure of the sector.[71] The target population covered both household and non-household units, and the qualifying criteria included persons who had undertaken weaving or allied handloom activity even for one day in the year preceding the date of survey, thus also covering a broad range of allied workers within the sector.[72] A limitation of the geographic area covered in this census, as acknowledged in the introduction, is that it included pre-identified concentrated villages or urban blocks having at least five handloom households; the reason behind this was to minimize the cost of data collection.[73]

Number of weavers, age distribution, gender distribution and nature of engagement

A total of 43.31 lakh persons were engaged in weaving, of which 36.3 lakh were located in rural regions while the remaining 7 lakhs resided in urban areas.[74] 38.47 lakhs or 88.8% of the workforce were adults (18 years and above), of which 75.6% were weavers while 24.4% were allied workers.[75]

In terms of gender participation in handloom weaving, among the adult workforce, male weavers constituted 22.1% of workers while female weavers constituted a whopping 77.9%.[76] In terms of participation in the kind of activity – weaving or allied work – male worker participation was more in weaving activity (24.3% male and 75.7% female) than in allied work (15.2% male and 84.8% female).[77] On their nature of engagement, 24.72 lakh weavers worked full-time and 13.75% worked part-time.

Handloom households, purpose of weaving

Of nearly 27.83 lakh handloom worker households, approximately 87% were operational in rural areas and the remaining 13% in urban areas.[78] Of these households, north-eastern States accounted for 60.5% of handloom households, of which Assam's singular share was 44.6% whereas West Bengal's share was 14.6%, while Gujarat shared merely 0.13% of such households.[79] Among these households, 53.1% worked solely for commercial purposes, 28.2% undertook weaving for domestic purposes and 15.8% were weaving for a mixture of domestic and commercial purposes.[80]

Education and employment status

A startling figure as to the education level of weavers was that 29.4% had never attended school.[81] Next, regarding the weavers' employment status (whether they worked independently or under master weavers/private owners or under some institutional structure such as a co-operative society etc.), the data revealed that 61.1% of weavers were independent workers whereas those working under master weavers or private owners and institutions accounted for 33.8% and 5.1% respectively.[82] In this, the proportion of independent workers belonging to the north-eastern States is more than the other States added together.[83]

Income

The average annual income for handloom households in terms of purely commercial production was ₹ 31,390 in rural areas and ₹ 28,343 in urban areas.[84] If one looks at the average annual income from handloom activity for those undertaking some level of commercial production – irrespective of whether a person only works for commercial production or a mix of commercial and domestic production – this is ₹ 11,465 across all households, ₹ 10,687 for rural households and ₹ 16,483 for urban households; evidently the income is low in both cases, even when income from handloom work by urban households is higher than the rural income.[85] In Gujarat, the average income for total handloom households was ₹ 24,006 and for urban households was ₹ 23,489.[86]

Membership of handloom co-operatives

A low membership trend was identified among weavers, with a mere 9.8% or 2.74 lakh households – of which 9.0% were rural and 15.6% urban households – being members of co-operative societies.[87] Such membership is concentrated in the States of Tamilnadu, Andhra Pradesh, the North-East, Orissa and West Bengal.[88]

Future of handlooms

This census probed a pertinent factor of whether young weavers or the youth of handloom households were interested in undertaking handloom weaving as their occupation. The majority of adult weavers (35.7%) were unsure, 24.5% responded that handloom weaving did not interest youth as a future occupation option and only 25.3% of respondents were sure of the youth pursuing this occupation, comprising mainly weavers from Orissa (70.3%) and the north-east (30.7%).[89]

Threat from power looms

A question on the perception of the threat posed by power looms was also put to the weavers. 16.8% of handloom households perceived power looms as a threat, 16.5% felt a moderate threat, 44% perceived no threat and 22.6% were unaware of the existence of any threat.[90]

Table 4.1 Handloom census summary and comparative figures

Sr. No.	*Particulars*	*1987–1988*	*1995–1996*	*2009–2010*	*Change from 1st to 2nd census (in %)*	*Change from 2nd to 3rd census (in %)*	*Change from 1st to 3rd census (in %)*
1.	Handloom units (lakhs)	29.97	25.24	27.83	–16	10	–7
2.	Weavers & allied workers (lakhs)	67.4	65.5	43.32	–3	–34	–36
3.	Gender distribution (included categories: men and women)	–	Men 30% Women 62%	Men 20% Women 69%	–	Men –10 Women 7	
4.	Number of handlooms (lakhs)	37.8	34.71	23.77	–8	–32	–37
5.	Share of idle looms to total looms						
6.	Man days worked by weaver households during the census year	–	197	234	–	19	–
7.	Share of weaver households contributing more than 60% income from handlooms and related activities	36%	31%	35%	–14	4	–1
8.	Share of handloom cloth to total cloth production	24%	23%	11%	–4	–12	–13
9.	Share of handloom in the export of total textiles	4.8%	1.3%	1.2%	–73%	–0.1	–3.6

Source: Gunti Amaravathi and K. Bhavana Raj, "India Handloom Sector – A Glimpse" (2019) 8 (6S4) International Journal of Innovative Technology and Exploring Engineering (IJITEE) ISSN: 2278-3075, 645–654, 648 accessed 2 March 2021.

4.4.4 Fourth all-India handloom census (2019–2020)

Objectives, geographical coverage, limitations

Acknowledging the potential of handlooms to generate livelihoods for a large population base, the fourth handloom census was an attempt at uncovering data on weavers, their requirements and policy impact assessment.[91] This census covered as many as 31 States and Union Territories that practice the art of weaving.[92]

Number of weavers, age distribution, gender distribution and nature of engagement

The total number of handloom workers in the fourth census is 35.2 lakh, of which 30.5 lakh workers reside in rural India and the remaining 4.6 lakh workers in urban India.[93] Of this total, the number of adult (aged 18 years and above) workers constitute 96.9%.[94] Of the 35.2 lakh workers, weavers constitute 26.7 lakh while allied workers make up 8.4 lakhs.[95] The ratio of full-time and part-time workers is almost equal at 50.8% and 49.2% respectively.[96]

Gender distribution among workers of handloom is males at 9.7 lakhs or 28%, females at 25.4 lakhs or 72.3% and transgenders a total of 494 (inclusion of transgender workers is a new feature added to this census).[97]

Handloom households, purpose of weaving

Of nearly 31.44 lakh handloom worker households, the majority of the weaver households are located in the following four States: Assam (10.9 lakhs), West Bengal (3.4 lakhs), Manipur (2.1 lakhs), and Tamil Nadu (1.7 lakhs).[98] The number of weaver households[99] stands at 25. 45 lakhs and the total number of weavers in these households is 26.73 lakhs.[100] 22.5 lakhs (88.7%) of weaver households are located in rural areas while 2.8 lakhs (11.3%) are in urban areas.

Among these households, 53.1% worked solely for commercial purposes, 28.2% undertook weaving for domestic purposes and 15.8% were weaving for a mixture of domestic and commercial purposes.

Education and employment status

The States with the most educated weavers (having completed high school or more) are Goa (68.2%), Maharashtra (60.6%), Manipur (40.6%), Telangana (33.6%) and Himachal Pradesh (32.6%).[101] 23% of workers of the total are uneducated,[102] meaning that nearly one in four weavers have not received any formal education while a further 14% have not completed primary level, and the education level among female workers is higher than for male workers.

Of the 35.2 lakh workers, 25.77 lakh are independent workers, followed by 6.8 lakh who work under master weavers and 2.2 lakh who work under the co-operative fold.[103]

Income[104]

The majority (66.3%) of the weaver households earn less than ₹ 5, 000 a month.[105] A little more than a quarter of the households earn between ₹ 5,000 and 10,000 a month while just 7.4% have a monthly income in excess of ₹ 10,000. Of weaver households from urban areas, 36.1% earn more than ₹ 5,000 a month as compared to only 25.1% living in rural areas. The States of Goa (95.5%), Uttarakhand (69.8%) and Maharashtra (60.3%) recorded 60% or more of the weaver households earning in excess of ₹ 5000 per month. The survey further reveals that earnings from handloom activities alone stand at less than ₹ 5,000 a month for 82.5% of weaver households. Given that for 66.3% of the households the overall household monthly income is less than ₹ 5,000, this would imply that for a sizeable segment of weaver households, weaving is the only income-generating activity.

Banking penetration and social security[106]

Out of the total of 26.73 lakhs weavers who have been enumerated, 23.3% have a bank account. Banking penetration among weavers is higher among urban households (41.8%) than those living in rural areas (only 20.8%). Further, penetration is higher among male weavers (37.8%) than female weavers (only 17.6%).

The survey data clearly indicates that at an aggregate level, insurance penetration (life or health) is very low among weaver households (3.8%). Though only 7%, the penetration of insurance among urban weavers is over double that of rural areas (3.3%). The States with the highest recorded insurance penetration among weavers are Telangana (12.7%), Odisha (10.5%), Kerala (10.4%), Chhattisgarh (10.1%), Andhra Pradesh (9.8%) and Maharashtra (9.8%).

Membership of handloom co-operatives

The States where weavers are organized under a co-operative society or under other non-household units include Goa (95%), Kerala (71%), Puducherry (91%) and Tamil Nadu (56%).

In fact, estimates show that of the 21,765 registered Primary Weavers' Co-operative Societies (which cover only around 15% of the weavers in the country), only 50% are functional and those too only partially, leaving about 85% of weavers in the country outside the co-operative fold.[107]

Awareness of schemes[108]

The survey reveals that the majority of weaver household members are not aware of various schemes available to support them in the allied activities of handlooms. The response on a lack of awareness on the existing schemes, trainings and other enablers is more than 65% for each of the listed items; in fact, for 9 out of the 13 listed schemes, awareness levels were below 15%.

Mere tagging a handloom as a Geographical Indication cannot aid its survival, which is sufficiently evident from the case studies in Chapter 2 as well as the handloom census statistics. Data from the handloom census is not exactly encouraging; however, it is a mirror reflecting the reality of the lagging handloom sector, which needs extensive, urgent and earnest interventions for a complete revival.

4.5 Five-year plans and consequent interventions

Various commonalities specific to the handloom sector can be detected through an understanding of the statistics collected under handloom censuses over the years, but the one common factor that is found consistently is the importance of the handloom sector in India's overall growth strategy. This sector has received attention right from the first five-year plan till the twelfth; however, an apt observation from these plans is that they lacked consistency in their approach towards handlooms as each of the 5-year plans focussed on a different aspect of the economy.[109] A comprehensive study of the crises crippling the handloom industry is made by Dr. M. Lakshmi Narasaiah, and Dr. Ch. Thandava Krishna's work[110] highlights briefly the objectives of the various 5-year plans India instituted from time to time in the post-independence period.

The first plan (1951–1956) treated the growth and development of the handloom sector as simultaneous with the agriculture sector due to its linkage with agriculture in terms of geographical locations, workforce profiles and inputs. This plan focused primarily on providing more labour absorption power to the agricultural sector through employment and crop production benefits, assuming that the handlooms would also benefit from strengthening of the agricultural industry. The second 5-year plan (1957–1961) aimed at re-building rural India and pursuing industrial progress by promoting small-scale industries and providing opportunities for unskilled and underprivileged sections of society to ensure a balanced, wholesome development across the nation. In the third 5-year plan, the emphasis was on integrating the handloom industry with the rural economy through rural industrialization by providing assistance such as skills improvement, technical guidance, better equipment and liberalized credit. However, this was a time when some problematic schemes seeped into the system whereby handlooms' conversion into power looms was being encouraged, providing impetus for the growth of power looms and leading handlooms towards their slow demise. These mechanized looms deeply damaged the market share and economic viability of the handloom industry by providing an alternate cloth for the people.[111] In fact, the growth of power looms had a negative effect on handlooms to such an extent that a report by the Sivaraman Committee (1974) for the fourth 5-year plan (1969–1974) found that for every two people employed by a power loom, 24 persons were being displaced.[112] This committee report was a brave attempt to outline the problems faced by the handloom industry as a significant sector in the nation's economic landscape. Post this report, the fifth and sixth 5-year plans (1974–1985) were able to deliver better schemes for the handloom sector. The seventh five-year plan (1985–1990) derived its strength from the Textile Policy, 1985 and pitched handlooms and power looms in competition but with certain items exclusively reserved for handloom production under the Handloom Reservation Act. However, the Textile Policy also carved out an opportunity for the registration, regularization and installation of power looms, creating a further divide between the collective capabilities of handlooms and power looms.[113] Following this 5-year plan, the share of handloom sector in cloth production declined from 24.98% in 1980–1981 to 19.05% in 1989–1990.[114] In the upcoming decade, India embraced economic liberalization and, as the phrase suggests, domestic practices of business were made liberal. The economic opening up attracted export-led growth, and with the swift growth of power looms, the deteriorating handlooms became mere torch-bearers of India's cultural heritage compared to their economy-boosting counterpart.

With this, we now turn to the eleventh and twelfth five-year plans, both of which have focussed on the tremendous value potential of handlooms, to discuss the most-recent schemes implemented by the governments with a view to reviving their condition.

4.5.1 Eleventh Five-year Plan (2007–2012) and Twelfth Five-year plan (2012–2017)

The 5-year plans have been an integral exercise merging the Indian economic and social development strategies. The transition from a traditional and subsistence economy in the 1950s to a modern, industrial and knowledge economy was largely the outcome of plan exercises spanning a total of ten 5-year plans and a few annual plans.[115] In order to achieve faster and more equitable socio-economic development, the eleventh 5-year plan aimed to improve the quality of life for the citizens of the State and contribute to the larger national goals of socio-economic development.[116]

The core aspects building the handloom industry, i.e. its prevalence in rural India, labour intensiveness, gender distribution etc., make it a vital growth engine for the nation's overall socio-economic development. Further, to encourage entrepreneurial spirit and promote it as a major tool for sustenance among the key participants in this sector, the requirement was to prioritize the inclusion of micro, small and medium enterprises (MSMEs) and to devise schemes benefiting such enterprises and their creators. Thus, while laying plans for this vital sector coupled with handicrafts, a systematic approach was undertaken, focusing on the arts as well as artisans and on moving from competitive to complementary relationships among the various sub-industries of the textile industry.[117]

A mid-term appraisal of the eleventh 5-year plan reveals observations about the effectiveness of policies and programmatic interventions for the handloom sector. A peculiar aspect of any organizational arrangement in India is its complex technical layout, especially when it comes to schemes and policies that are numerous in number, sometimes with a common target. However, if the beneficiary is a partially literate or completely illiterate person residing in rural India, it is barely possible to comprehend how benefits or the mere awareness of a scheme will reach its target population. Such is the anomaly of this vast arrangement of schemes and policies, the outcome of which is too small to be visible at the macro level.[118] Acknowledging this, during the eleventh plan period, 12 schemes in the tenth 5-year plan for the handloom sector were merged into 5 schemes: (i) the Integrated Handloom Development Scheme (IHDS), (ii) the Handloom Weavers Comprehensive Development Scheme, (iii) the Marketing and Export Promotion Scheme, (iv) the Diversified Handloom Development Scheme, and (v) the Mill Gate Price Scheme (MGPS).[119]

In order to lay a relevant road-map for handlooms as part of the twelfth 5-year plan (2012–2017), a steering committee was commissioned ahead of the plan to assess the following aspects of weavers' and ancillary workers' lives: i) the overall standard of living, ii) the welfare situation, iii) technological improvement, iv) distribution and marketing networks, and v) demarcation of areas for assistance from government and NGOs or other such organizations.[120]

Consequently, the twelfth plan's National Handloom Development Programme (NHDP) was formulated to be implemented as a centrally sponsored plan scheme approved by the Planning Commission, merging, with or without modifications, the Revival, Reform and Restructuring (RRR) Package, the Institutional Credit component of the Integrated Handlooms Development

Scheme (IHDS) as Concessional Credit and Comprehensive Handlooms Development Scheme (CHDS). CHDS, a component of NHDP, has been formulated by merging three plan schemes i.e., the Integrated Handlooms Development Scheme, the Marketing and Export Promotion Scheme and the Diversified Handlooms Development Scheme implemented during the eleventh plan.

4.5.2 Integrated Handlooms Development Scheme (IHDS)

The Integrated Handlooms Development Scheme (IHDS) is divided into four components:

(i) The Cluster Development Programme provides need-based inputs to clusters of 300–500 handlooms over a 3-year period through grants of financial assistance of up to ₹ 60 lakh per cluster, for meeting expenditure on the formation of Self Help Groups (SHGs), setting up yarn depots, design development, setting up Common Facility Centres (CFCs) or dye houses, margin money for working capital, new looms and accessories and construction of worksheds, skill upgrading and marketing opportunities.[121]

(ii) The Group Approach supports the handloom weavers not covered by the clusters, in groups of 10 or more and up to 100 weavers, by providing financial assistance for basic inputs; training in weaving, dyeing, designing and managerial disciplines; and the construction of worksheds. Per beneficiary cost is in the range of ₹ 10,000 to ₹ 30,000.[122]

(iii) Marketing incentive is given to handloom corporations, apex organizations and primary weaver co-operative societies at the rate of 10% (shared 50:50 between the central and the State governments) for promoting the marketing of handloom products, largely through the promotion of investment in infrastructure.[123]

(iv) Up to 10% of funds under the scheme are for innovative ideas, and up to 2% is allocated for publicity, monitoring, supervision, and training of officials of the Office of Development Commissioner for Handlooms and State Directors of Handlooms as well as for evaluation of the scheme.[124]

Moreover, the Integrated Handloom Cluster Development Scheme (IHCDS), a central sector scheme for holistic and integrated development of 20 handloom clusters, introduced in 2006–2007, was also continued in the eleventh plan, covering about 5,000 handloom weavers in each cluster, with the Government of India's contribution being up to ₹ 2 crore per cluster over a period of 5 years.[125]

4.5.3 *Comprehensive Handloom Cluster Development Scheme*

A Comprehensive Handloom Cluster Development Scheme (CHCDS) was also introduced as a central sector scheme under the Ministry of Textile's Mega Cluster Scheme in 2008–2009, which covers clearly identifiable geographical locations with at least 25,000 handlooms, in which the central share is up to ₹ 70 crore per cluster over a time period of 5 years.[126] The objective was to support the weavers by providing a corpus for raw materials; credit for working capital; the construction of worksheds; skill upgrading; technology upgradation; a design studio marketing complex; value addition, such as the setting up of garment units; common infrastructure; and publicity.[127] Four such mega clusters were sanctioned at Varanasi (UP), Sivasagar (Assam), Virudhunagar (Tamil Nadu) and Murshidabad (West Bengal), and 20 clusters, each covering a target group of about 5,000 handloom weavers, were also sanctioned with a Government of India contribution of ₹ 2 crore for each cluster.[128]

4.5.4 *Marketing and Export Promotion Scheme*

The Marketing and Export Promotion Scheme, aimed at developing and promoting marketing channels in domestic as well as export markets, has two components:

(i) The Marketing Promotion Programme was designed to assist in the sale of handloom products by organizing exhibitions at national, regional, State and district levels; providing facilities to consumers to purchase genuine handloom products under one umbrella; promoting awareness about the latest designs and varieties of handlooms; providing marketing infrastructural support; encouraging innovation in designs and techniques; preserving and promoting traditional skills and designs; fostering brand identity and technological developments among weavers; providing assistance for organizing special expos, craft melas, urban haats and marketing complexes; granting National Awards and National Merit Certificates; registering special designs/techniques under the Geographical Indication (GI) Act; and establishing brand images for handloom products through the Handloom Mark.[129]
(ii) The Handloom Export Promotion Programme's objective was to identify and assist suitable apex/primary handloom co-operative societies and corporations in developing export-worthy products through interventions such as engaging professional designers and marketing consultants; upgrading skills; enabling market penetration through participation in international fairs/exhibitions, buyer–seller meets and brand development through the Handloom Mark; and setting up design studios.[130]

A study report by the Bankers Institute of Rural Development (BIRD) States that a dearth of innovation and limited dynamism is associated with the handloom sector, particularly in the field of marketing. A lack of adequate investment and participation or stake-holding on the part of the private sector is also a factor impeding the marketing and supply chain infrastructure.[131] Quoting data from the third handloom census, the report further States that as 61.1% of the total weaver workforce comprises independent workers, a majority of the weavers necessarily bear all the risks associated with the business of procurement, marketing and sale, with obvious consequences.[132] Building reliable and sustainable marketing networks, with participation from the private sector, could be a way to absolve the sector from such challenges.

Unfortunately, in the last 5–10 years, several apex societies/handloom corporations have become dormant due to a host of reasons such as financial losses, lack of professional management, over-staffing and poor marketing and distribution channels. These organizations are, therefore, not able to arrange for sufficient work for the weavers' communities, which has further adversely affected the health of the Primary Weavers' Co-operative Societies. Estimates show that of the 21,765 registered Primary Weavers' Cooperative Societies (which cover only around 15% of the weavers in the country), only 50% are functional, and those too only partially.[133] Moreover, about 85% of weavers in the country are outside the co-operative fold, as they work either under master weavers/traders or independently.

4.5.5 Mill Gate Price Scheme

Yarn is an essential raw material, the continuous supply of which at reasonable rates is a must if the handloom sector is to be sustained. However, sourcing raw materials (yarns, dyes and chemicals) which are the basic supplies required for handloom production has also been a key issue for the sector, the problem being far more acute for individual weavers.[134] In around 2010, cotton yarn prices rose steeply due to a shortage of yarn, with capacities shrinking and acute power and labour shortages in areas with good quality spinning capacity.[135]

The Government of India introduced the Mill Gate Price Scheme (MGPS) during 1993–93, with the objective of providing all types of yarn to handloom weavers' organizations at the prices at which yarn was available in mills.[136] This scheme facilitates i) a regular supply of basic raw material to individual weavers through the yarn depots and ii) assistance for the reimbursement of transportation expenses in the supply of yarn; for expenses related to operating the yarn depots; and service charges to National Handloom Development Corporation (NHDC) for its role as nodal agency for implementation of the scheme.[137] In 2011–2012, a component was added to this scheme to mitigate the price disadvantage which had arisen for the handloom sector after the Central Value Added Tax (CENVAT) of 9.2% on all varieties of cotton yarn was abolished in July 2004.[138]

A sharp increase in cotton prices created major inconvenience for the handloom sector. This situation was further fuelled by a lack of proper delivery systems, the closure of spinning mills in some handloom-producing States and the non-fulfilment of the Hank Yarn obligation by the organized mill sector. Under the MGPS, yarn and dyes are supplied by National Handloom Development Corporation (NHDC) through over 660 yarn depots functioning in weaver clusters.[139] This scheme is popular largely because it is the only scheme that deals with the supply of the most vital raw materials, i.e. yarn and dyes, required by handlooms. However, the NHDC is able to supply barely 18% of the total yarn needed.[140] Moreover, as this delivery of the yarn is in bulk, independent weavers who place small quantities face difficulty.

4.5.6 Handloom Weavers Comprehensive Welfare Scheme

This scheme was an important initiative aimed at providing social welfare facilities to weavers and ancillary workers, consisting of two separate sub-schemes:

(i) The Health Insurance Scheme (HIS) for providing health insurance for weavers and their families was introduced in 2009–2010 but this scheme has been discontinued. However, considering the strenuous work of weaving, it is essential that such a scheme is in place.
(ii) The Mahatma Gandhi Bunkar Bima Yojana (MGBBY) scheme was established to provide life-insurance cover to handloom weavers/workers in case of natural death (₹ 60,000), accidental death and total disability due to accident (₹ 1, 50,000) and partial disability due to accident (₹ 75,000).[141] This scheme was downgraded from 2017 to restrict new enrolments and is confined to renewals. This scheme has now been subsumed under the two newly launched schemes, the Pradhan Mantri Jeevan Jyoti Bima Yojana (PMJJBY) and Pradhan Mantri Suraksha Bima Yojana (PMSBY) schemes. In effect, from 2017, there has been no dedicated life-insurance scheme for handloom weavers. Also, as the PMJJBY and PMSBY schemes are meant for the general public, they do not consider the issue of occupational disability, which had been the case with the earlier version of MGBBY.

Further, from the published figures in the latest census, average insurance penetration is as low as 3.8% among weaver households.

Currently, several welfare schemes for handloom weavers have been either downgraded or done away with. MUDRA (THE Micro Units Development and Refinance Agency), an existing flagship programme to offer loans to small business enterprises at relatively low interest rates, is applicable to handloom weavers, but only 23.3% weavers across the country possess bank accounts, as per the fourth census, effectively excluding a large pool of weavers from the purview of MUDRA loans because the scheme is envisaged as a direct cash transfer to the beneficiaries' bank accounts.

4.5.7 Diversified Handloom Development Scheme

The Diversified Handloom Development Scheme (DHDS) provides assistance for technological and skill upgrading of weavers, and it offers design inputs and product development through 25 Weavers' Service Centres (WSCs) and 5 Indian Institutes of Handloom Technology (IIHT), aimed at improving the productivity and earnings of the weavers. The IIHTs included in the initial years of this scheme were located at Varanasi, Salem, Jodhpur, Guwahati and Bargarh (Odisha), while additional IIHTs were being set up in the State sector at Champa (Chhattisgarh) and Kannur (Kerala).[142] Besides the National Centre for Textile Design (NCTD) set up in January 2001, other components of DHDS include facilitating design exhibitions-cum-dyeing workshops and research and development activities (studies and need-based surveys), conducting the Handloom Census and issuing photo identity cards.[143]

4.5.8 Revival, reform and restructuring package

The Scheme aimed to revive the handloom sector through a one-time write-off of loans extended by banks to individual weavers and also open the choked credit lines for the handloom weavers' co-operative societies, to facilitate future access to credit by the handloom weavers at a lower cost.[144] NABARD was the designated implementing agency for the Scheme.[145]

A challenge here is that major institutions providing inputs (credit, research, technology, management and market development, etc.) are largely centralized and hence unable to reach the dispersed and largely home-based weavers. There has been limited information flow between buyers and sellers, and as such, weavers are often not familiar with the variety in the usage of fabrics and thus find themselves unable to respond to dynamic market trends or suggestions by designers/marketing agencies.

4.5.9 Integrated Skill Development Scheme

The Integrated Skill Development Scheme (ISDS) was launched in 2010 to address the training needs of textiles and related segments. For the handloom sector, the target was to train 1.55 lakh persons over a period of 5 years wherein all facets of skill development were to be covered, namely basic training, skill upgrading, advanced training, training of trainers, retaining and entrepreneurship development.

Weighing the target figure against the number of weavers employed in the handloom sector as per the third census, the scheme aimed to develop skills among merely 3.6% of the relevant population.

4.6 Concluding observations

Understanding the massive share of both the handloom and handicrafts sectors in India's development as well as their employment-generating capacity, the Government of India along with State governments have time and again made programmatic interventions. The policy initiatives have mainly been aimed at generating sustained, productive and gainful employment with decent working conditions for the entire weaver population. Although certain programmes have yielded positive results, the work is far from complete even at present. Policy initiatives since the early pre-independence years have aggressively pushed to revive the sector, but such revival efforts that have lasted for more than 70 years cannot be called the most suitable solution, which is why we see that the handloom industry has failed to travel beyond rural areas and is reduced to a mere form of art in need of preservation. In fact, treating the weavers on a par with any other entrepreneur is essential in order for them to secure confidence in their financial independence, which can also lead to other kinds of independence, such as working under a master weaver. With policies that are scattered and non-uniform as well as the disbursal of funds being sporadic and inconsistent, the change as envisioned cannot be achieved. Therefore, a need has emerged to consolidate policies and schemes that vary from State to State under a clear central arrangement to avoid some of the core features of the handloom industry, such as its prevalence in rural areas, lack of industrial organization etc., which act as impediments to its prosperity.

Further, bolder implementation of the Handloom Reservation Act is required. There has been a strong push for redefining the term *handloom* in such a way that semi-power looms can be included under it. Attempts are also made to remove reserved items like sarees. However, such changes will only increase the power loom's prominence and give it a free ride over handlooms, rendering massive unemployment among weavers as sarees boost the demand for handlooms. Even if such changes are made to the Act, in its current form it is still a law that clearly lacks the power to curb the entry of power looms into the production of items reserved exclusively for handlooms.

Over and above factors like demographic, social, technical and cultural aspects, the immense popularity of low-cost, eye-catching synthetic materials over traditional handloom products has led to a situation of partial turnaround in the sector. The handloom sector, being spread across all regions of the country – albeit not equally, but mainly in rural India – makes it uniquely challenging for policy and programme interventions to be implemented effectively. Moreover, the fact that the sector is decentralized only adds to the enforcement and implementation challenges. Consequently, the creation of sustainable livelihoods in the sector remains a major concern, making the situation only slightly better than in post-independence days. Statistically, according to the first Handloom Census carried out in 1987–1988, the total number of weavers across the country was 67.39 lakh, and as per the second handloom census conducted in 1995–1996, this number was almost stable at 65.5 lakh. However, in the third and fourth census exercise, the number reduced significantly to 43.31 lakh and 35.2 lakh respectively. The cause of this fall in handloom weavers' numbers cannot be attributed to a single factor rather to a combination of factors that equally contribute to the decline. Through this chapter, we attempted to draw out a design of factors negatively affecting the handloom industry by understanding and assessing the impact of policies structured to sustain the cultural heritage.

Notes

1 Seemanthini Niranjana and Soumya Vinayan, Planning Commission, *Report on Growth and Prospects of the Handloom Industry*, 2001, 5. This report was commissioned by the Planning Commission of India to Dastkar Andhra, an NGO dedicated to sustain handloom weaving as a viable rural livelihood, to collect field data necessary for planning and initiating relevant policies.

2 "Highlights, Fourth All India Handloom Census 2019–20" (*Office of the Development Commissioners of Handlooms, Ministry of Textiles, Government of India*, 2019) 14 <http://handlooms.nic.in/writereaddata/3736.pdf> accessed 1 March 2021.

3 NITI AAYOG, *Handlooms – A Large Employment Generating Sector, Report of the Working Group on Handlooms for the 12th Five Year Plan* (2012–2017) 24 <https://niti.gov.in/planningcommission.gov.in/docs/aboutus/committee/wrkgrp12/wg_emp_planing.pdf> accessed 1 March 2021.

4 Ibid.

5 Siddharth Joshi, "A Brief History of Handloom Reservation Act" (*Network of Rural Agrarian Studies* 2016) 1 <http://ruralagrarianstudies.org/wp-content/uploads/2016/03/Paper.pdf> accessed 1 November 2020.

6 Seemanthini Niranjana and Soumya Vinayan (n 1).

7 Ibid.

8 Ibid.

9 Ibid.

10 Invented by James Hargreaves, the spinning jenny was the first machine to improve upon the spinning wheel. At the time, cotton producers had a difficult time meeting the demand for textiles, as each spinner produced only one spool of thread at a time. Hargreaves found a way to ramp up the supply of thread with this invention <https://www.thoughtco.com/who-invented-the-spinning-jenny-4057900> accessed 1 November 2020.

11 Dr. M. Soundarapandian, National Bank for Agriculture and Rural Development, *Growth and Prospects of Handloom Sector in India* (2002) ix <https://www.nabard.org/demo/auth/writereaddata/File/OC%2022.pdf> accessed 2 March 2021.

12 Siddharth Joshi (n 5).

13 Peter Harnetty, "'Deindustrialization' Revisited: The Handloom Weavers of the Central Provinces of India, c. 1800–1947" (1991) 25 (3) *Modern Asian Studies*, 455–510 <https://www.jstor.org/stable/pdf/312614.pdf?refreqid=excelsior%3Ad79369a5b3364caa4f30b3f46bdb6c27> accessed 2 March 2021.

14 Dr. M. Soundarapandian (n 11) ix.

15 Ibid.

16 Ibid.

17 Bankers Institute of Rural Development (BIRD), Lucknow, *Study Report on Problems and Prospects of Handloom Sector in Employment Generation in the Globally Competitive Environment* (2016) 49 <http://www.birdlucknow.in/wp-content/uploads/2016/04/Study-Report-on-Probelms-Prospects-of-handloom-Sector-by-BIRD-Lucknow1.pdf> accessed 2 March 2021.
18 Siddharth Joshi (n 5).
19 BIRD Report (n 17).
20 Kausalya Santhanam, "Reviving Textile Traditions" (*The Hindu*, 16 February 2012). <https://www.thehindu.com/arts/crafts/reviving-textile-traditions/article2899650.ece> accessed 2 March 2021.
21 Ibid.
22 "List of Weavers' Service Centres" (*Office of Development Commissioner (Handlooms)*). <http://www.handlooms.nic.in/writereaddata/Address%20and%20contact%2028%20WSCs635725578191936271.pdf> accessed 2 March 2021.
23 Pheroze L. Vincent, "Boards that Gave Artisans a Voice Scrapped" *Telegraph India* (New Delhi, 8 August 2020). <https://www.telegraphindia.com/india/all-india-handloom-board-and-the-all-india-handicrafts-board-scrapped/cid/1788527> accessed 2 March 2021. The board was first set up with limited objectives of supplying raw materials and assisting in marketing the handloom products. In its later version, the board's functions were widened to include financial assistance, credit facilities, bringing weavers into the cooperative fold, technical assistance, etc.
24 Ibid.
25 "Advisory Bodies" (*Ministry of Textiles*, 2021). <http://texmin.nic.in/about-us/advisory-bodies> accessed 2 March 2021.
26 "Indian Institute of Handloom Technology, Salem" <http://www.iihtsalem.edu.in/about-us/> accessed 2 March 2021.
27 BIRD Report (n 17).
28 "Handloom Export Promotion Council" <https://www.hepcindia.com/page/about_hepc> accessed 2 March 2021.
29 "Office of the Development Commissioner (Handlooms)" <www.handlooms.nic.in> accessed 2 March 2021.
30 Dr. M. Soundarapandian (n 11)15.
31 Dr. M. Soundarapandian (n 11) 11.
32 Ibid., 12.
33 Ibid., 12.
34 Ibid., 12.
35 Prafull Anubhai, "Sickness in Indian Textile Industry: Causes and Remedies" (1988) 23 (48) *Economic and Political Weekly*, M147–M157, 147 <https://www.epw.in/journal/1988/48/review-industry-and-management-uncategorised/sickness-indian-textile-industry-causes> accessed 20 February 2021.
36 Ibid.
37 "Statement of Objects and Reasons, The Handlooms (Reservation of Articles for Production) Act, 1985" (*Ministry of Law and Justice, Government of India*, 1985). <http://handlooms.nic.in/writereaddata/UploadFile/Act%201985.pdf> accessed 2 March 2021.
38 Siddharth Joshi (n 5).
39 *Parvej Aktar vs. Union of India and Ors.*, 1993 SCR (1) 803.
40 Ibid.
41 Siddharth Joshi (n 5).
42 Ibid.
43 Ibid.

44 Ibid.
45 Ibid.
46 Ibid.
47 Ibid.
48 Ibid.
49 "Message from Dayanidhi Maran, Third National Handloom Census of Weavers and Allied Workers, 2009–10" (*National Council for Applied Economic Research, Development Commissioner (Handlooms) Ministry of Textiles, Government of India*, 2010). <http://handlooms.nic.in/Writereaddata/Handloom%20report.pdf> accessed 1 March 2021.
50 Four handloom censuses have been undertaken to date, in 1987–1988, 1995–1996, 2009–2010 and the latest in 2019–2020.
51 "Preface by Suman K-Bery" (n 41).
52 Ibid.
53 "Examining Employment Figures in the Handloom Sector" (*The All India Artisans and Craftworkers Welfare Association*, 2006) 5 <https://www.aiacaonline.org/wp-content/uploads/2018/08/research-NCAER-study-employment-figures-handloom-sector.pdf> accessed 1 March 2021.
54 Ibid., 5.
55 Ibid., 5.
56 Ibid., 5.
57 Ibid., 5.
58 Ibid., 5.
59 Ibid., 5.
60 Ibid., 10.
61 Ibid..
62 Ibid., 11.
63 Ibid.
64 Ibid.
65 A handloom household unit is defined as one in which any member undertakes handloom-related work (either weaving on the loom, or as pre-loom or post-loom allied activity, other than marketing) even for one day in the last year (preceding the survey date), either within the premises of the house or outside the household premises.
66 A handloom non-household unit is an establishment which could be run by a private owner or a society, such as a master weaver, co-operative societies, handloom development corporation, etc. These could be placed in worksheds in the premises of non-household units, or else they could be distributed in the houses of the hired weavers.
67 "Examining Employment Figures in the Handloom Sector" (n 45) 11.
68 Ibid.
69 Ibid.
70 Third National Handloom Census of Weavers and Allied Workers (n 41) 1.
71 Ibid., 2.
72 Ibid., 2.
73 Ibid., 2.
74 Ibid., 18.
75 Ibid., 18.
76 Table B3: Distribution of Adult (18 years and above) Handloom Workers by Gender (n 41) xvii.
77 Ibid., 19.
78 Ibid., 9.
79 Ibid., 9.

80 Ibid., 35.
81 Ibid.
82 Ibid., 21, 23.
83 Ibid., 23.
84 Ibid., 35.
85 Ibid.
86 Ibid.
87 Ibid., 36.
88 Ibid.
89 Ibid., 37.
90 Ibid., 37.
91 "Message from Smriti Zubin Irani, Fourth All India Handloom Census (2019–20)" (*Ministry of Textiles, Government of India*, 2019). <http://handlooms.nic.in/writereaddata/3736.pdf> accessed 1 March 2021.
92 Ibid.
93 "Table 5, Number of Handloom Workers by age group" (n 84) 9.
94 Ibid.
95 "Table 10, Number of Handloom Workers by Type" (n 84) 11.
96 "Table 13, Number of Handloom Workers by Nature of Engagement" (n 84) 11.
97 "Table 7, Number of Handloom Workers by Gender" (n 84) 10.
98 32 and 33.
99 Weaver household: Such a unit is defined as one in which any member has operated a loom in the last one year, either within the premises of the house (classifying the household as a "with loom household") or outside the household premises (classifying the household as a "without loom household").
100 "Fourth All India Handloom Census" (n 84) 32.
101 "Fourth All India Handloom Census" (n 84) 34.
102 "Table 9, Number of Handloom Workers by Level of Education" (n 84) 10.
103 "Table 16, Number of Handloom Workers by Employment Typology" (n 84) 12.
104 "Fourth All India Handloom Census" (n 84) 35.
105 Ibid.
106 "Fourth All India Handloom Census" (n 84) 35.
107 BIRD Report (n 17).
108 "Fourth All India Handloom Census" (n 84) 39.
109 Shambhavi Sawhney, "'Make in India' and its Economic Impact on the Indian Handloom Sector" (*Lampert Institute for Civic and Global Affairs*, 2016) 1–33, 10.
110 "Crises of Handloom Industry" (Discovery Publishing House 1999) 17.
111 Shambavi Sawhney (n 102) 11.
112 L. C. Jain, "1985 Textile Policy: End of Handloom Industry" (1985) 20 (27) *Economic and Political Weekly* 1121 <https://www.epw.in/journal/1985/27/our-correspondent-columns/1985-textile-policy-end-handloom-industry.html> accessed 1 March 2021.
113 Shambavi Sawhney (n 102) 12.
114 Ibid.
115 "Approach and Salient Features of the Eleventh Five Year Plan" (*Planning Commission*, 2007) 30 <http://mpplanningcommission.gov.in/fiveyearplan/VolumeIsep07/Chapter-4-salient%20features%20final.pdf> accessed 1 March 2021.
116 Ibid., 31.

117 While this approach may be required, its viability should be tested given the heterogeneity and differential needs of the handloom sector as compared with other sub-industries, for example the powerloom sector.
118 "Chapter 10, Handlooms and Handicrafts" (*NITI AAYOG*) 222 <https://niti.gov.in/planningcommission.gov.in/docs/plans/mta/11th_mta/chapterwise/chap10_handloom.pdf> accessed 20 February 2021.
119 Ibid., 223.
120 VSE Division, Planning Commission, Government of India, *Report of the Steering Committee on Handlooms and Handicrafts Constituted for the Twelfth Five-Year Plan (2012–17)* 8 <http://handicrafts.nic.in/CmsUpload/22342016043422str_handloom0305.pdf> accessed 1 March 2021.
121 Ibid., 19.
122 Ibid.
123 Ibid.
124 Ibid.
125 Ibid., 20.
126 NITI AAYOG, *Handlooms – A Large Employment Generating Sector, Report of the Working Group on Handlooms for the 12th Five Year Plan* (2012–17) 45 <https://niti.gov.in/planningcommission.gov.in/docs/aboutus/committee/wrkgrp12/wg_emp_planing.pdf> accessed 1 March 2021.
127 Ibid.
128 Ibid.
129 *Marketing and Export Promotion Scheme in Report of the Steering Committee on Handlooms and Handicrafts Constituted for the Twelfth Five-Year Plan (2012–17)*, (n 113) 20.
130 Ibid.
131 BIRD Report (n 17) 40.
132 Ibid.
133 BIRD Report (n 17) 76.
134 BIRD Report (n 17) 39.
135 "Cotton Yarn Price Increase and Shortage: Reasons and Solution" (*Textile Magazine*, 2010). <https://www.indiantextilemagazine.in/industry-news/cotton-yarn-price-increase-and-shortage-reasons-and-solution/> accessed 2 March 2021.
136 *Mill Gate Price Scheme (MGPS) in Report of the Steering Committee on Handlooms and Handicrafts Constituted for the Twelfth Five-Year Plan (2012–17)*, (n 113) 21.
137 Ibid.
138 Ibid.
139 BIRD REPORT (n 17).
140 Ibid., 55.
141 "Mahatma Gandhi Bunkar Bima Yojana" *(Ministry of Textiles*, 2021). <https://pib.gov.in/PressReleasePage.aspx?PRID=1607362> last accessed 4 March 2021.
142 *Diversified Handloom Development Scheme in Report of the Steering Committee on Handlooms and Handicrafts Constituted for the Twelfth Five-Year Plan (2012–17)*, (n 113) 22.
143 Ibid.
144 *Revival, Reform and Restructuring Package in Report of the Steering Committee on Handlooms and Handicrafts Constituted for the Twelfth Five-Year Plan (2012–17)*, (n 113) 23.
145 Ibid.

5

CONCLUSIONS

Mapping the road ahead

> Law is not a mausoleum. It is not an antique to be taken down, dusted, admired and put back on the shelf. It is like an old but vigorous tree, having roots in history, yet continuously taking new grafts and putting out new sprouts and occasionally dropping dead wood. It is essentially a social process, the end product of which is justice and hence it must change with changing social values. Otherwise there will be estrangement between law and justice and law will cease to have legitimacy.
>
> – Justice P. N. Bhagwati[1]

5.1 Note for readers

Taking inspiration from the words of a legal luminary of the Indian judiciary, we agree that the legitimacy of law cannot be established unless the purpose of justice is served. This principle is sacrosanct irrespective of any law, customary or contemporary, and the law protecting Geographical Indications is no exception.

Goods with a specific geographical origination, having unique characteristics solely attributable to them, are protected under the law of GI via a formal registration process. A bundle of legal rights is attached to such recognition. However, the legal right in the absence of effective enforcement remains only as a part of the letter of the law. Thus, without bridging this gap between *law in text* and *law in context*, any legal instrument, howsoever noble in its intentions, remains inadequate. The law on Geographical Indications in India is on the verge of completing nearly two decades of existence, having been legislated with the intention to secure the nation's traditional and cultural heritage. Looking at the increasing number of registrations, a question on the efficacy of GI law in India arose in our minds. Has the Act fulfilled its objective? Has it achieved the desired protection envisaged through the legal provisions? In order to answer these questions, we studied the system of GI law, employing doctrinal and empirical research methodologies. However, during the study, we stumbled upon eye-opening

DOI: 10.4324/9781003002147-6

realities leading us to conclude that in fact there exist conspicuous gaps between recognition and the realization of rights. This primary knowledge encouraged us to conduct a specific inquiry into the reasons for such gaps. It is pertinent to mention that this probe would have been incomplete without the inclusion of policy initiatives and other programmatic interventions by the government, as the success of this law is heavily dependent on the crucial role played by the State through such measures. This research study is spread over four chapters, consisting of an overview of the Geographical Indications systems, including international instruments, as well as the Indian law on GIs; a doctrinal compilation of case studies of selected handloom products across India, followed by an analysis of empirical outcomes of a study conducted on two handlooms from Gujarat; and finally a comprehensive layout of government schemes and policies targeted towards the handloom sector.

5.2 Summary of chapters

A summary of conclusions drawn from the preceding chapters is presented here. While assessing the evolution and rationale of the GI system, we take away that the conceptual status of GIs goes beyond being merely a legal instrument. In fact, what sets it apart from other laws is evident from its meaning, nature, characteristics and functions. Though the term *Geographical Indications* is fairly recent in the international IP regime, the concept is not. Rooted in French locals' deep belongingness to traditions nurtured on their land, the current concept was gradually developed through the idea of *terroir*, later taking the shape of Appellations of Origin and Indications of Source, among many others.[2] With TRIPS, these domestic terms acquired substantial recognition as *Geographical Indications*. Although the earlier terms are still in practice, the Indian system legally recognized the contemporary term through the Geographical Indications of Goods (Registration and Protection) Act, 1999; and this has assumed increased importance in our developing economy, which is also home to a vast variety of traditional knowledge–based products. These products are not only marks of distinct Indian traditions, culture and heritage but also have potential for large-scale revenue generation. Thus, by recognizing such traditional products as GIs, the domestic legislation protects heritage as well as adds value to the economy. With this Act, India created a *sui generis* system in line with the EU system of protection, distinct from the US-led system protecting GIs as conventional trademarks.

With the objective of assessing the efficacy of GI law in the handloom sector in India, Chapter 2 discussed case studies which are apt illustrations of regional diversity and traditional heritage. One of the major observations here is that the handloom sector is territorially dispersed and unorganized yet is the second-most employment-generating industry in the country, and is mainly practiced in rural areas by local communities that are socially, economically and educationally backward. Due to the nature of the industry, statistical data that can be analyzed to draw quantitative conclusions on the impact created by the law is almost unavailable. Thus, taking our cue from secondary resources, we traced the GI registration journey of the selected handlooms that offered the following essential insights.

Registration is the first, formal step towards recognition of the product as a GI, which, in a few cases, as observed, has even served the purpose of reviving the craft, such as Kota Doria and Tangaliya shawls.[3] It is interesting to note that a Geographical Indication, unlike other forms of IP, is a recognition of products that are age-old, already established and available to the public. Thus, their recognition is not solely attributable to their GI status. Likewise, granting of GI status does not mean an automatic betterment in the socio-economic condition of the weavers of the handloom sector. They need extensive support for marketing, branding and sales of the registered product, which also means that a market demand for such valued products must be created among the end-users. This support system may not work effectively in the absence of adequate post-grant benefit-sharing mechanisms, and for such a system to operate at all rural levels, the government needs to be proactive. External actors such as non-governmental organizations (NGOs), government agencies and educational institutes have a pivotal role to play in the overall protection of GIs for example, not only facilitating registration but also making the weavers understand the benefits of such registration.

GI registration is granted as a community right to an association of producers; however, in the majority of cases, there are in fact many weavers who are left out of this fold. The Act also facilitates such weavers through Section 17 to be registered as Authorized Users of the GI tag, but as observed in the case studies, only a few weavers have taken advantage of this provision.[4] The reason behind this is a lack of awareness as well as a striking disconnect between weavers and external agencies. The unfortunate reality of existing handloom products is that despite their GI status, powerloom products have taken over the originally handcrafted fabric and sarees, due to which the weaving community has lost a lot of work.

The system as prescribed through the legal provisions is certainly not entirely weak by nature. On a positive note, we see the GI Register growing at a rapid speed with many States racing to protect as many products as possible. While we draw a conclusion on this work, India has reached a mark of 370[5] registered GIs, which is worthy of appreciation, considering the lengthy registration procedure. However, as observed through the doctrinal research carried out on selected handloom products, it is crystal-clear that registration is not the end of the story but a beginning to a perpetual legal recognition.

The empirical study conducted by us, wherein data relating to weavers of Tangaliya and Kutch shawls was collected, revealed that though these products were registered as GIs in 2009–2010 and 2011–2012 respectively, this has not achieved the objective as envisaged for the reasons listed here.

Weavers are unaware on several fronts ranging from pre-registration, i.e. about the term *Geographical Indications*, the rights granted through it and its benefits, to post-registration, i.e. the mechanism for the enforcement of rights. This lack of awareness equally affects the benefits that can be accrued from government schemes and policies. The following reasons are identified for the insufficient realization of legal rights granted under the GI Act:

1. Weavers face difficulty in marketing and selling their products despite GI registration.
2. The GI tag could not generate a sufficient market, leading to difficulty in creating demand for and sales of such genuine products.
3. Owing to various challenges, weavers are leaving the craft to work as full-time labourers on farms or construction sites.
4. Young family members are reluctant to continue weaving despite GI registration.
5. Weavers were not part of the last National Handloom Census carried out in 2009–2010.
6. Weavers invest a considerable amount of time and energy in weaving one genuine shawl, as opposed to a powerloom shawl; this goes unnoticed due to lack of general awareness about the value of GI products.
7. There exists a noticeable disconnect between weavers and the associations/organizations/NGOs responsible for acquiring the GI registration of the selected handlooms.
8. There is a partial awareness among weavers about GI. There are weavers who have heard the term but are unaware of what it means. Weavers are not aware that their handloom product is legally recognized and protected as GI.
9. There is a lack of awareness about the government schemes for weavers.
10. Some weavers are not familiar with the India Handloom Brand.
11. There is a lack of awareness about the ongoing cluster development scheme for Tangaliya handloom.
12. There is a lack of awareness about the Yarn Supply Scheme, which adds to the difficulties being faced by the weavers in the procurement of raw material under the said scheme.

To complete the full circle of inquiry, our investigation took us beyond the legal provisions into other government interventions because, as explained previously, the success of this Act, especially in the handloom sector, depends on adequate assistance from schemes and policies. In fact, some of these policies and interventions were in place long before the law, which means the sector's importance has not been unknown to the government. These interventions have come from time to time, first through 5-year plans and now on the suggestions of the NITI Aayog, of course not without guidance from expert bodies. Most of the efforts to date have been two-fold: to ensure the generation of profitable and sustainable employment and to provide for a socially and economically sound standard of living. Other factors like educational support, health assistance etc. are also part of the larger schematic arrangement. Apart from these interventions, India has devised an innovative model of data collection through the Handloom Census initiative, the 2019–2020 edition being the latest, to provide statistical insights into the sector's health. However, it is rather disheartening to go through dwindling numbers of handloom weavers, most of who are uneducated or poorly educated with little awareness of how valuable their contribution is to the Indian economy. According to the first Handloom Census of 1987–1988, the total number of weavers across the country was 67.39 lakh, which, as per the second handloom census conducted in 1995–1996, remained almost stable at 65.5 lakh, but the figure significantly reduced in the third and fourth census exercises to 43.31 lakh and 35.2 lakh respectively.[6] A dearth of basic resources like hassle-free financial assistance, health insurance, banking facilities etc. makes this sector not lucrative enough for young weavers to be motivated to continue their traditional legacy.

Further, among a host of governmental interventions made towards protection and sustenance of the handloom sector, the Handlooms (Reservation of Articles for Production) Act, 1985 is a key outcome of several expert bodies' deliberations.[7] As the title suggests, this legislation was enacted in order to give handloom producers an exclusive right to the production of certain items, thus legally keeping out the power looms that have been a major competition to the handloom sector. Yet, 36 years into its enforcement, this legislation is yet to make its mark. In fact, the 22 articles reserved in the initial years of this legislation were later reduced to 11, which further enunciates the dire condition of our handloom industry. So, how did we severely fail this sector? The answer lies in not a single factor but a multilevel debacle involving several external authorities. As elucidated in the earlier chapters, the success of GI cannot be attributed to mere registration, likewise any single authority cannot produce the desired result behind enacting the GI law and building a policy structure. All the stakeholders involved must sufficiently play the roles assigned to them in order to implement the law and policies better than the present scenario. The situation of the handloom sector necessitates a synergy of law and policy to be effectuated by those involved with the sector – directly or indirectly – with the right amount of passion to save the looms and their weavers from age-old problems.

5.3 Gaps located between legal right and real right

Based on the broad conclusions from the doctrinal and empirical research studies, we further focused in on gaps between the legal and real rights that are common to the Indian handloom sector in the context of the GI system.

5.3.1 Lack of awareness

The efficacy of any law is dependent on awareness among its stakeholders. This becomes more relevant when such stakeholders range across various categories such as producers, consumers and the government as well as other external actors like NGOs, educational institutes etc. which is the case here. The law of GIs, as we have discussed, is meant to serve as a tool for rural development, consumer protection and the preservation of traditional knowledge by way of recognizing the reputation and unique characteristics of origin-bound products. But these functions cannot fulfil their purpose unless all the stakeholders involved are well aware of the benefits. The conclusions drawn from our study, as discussed at length, mainly point at a lack of awareness on the part of the producers and weavers, which creates a considerable gap between them and the system. Further, this gap is found at all stages of the process from pre-registration to post-registration. Being unaware of the benefits of registration, producers and weavers miss out on the opportunity of earning recognition for their unique, invaluable craft. Even the external agencies, as evidenced from the case studies, had to struggle to bring together these producers and weavers in the form of an association while assisting them in registering their handloom as a GI mainly due to this rampant unawareness. This widespread lack of awareness can be viewed as a root cause of the remaining gaps discussed below.

5.3.2 Non-functional inspection bodies

Under the registration requirements of the GI Act and Rules, it is mandatory to provide particulars of inspection body. The underlying objective of such a body is to maintain the quality and regulate the use of GI products by establishing an independent, neutral agency. Following details from the handloom case studies conducted in Chapters 2 and 3 are apt to be considered while comparing the situation on paper vis-à-vis on ground.

Three broad categories of inspection body emerge out of the list of studied handlooms as elaborated in Table 5.1. The first category refers to those products where the inspection body is proposed to be established. The second category of products is where a set structure of the inspection body is mentioned. The third and final category is where the purpose, functions and responsibilities along with the composition of the inspection body is clearly Stated. Out of the 14 products we studied, 3 fall in the first category, 10

Table 5.1 Inspection bodies of select handlooms

Sr. No.	*Product*	*State*	*Inspection body*
1.	Pochampally ikat	Telangana	The applicants have Stated that they are moving towards the establishment of an inspection structure in consultation with the following: Textile Committee under MoT, GoI Weavers' Service Centre, GoI Govt. of Andhra Pradesh
2.	Chanderi saree	Madhya Pradesh	State Government of Madhya Pradesh with no specific distribution of roles and responsibilities
3.	Kota Doria	Rajasthan	Kota Doria Development Hadauti Foundation with no specific distribution of roles and responsibilities
4.	Kancheepuram silk	Karnataka	State Government of Tamilnadu with no specific distribution of roles and responsibilities
5.	Muga silk	Assam	The inspection body comprises the following: i. Department of Sericulture, Govt. of Assam ii. Representative Committee iii. Central Silk Board of India iv. Weavers' Association v. Weavers' Service Centre vi. ARTFED vii. District Industry Officer viii. Representative of Department of Sericulture ix. PIC/ASTEC x. Institute of Advanced Studies in Science & Technology, Asom-Laboratory and Certification with no specific distribution of roles and responsibilities
6.	Kullu shawls	Himachal Pradesh	The inspection body comprises the following: i. Co-ordinator, H.P. Patent Information Centre, State Council for Science, Technology and Environment, H.P. ii. General Manager, District Industries Centre, Kullu or his representative

(*Continued*)

Table 5.1 (Continued)

Sr. No.	*Product*	*State*	*Inspection body*
			iii. Managing Director, Himbunkar, Bhunter, District Kullu iv. President, Kullu Shawl Weavers' Association, Kullu. v. Assistant Registrar, Co-operative Societies, Kullu vi. H. P. Handicraft and Handloom Corporation vii. In charge, Central Wool Development Board, Kullu viii. One expert in textile technology/ design
7.	Kashmir pashmina	Kashmir	The applicant is taking steps to set up a suitable and effective inspection body
8.	Banaras brocades and sarees	Uttar Pradesh	The inspection body comprises the following: i. The Department of Handlooms, Government of Uttar Pradesh ii. Development Commissioner (Handlooms), Government of India iii. The Weavers' Service Centre, Government of India, Banaras is also providing technical and design related services to the weavers iv. Master weavers v. The Textiles Committee, Ministry of Textiles, Government of India with no specific distribution of roles and responsibilities
9.	Paithani sarees	Maharashtra	The inspection body comprises the following: i. The Department of Powerloom, Handloom & Textiles, Government of Maharashtra ii. Development Commissioner (Handlooms), Government of India iii. Maharashtra Handloom Development Corporation iv. Maharashtra State Small Scale Industrial Development Corporation (MSSIDC)

(*Continued*)

Table 5.1 (Continued)

Sr. No.	*Product*	*State*	*Inspection body*
			v. A mix of artisans, experts from the Ministry of Textiles and traders of Paithani are suggested to be added with no specific distribution of roles and responsibilities
10.	Mysore silk	Karnataka	Karnataka Silk Industries Corporation with no specific distribution of roles and responsibilities
11.	Kutch shawls	Gujarat	Inspection structure will be established comprising the master artisans, experts from the handloom sector, designers, members of government and non-government organizations etc.
12.	Tangaliya shawls	Gujarat	The inspection body comprises of craftsmen from Tangaliya, experts from the National Institute of Fashion Technology (NIFT), Gandhinagar and experts from the National Institute of Design with no specific distribution of roles and responsibilities
13.	Patan patola	Gujarat	The inspection body comprises the following: Two-tier inspection system i. Initial inspection by expert artisans ii. Inspection by inspection committee consisting of two members of the association and one expert independent agency as appointed from time to time with no specific distribution of roles and responsibilities
14.	Rajkot patola	Gujarat	The inspection body comprises expert artisans and Rajkot District Weavers Association with no specific distribution of roles and responsibilities

Source: Compiled from GI Registry at www.ipindia.nic.in

fall in the second category and only 1 i.e. Kullu Shawl in the third category. This is suggestive of establishment of inspection body being just part of the application formality. In order to be functional, prescription of the roles and responsibilities of inspection body members is the key. In an attempt to verify on-field information, we tried reaching out to each registered proprietor of the handlooms on the current status of inspection body. However, in most cases such information could not be gathered as the same is not available. More painful was to observe a complete lack of awareness on part of Kutch and Tangaliya Shawl weavers' associations regarding setting-up of an inspection body. Thus, it is safe to conclude that such inspection bodies are mere paper-entities and have failed to fulfil the requirement of regulating use of GIs. It is worthy to note that Kullu Shawl and Kashmir Pashmina have developed an online presence post registration i.e. their inspection body- structure, functions, roles and responsibilities as well as quality control details are well in place.

5.3.3 Absence of code of practice

As prescribed under TRIPS, GI is granted for a product which carries unique, qualitative characteristics attributable to a specific geographical origin, thus giving an assurance to the end-user of its quality and reputation. In order to supply to the market products of a certain quality, an effective standard operating procedure must be established. Such standard operating procedures and other management set-ups are widely used by the European nations under the title *Code of Practice* (CoP). This code is a document establishing rules for the use of a Geographical Indication. Its elaboration is a very important step, leading to the voluntary "standard" or specifications with which local producers who want to use the GI have to comply.[8] The objective behind establishing a CoP can be two-fold: 1) to facilitate the producers by prescribing the norms for quality maintenance of the GI tagged product; and 2) to in turn ensure that a quality-checked product will reach the consumer.

A Code of Practice prescribes rules for the use of GI among producers which further ensures the involvement of all stakeholders in the value chain of the GI product. A Code of Practice, though not mandatory, is a tool that can be prescribed for communicating several characteristics as well as for the quality assurance of each product that is produced by these weavers. Mere registration in the absence of a Code of Practice again may not aid the producers in creating the desired market. The significance of creating a CoP is evident from examples like Parma ham from Italy, Champagne from France and Tequila from Mexico.[9] A laudable example closer to India is the Thai system, where the government and the Department of Intellectual Property (DIP) are actively involved in creating manuals of production and methods for tracing the origins of each product, assisted by the Thai Industrial Standard Institute (TISI) and the National Bureau of Agriculture Commodity and Food Standard (ACFS).[10]

In the Indian context, through the Statement of Case filed with a GI application, several details of the art, such as its geographical origin, its historical evolution, the characteristics that make the art unique, the raw materials used accompanied by a description of the entire weaving process etc., is currently provided. However, institutional governance of the GI registered products through the establishment of a CoP is a missing link that could build a system of reputation and value for such products.

5.3.4 Minimal logo registrations

A logo can be used as an excellent tool for marketing and branding GI products and can transform their rural identity into an international one. However, the data currently available through the GI Registry website does not paint a motivating picture. It reveals that out of 74 handlooms registered as GIs, only 7 have also registered their logos as GIs separately. 15 products have their logos as part of their application; 20 applications show only pictures of the respective product, which cannot be considered a logo; and 31 applications have neither a picture nor a logo. Among the logos registered separately, it is interesting to note that registration of Kota Doria was valid only until 2019 and action on its renewal has not been taken, while in the case of Muga silk, a separate inspection body structure is prescribed for the product and its logo. Thus, such cases of non-uniformity or no-action do nothing to strengthen the GI system.

Considering the unawareness among producers of GI registered products as well as consumers of the end products, an information asymmetry arises which can be mitigated through an added authentication process using a logo. As discussed here, currently a negligible percentage of products have registered separate logos in the case of handloom GIs, with no verifiable source of such logo being put to use successfully. Under such situations, a common logo can benefit the entire community of GI proprietors. To tackle this, the Department for Promotion of Industry and Internal Trade (DPIIT), in order to encourage the promotion and marketing of Indian products registered as Geographical Indications, launched a common GI logo and tagline.[11] The GI logo will act as a certifying mark that can be used to identify all Indian products registered as GIs, irrespective of their categories, which makes it convenient for the consumers to recognize authentic GI products, thereby protecting the interests of genuine GI producers.[12] However, in the absence of an institutionalized mechanism to identify the value chain, the strategic use of the GI logo and tagline is largely missing.

5.3.5 Insufficient registration of authorized users

As discussed in Chapter 2, the concept of Authorized User (AU) is a legal innovation of the Indian GI Act.[13] Considering the nature of the GI right, which is a community right, the same cannot be transmitted, licensed or assigned. However, a property right is underutilized in the absence of such commercial arrangements. Therefore, the Act prescribes for the registration of Authorized Users. Under the system, over and above the registered proprietor of a GI, any individual, i.e. a producer, manufacturer, dealer, trader or exporter,[14] can apply for the status of an Authorized User, which enables him to make use of the GI tag as well as initiate actions against infringement.

From the basic details available from the GI Registry, it is understood that weavers' associations do not make the applications for GI registration. Here, external agencies like the Himachal Pradesh Patent Information Center for Kullu Shawl or the Assam State's Patent Information Center for Muga Silk have applied and are the registered proprietor of the same. In such cases, it becomes imperative that weavers, producers, traders, manufacturers, dealers and exporters must individually apply for registration as Authorized Users under the Act. However, as discussed in Chapter 2, such registration is minimal or completely absent. Quoting the data of registered AUs, it can be seen that Pochampally ikat has 2, Patan patola has 14, Kota Doria has 15 and Kancheepuram silk has 34,[15] Banaras brocade and sarees has 117 registrations, Kullu shawls has 134, Kashmir pashmina has 251 and Muga silk has 286 registrations. In some cases like chanderi, paithani saree, Rakjot patola, Mysore silk, Tangaliya shawls and Kutch shawls there are no authorized users, further proving how under-used the legal provisions are.

5.3.6 Sparse infringement cases

Finding an imitation GI product in the domestic or international market is not unusual. A customer searching for a "pure" Banarasi silk saree may end up buying an artificial look-alike product made from Chinese silk on a power loom.[16] This goes against the very objective, as mentioned earlier, of the GI law to create a niche market for genuine products. The reasons behind such rampant infringement are many and not limited to lack of awareness about legal rights, the absence of and inspection body and CoP, the non-recognition of the value chain, insufficient numbers of Authorized Users and the lack of a post-registration enforcement mechanism. A law without enforcement is definitely in a miserable State, which is the case with the GI Act. To date, a handful of infringement cases have reached the Court, the most noteworthy being that of Darjeeling tea and Pochampally ikat. However, these cannot be considered as precendents as most of the Darjeeling Tea GI infringement matters were fought in foreign jurisdictions while the the Pochampally Ikat dispute got settled outside of the Court. In the first case, *Tea Board of India vs. ITC Ltd.*,[17] the plaintiff, who was the registered proprietor of GI Darjeeling Tea, alleged fraudulent use of the GI registered "Darjeeling Tea" by the defendant in naming one of its business premises the "Darjeeling Lounge". In using this name, the plaintiff argued that the defendant has misled its customers by suggesting that the goods which it sells at the said premises originate in the said geographical area. Such activity of using the name for the purpose of the lounge threatened the commercial activities of persons actually in the business of producing Darjeeling tea. Addressing the matter on merits, the Court observed that rights in the registered GI "Darjeeling Tea" are applicable only to goods, particularly to tea, and not to services. The defendant's lounge does not qualify as goods. As to the issue of unfair competition, the Court opined there is no competition between the plaintiff and the defendant in any industrial or commercial matters, and therefore the issue of unfair competition within the meaning of the GI Act does not arise at all.[18]

The legal rights as prescribed under the Act cannot be viewed as ineffective when the remedial measures of the legal provisions are not invoked against cases of infringement. Taking a clue from Chapter 3, from our interaction with the weavers it is clear that they are barely aware of their legal rights flowing from the GI registration. When this is the situation, it is unreasonable to expect them to be vigilant as to the infringement of such legal rights. In addition, there are individual weavers who are aware both of the GI right, if only partially, and that infringement of their handlooms frequently takes place, but they lack the legal, technical and financial strength to fight a legal battle.

5.3.7 Ineffective organizational arrangement of government schemes and policies

In Chapter 4, we highlighted the prominence of the handloom sector through various government schemes and policies that have been in place prior to the *sui generis* system of GIs that India adopted in 1999.[19] Policy initiatives and other programmatic interventions together form an important facet of a successful GI protection system, without which effective enforcement of the rights granted through registration seems to be a distant dream. Our effort to understand these schemes and policies, together with the data collected empirically and doctrinal case studies, led us to conclude that although aimed at sustaining the handloom sector among a variety of challenges, these schemes and policies have not achieved the same. Not only have the number of handloom workers reduced but the situation of the entire sector also remains dire on various fronts, as enunciated by the Handloom Census data. A weaver household making as little as ₹ 5,000 per month will definitely lack the will to continue practicing the art, which cannot bring them long-term sustainability. Besides, factors like a lack of education, meagre penetration of basic banking and insurance facilities, employment status etc. contribute majorly in bringing down this priceless sector, making the primary stakeholders, i.e. the weavers, not independent entrepreneurs but dependent workers.

The innate challenges of a widely dispersed handloom sector such as rising input costs, sparse credit coverage, marketing bottlenecks, poor institutional management, poor policy dissemination, information and resource gaps, infrastructural gaps, the unavailability of an adequate and dedicated database, the absence of robust monitoring and evaluation systems, the lack of technical and technological upgrades and the non-inclusion of research and training in the formal educational system continue to contribute towards the widening gap between legal right and real right in the case of GI-registered products.

5.3.8 Lack of post-registration enforcement mechanism

Beginning on a positive note, India under its *sui generis* GI law has identified and registered more than 370 unique products, including 15 foreign products like Champagne, Prosecco and Cognac. While conducting this research, multiple challenges and concerns in the overall system of GIs protection have been noted, the biggest of them being an almost-absent post-registration enforcement mechanism. This mechanism should essentially work towards two broad goals: i) to facilitate the establishment of a niche market for GI products and ii) to enable the producers in demystifying their grievances, especially the violation of legal rights.

The post-registration enforcement mechanism is expected to address concerns like setting up a Code of Practice, creating domestic and export-oriented markets through effective branding and building a premium value for quality-assured GI products. Such absence is prominently evident from the case of Tangaliya shawls, where the GI registration lapsed in 2018.[20] Even the producers' association is unaware of this lapse, and such information has not been brought to their notice even by the external agencies who played an instrumental role in reviving this handloom through GI registration in 2008.

In absence of a sound post-registration enforcement mechanism, the objective, of enacting the GI law, to improve domestic and export-oriented markets for unique, origin-bound products cannot be fulfilled. The need for such a mechanism is heightened particularly in the context of the handloom sector, which, as seen in Chapter 4, employs mostly socially, educationally and economically backward sections of Indian society. Such factors make it essential for hand-holding in the form of a post-registration enforcement mechanism, which not only facilitates the creation of a market but also extends to playing the role of a watch-dog agency in case of misappropriation. For example, the rampant plagiarism of Banarasi sarees can be effectively arrested with a procedural investigation so that a genuine GI tagged Banarasi saree produced in the specific territory can earn its real value.[21]

5.4 Recommendations: Mapping the road ahead

Resolving a problematic situation has to be three-phased, involving i) identifying the problem; ii) locating the issues and challenges requiring a solution; and iii) adopting a solution and moving towards enforcement. Based on the substantive discussions in Chapters 1–4 and the gaps highlighted in this chapter, it is well-established that the current system and structure of Geographical Indication protection in India has not been as successful as envisaged in its objectives. Such a failure cannot be attributed to just one stakeholder but to the entire institution in place. Further, analyzing the efficacy of the enforcement of GI law is a complex issue due to the involvement of multiple factors ranging from social, economic, cultural, and educational aspects to gender participation and more, which present challenges to the functioning of the system. Hence, collective action on the part of each involved stakeholder will certainly take India down the path of the desired realization of legal rights. The following are some recommendations we present based on the unique issues and challenges raised by the deliberations on the GI products from the Indian handloom sector. However owing to the vastness of the sector and the complexity of its issues that often spillover to other sectors these recommendations should be merged with other workable solutions to specifically target the betterment of Indian handlooms.

- **Adequate and effective pre- and post-registration policies and schemes to promote GI**
  GI as a form of intellectual property has a significant role to play in socio-economic benefits and rural development. However, mere granting of GI tag does not help artisans earn a livelihood from it. In the domestic context, GI's scope is not limited to protecting origin-based products but is extended to the protection of traditional knowledge and traditional cultural expressions as well. In a geographical terrain as vast and diverse as India's, where a wide range of agricultural, handicraft and handloom products etc. are found in each State, it is essential to adopt a scheme that is sector-specific, holistic and development oriented. Adopting such a scheme becomes necessary also because the population attached to major GIs belong to weaker sections of the class system. Thus, targeting to strengthen them educationally, financially, technologically and skill-wise while providing assistance with marketing, quality control set-up and product distribution, including export development, will enable India to create success stories of the GIs unique to the nation. The gap between legal right and real right will be appropriately bridged with an operational post-grant mechanism.
- **Establishment of GI Protection and Promotion Council**

The Indian Government's initiative in establishing Cell for IPR Promotion and Management (CIPAM), a professional body under the aegis of the Department for Promotion of Industry and Internal Trade (DPIIT) which ensures focused action on issues related to IPRs and addresses the seven identified objectives of the National IP Policy,[22] is appreciated. However, the system needs further streamlining with a focused approach to GIs, which can be undertaken by establishing a nodal agency, i.e. a GI Protection and Promotion Council (GPPC) at the national level along with sub-committees at the State level. This council should be established under the GI Registry, Chennai. The council would consist of experts from relevant ministries, committees/commissions, bankers, independent researchers and members of academia as well as including adequate weavers' representation to get a holistic idea of the issues and challenges that remain within the handloom sector and deliberate upon resolving them.

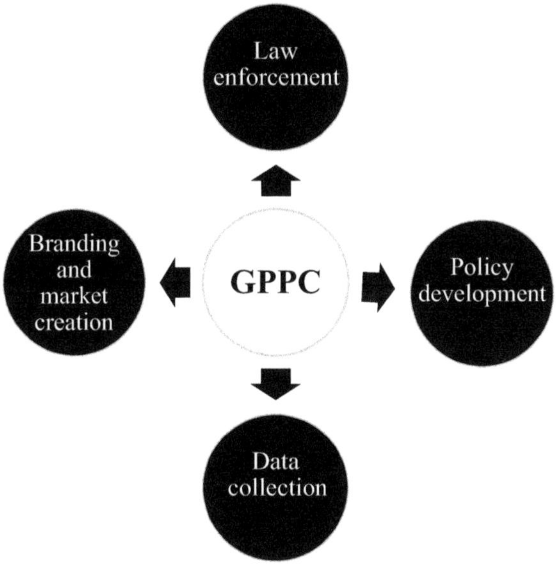

Figure 5.1 Focus area for GPPC functioning. (Source: Developed by the authors)

Looking at the handloom sector's current situation, it is in decline mainly due to a lack of law enforcement, a loosely strategic policy infrastructure, poor branding and market creation and sporadic/insufficient data collection. Thus, these are the four broad areas the GPPC must primarily target. The council must also work towards compulsory registration of all registered GI associations for better enforcement of existing GIs, which also include re-registration processes. It must also undertake systematic studies to investigate the real impact of registered GIs on producers and consumers.

Conducting regular handloom census and creating online databases

Launching targeted policies without having an accurate database can spell doom for such initiatives right from the beginning. Although the handloom census is a unique form of identifying various factors of the relevant handloom sector, the timeline under which it is conducted (at an interval of 10 years) may be too long to evaluate policies in place and understand the future requirements. Also, considering the overall health of the sector, it is necessary to keep updating the numbers. However, also taking into consideration the cost and time involved in gathering such data through a national exercise, a State-specific database can be created by the State Committees under the GPPC in order to assess such numbers from time to time.

A time-bound calculation of the people involved in the handloom sector will also assist with increasing registration of authorized users who are not within the fold of the association that is granted the GI tag as the registered proprietor. Here again, considering the educational background of weavers, where a majority of them lack basic acquaintance with English/Hindi, any such database should be made accessible under the local language through appropriate mechanisms for its dissemination.

Establishment of an Indian Institute of Handloom Technology in Gujarat

In order to add life to dying arts like Tangaliya and Kutch work shawls, it is essential to motivate the younger generation to become technically qualified. To provide technically qualified personnel for the development of the handloom industry, the Indian Institutes of Handloom Technology (IIHT) have been set up. There are six IIHTs under the Central Sector under the administrative control of O/o D.C. (Handlooms), and these are situated at Salem (Tamilnadu), Varanasi (Uttar Pradesh), Guwahati (Assam), Jodhpur (Rajasthan), Bargarh (Odisha) and Shantipur (West Bengal). Moreover, 4 IIHTs under the State Sector are also operating under the administrative control of respective State governments, situated at Venkatagiri (Andhra Pradesh), Gadag-Betgeri (Karnataka), Champa (Chattisgarh) and Kannur (Kerala). Considering the rich handloom traditions of Gujarat, we recommend establishment of an IIHT in the State.

Mass awareness camps

Awareness of GI can certainly play a vital role in realizing the objective of its protection. The system of GI protection demands awareness at every level including the pre- and post-registration phases. While producers of GI registered products will benefit from the awareness of their rights and the ways in which they can be enforced, the consumers, when made aware of the characteristics that are attributable to the uniqueness of the product, will recognize the significance of Geographical Indications. Building awareness is also inevitable to reduce instances of infringement and free-riding. Such increased awareness will in turn boost the commercial utilization of GIs. Awareness campaigns are required to be undertaken at national as well as State levels; hence, the same should be conducted under the supervision of government machinery. As recommended earlier, the GI Protection and Promotion Council could establish a three-tier system at national, State and regional levels for undertaking this herculean task looking at the breadth and length of the country. Further, these awareness camps could highlight the organic, environmentally friendly aspects of handlooms among customers, which will not only make them familiar with such unique attributes but also will influence their purchase preferences.

Better reach of Cluster Development Programme

After observing the current State of affairs through our empirical outing, we have concluded that schemes and programmes are being run with a negligible outcome on several beneficiaries. In fact, the data is suggestive of widespread unawareness of the schemes and policies run by the government for weavers. One such example is the Cluster Development Programme, under which prominent handloom clusters across the nation have been identified for technical and technological upgrades and skill development along the lines of the latest market trends etc., but the execution of the same lacks strength. Thus, the existing Cluster Development Programme needs to be redesigned with a better alignment towards weavers' needs, which should be the prime consideration.

All-inclusive approach to brand promotion of GI

An all-inclusive approach to brand promotion of GI should be undertaken by involving various public stakeholders. Public institutions involved in the agricultural, food and handloom-handicraft sectors can play an active role in defining and enforcing GI policies. The strategy should be to convert GI from being just an origin-based indicator to being a brand. Marketing strategies should be developed to target brand creation and recognition. From concept to commercialization, at every stage the objective of brand promotion should be highlighted. Appropriate brand promotion will significantly contribute towards creating a better export market and will help local products achieve global fame.

Establishment of a National Repository of Handlooms

Understanding the significance of the invaluable handloom treasures spread far and wide across India and taking inspiration from the GI tagline *Atulya Bharat ki Amulya Nidhi* (Invaluable Treasures of Incredible India), we recommend the creation of a National Handlooms Digital Library (NHDL). This digital repository will be inclusive of not just the GI registered handlooms but also those handlooms that are not granted such registration. Documenting this national treasure will assist in promulgating its value and protecting inter-generational craft that may be losing its vigour with the dwindling number of weavers. The scope of such a digital repository can further be widened to include registered Geographical Indications across all categories to enunciate their importance and value.

Pro-active role of government and other agencies

The discussion in previous chapters sufficiently clarifies the fact that a comprehensive legislative framework does not give rise to enhanced GI protection. On-the-ground enforcement of the law coupled with targeted schemes can bring the desired protection. The GI journey of a product is divided into two phases, pre- and post-registration, where multiple stakeholders are involved in different capacities. Even among the stakeholders, categories and sub-categories can be identified, such as producers, manufacturers, traders, dealers, exporters and retailers; master weavers, weavers paid a piecemeal rate, daily wage-earning weavers and independent weavers; and external agencies such as non-profit organizations government and academic institutes. This complex structure of multiple stakeholders often leads to non-trickling down of solutions to the roots, which is why we see that the issues with the handloom sector remain unresolved. An amalgamation of stakeholders and their roles at both stages of the GI journey is thus an urgent requirement.

Data available from the GI registry shows that the government through its agencies is not only directly involved in the registration procedure but also plays a pivotal role as a member of the inspection bodies. Considering the fact of the widespread unawareness about GI, such direct involvement of external agencies is a necessity; however, this hand-holding should be only until a sustainable marketing and distribution model for each GI registered product is in place. Otherwise, once dependent, the weavers will continue to be so, as in the case of Tangaliya shawls, whose revival and registration was due to the role played by the National Institute of Fashion Technology, Gujarat, but the registration of which has now lapsed. The weavers' association formed at the time of registration is completely unaware of the same. Thus, until weavers are ready to shoulder the weight of the entire process of production, marketing, selling etc., external agencies must continue assisting them.

Creating a Code of Practice, establishing inspection bodies and infringement monitoring authorities are specific tasks which demand that these external agencies take a proactive role. To bring these into existence and ensure their actual functioning, the GPPC, as recommended, can act as the nodal agency.

In conclusion, Geographical Indications in India is a complex network ensuring proprietary right as a unique form of intellectual property. This network is a combination of stakeholders, diverse cultural practices and inter-woven socio-economic and educational backgrounds dispersed across a vast territory. Against this backdrop, it is a noteworthy achievement to have identified and registered more than 370 goods with unique characters and reputations owing to their geographical origin. Registration trends also show enthusiastic participation from most States and Union Territories in

India. Yet, keeping in mind the object of the law, which travels beyond mere registration, the post-registration phase is equally crucial for its success. This phase, involving quality monitoring, standard maintenance, brand promotion, market creation, trust building and infringement checks, remains to be addressed.

Notes

1 *Motilal Padmapat v State of Uttar Pradesh* AIR 1979 SC 621, 118 ITR 326.
2 See Chapter 1, 1.1.2.
3 "Meeting of Consultative Group for Registration of Tangaliya Craft under Geographical Indication" (*Geographical Indications Registry*, 2008). This document created by NIFT is part of the GI Application for Tangaliya shawls <http://ipindiaservices.gov.in/GIRPublic/Application/Details/127> accessed 2 February 2021.
The Kota Doria Development Hadauti Foundation, with the help of the United Nations Industrial Development Organisation (UNIDO), applied for GI registration of the handloom, which was granted successfully in 2005; Karl M. Rich, "Trajectories of Value Chain Governance and Geographical Indications: Issues for Upgrading Handicraft Goods in India" (2011) CUTS CITEE Working Paper No. 1/2011 <https://www.cuts-citee.org/pdf/WP11-01.pdf>accessed 1 March 2021.
4 See Chapter 2, "Concluding Observations".
5 "State-Wise Registration Details of GI Applications" (*Geographical Indications Registry*, 2021) <https://ipindia.gov.in/writereaddata/Portal/Images/pdf/GI_Application_Register_10-09-2019.pdf> accessed 2 March 2021.
6 See Chapter 4,"Government Actions to Preserve the Handloom Sector of India – A Factual Insight".
7 Ibid.
8 Food and Agriculture Organization of the United Nations, *Linking People, Places and Products*, 51 <http://www.fao.org/3/i1760e/i1760e02.pdf> accessed 26 February 2021.
9 L. Narayanan and S. Vinayan, *Regional Products and Rural Livelihoods* (OUP 2019) 52.
10 Chuthaporn Ngokkuen and Ulrike Grote, "Challenges and Opportunities for Protecting Geographical Indications in Thailand" (2012) 19 (2) Asia-Pacific Development Journal 93, 107 <https://www.unescap.org/sites/default/files/chap-5-Ngokkuen.pdf> accessed 26 February 2021.
11 "Department for Promotion of Industry and Internal Trade Guidelines for Permitting the Use of Geographical (GI) Logo and Tagline, 2019" (*Department for Promotion of Industry and Internal Trade*, 2019) <https://dipp.gov.in/sites/default/files/GI_Guideline_Finalised.pdf> accessed 1 March 2021.
12 Ibid.
13 See Chapter 2, "Concluding Observations".
14 "Manual of Geographical Indications Practice and Procedure" (*Office of the Controller General of Patents, Designs and Trademarks & Registrar of Geographical Indications*, 2011) 36 <https://www.ipindia.gov.in/writereaddata/Portal/IPOGuidelinesManuals/1_31_1_manual-of-geographical-indications-practice-and-procedure.pdf> accessed 24 February 2021.
15 See more Chapter 2, "Concluding Observations".

16 Shefalee Vasudev, "Ground Report | The Banaras Bind" *Live Mint* (23 November 2013) <https://www.livemint.com/Leisure/5h1lnyORjhtn9Pr0Z4wiXL/Ground-Report--The-Banaras-bind.html> accessed 24 February 2021.
17 MANU/WB/077/2019.
18 Ibid.
19 The handloom sector features as one of the key sectors in focus for India's 5-year plans (1951–2017). See also Chapter 4, "Five Year Plans and Consequent Interventions".
20 "Certificate of Registration" (*Geographical Indications Registry*, 2009) <http://ipindiaservices.gov.in/GIRPublic/Application/Details/127> accessed 25 February 2021.
21 Omar Rashid, "WhatsApp Worsens Varanasi Weavers' Woes" *The Hindu* (Varanasi, 30 March 2014) <https://www.thehindu.com/news/national/other-States/whatsapp-worsens-varanasi-weavers-woes/article5851933.ece> accessed 24 February 2021.
22 "National Intellectual Property Rights Policy 2016" (*Ministry of Commerce and Industry, Department of Industrial Policy and Promotion (DIPP)*, 2016) <https://dipp.gov.in/sites/default/files/National_IPR_Policy_English.pdf> last accessed 2 March 2021.

REFERENCES

Journal Articles (print)

Addor F, 'Geographical Indications beyond Wines and Spirits—A Roadmap for a Better Protection for Geographical Indications in the WTO TRIPS Agreement' (2002) 5 The Journal of World Intellectual Property 865.

Aggarwal R, Singh H and Prashar S, 'Branding of Geographical Indications in India' (2014) 56 International Journal of Law and Management 431.

Ailawadi K L, Neslin S A and Gedenk K, 'Pursuing the Value-Conscious Consumer: Store Brands versus National Brand Promotions' (2001) 65(1) Journal of Marketing 71.

Amaravathi G and Bhavana K, 'Indian Handloom Sector-A Glimpse' (2019) 8 International Journal of Innovative Technology and Exploring Engineering 645.

Anderson J C and Gerbing D W, 'Structural Equation Modeling in Practice: A Review and Recommended Two-Step Approach' (1988) 103(3) Psychological Bulletin 411.

Broude T, 'Taking "Trade and Culture" Seriously: Geographical Indications and Cultural Protection in WTO Law' (2005) 26(4) University of Pennsylvania, Journal of International Economic Law 623.

Buaprommee N and Polyorat K, 'Intention to Purchase Traceable Meat: The Impacts of Perceived Information Asymmetry, Informativeness, Usefulness, and Norm' (2016) 9(1) Asia Pacific Management Review 141.

Calamari T, Price J and Sawhney A P S, 'A Successful Weaving Trial with a Size-Free Cotton Warp' (2004) 29 Indian Journal of Fibre and Textile Research 117.

Chong B, 'Why Culture Matters for the Formation of Consumer Trust? A Conceptual Study of Barriers for Realizing Real Global Exchange in Hong Kong' (2003) 8(2) Asia Pacific Management Review 217.

Deselnicu O C, Costanigro M, Souza Monteiro D M and Thilmany McFadden D, 'A Meta-Analysis of Geographical Indication Food Valuation Studies: What Drives the Premium for Origin-Based Labels?' (2013) 38(2) Journal of Agricultural and Resource Economics 204.

Farley C, 'Conflicts between U.S. Law and International Treaties Concerning Geographical Indications' (2000) 22 Whittier Law Review 73.

Fornell C and Larcker D F, 'Evaluating Structural Equation Models with Unobservable Variables and Measurement Error' (1981) 18(1) Journal of Marketing Research 39.

Fotopoulos C and Krystallis A, 'Quality Labels as a Marketing Advantage' (2003) 37(10) European Journal of Marketing 1350.
Geuze M, 'The Provisions on Geographical Indications in the TRIPS Agreement' (2009) 10 The Estey Journal of International Law and Trade Policy 50.
Goebel B, 'Geographical Indications and Trademarks - The Road from DOHA' (2003) 93 The Trademark Reporter 964.
Gurjar S, Joshi K D and Soni R, 'Study of Multiple Aspects of Kota Doria' (2020) 10 International Journal of Textile and Fashion Technology 21.
Hilde J C, Janneke D J, Lynn J F, Kher S V, Meike W, Niels B L L and Olivia H D, 'Experts' Perspectives on the Implementation of Traceability in Europe' (2010) 112(3) British Food Journal 261.
Huysmans M and Swinnen J, 'No Terroir in the Cold? A Note on the Geography of Geographical Indications' (2019) 70(2) Journal of Agricultural Economics 550.
Jain L, 'Textile Policy: End of Handloom Industry' (1985) 20(27) Economic and Political Weekly 1121.
Jiang Z and Benbasat I, 'Virtual Product Experience: Effects of Visual and Functional Control of Products on Perceived Diagnosticity and Flow in Electronic Shopping' (2004) 21(3) Journal of Management Information Systems 111.
Keh H T and Sun J, 'The Differential Effects of Online Peer Review and Expert Review on Service Evaluations: The Roles of Confidence and Information Convergence' (2018) 21(4) Journal of Service Research 474.
Kempf D S and Smith R E, 'Consumer Processing of Product Trial and the Influence of Prior Advertising: A Structural Modeling Approach' (1998) 35(3) Journal of Marketing Research 325.
Kendall E L and Sprotles G B, 'A Methodology for Profiling Consumers' Decision-Making Styles' (1986) 20(2) Journal of Consumer Affairs 267.
Kukar-Kinney M, Monroe K B and Weisstein F L, 'Determinants of Consumers' Response to Pay-What-You-Want Pricing Strategy on the Internet' (2016) 69(10) Journal of Business Research 4313.
Kumar N K, 'Geographical Indications Laws in India: Issues and Challenges' (2020) 3(1) Journal of Intellectual Property Rights Law 12.
Menozzi D, 'Economic Aspects of Labelling Regulations for Consumer Protection' (2006) 8 Progress in Nutrition 157.
Ngokkuen G and Grote U, 'Challenges and Opportunities for Protecting Geographical Indications in Thailand' (2012) 19(2) Asia-Pacific Development Journal 93.
Oubiña J, Rubio N and Villaseñor N, 'Brand Awareness – Brand Quality Inference and Consumer's Risk Perception in Store Brands of Food Products' (2014) 32 Food Quality and Preference 289.
Rahmah M, 'The Protection of Agricultural Products under Geographical Indication: An Alternative Tool for Agricultural Development in Indonesia' (2017) 22(2) Journal of Intellectual Property Rights 90.
Rangnekar D, 'Geographical Indications UNCTAD-ICTSD Project on IPRS and Sustainable Development Intellectual Property Rights and Sustainable Development' (2004) 4 Intellectual Property Rights and Sustainable Development 1.
Sawhney S, 'Make in India- and Its Economic Impact on the Indian Handloom Sector' (2016) JEL classification: R28, R58, O13, O14. Lampert Institute for Civic and Global Affairs, New York, 1.

Simanjuntak Y, 'Protection of Geographical Indications: Role of Local Governments and Communities' 307 Advances in Social Science, Education and Humanities Research 614.

Vats N K, 'Geographical Indication-The Factors of Rural Development and Strengthening Economy' (2016) 21(5/6) Journal of Intellectual Property Rights 347.

Verma S and Mishra N, 'Recognition and Marketing Opportunities of a "GI"' (2018) 23 Tag in Handloom Product: A Study of Banaras Brocades and Sarees 101.

Articles (Online Journal and Open Source)

Adinolfi F, Iddrisu A, Rosa M and Vecchio Y, 'Geographical Indication to Build Up Resilient Rural Economies: A Case Study from Ghana' (2020) 12 Sustainability 2052 <https://www.mdpi.com/2071-1050/12/5/2052> accessed 26 September 2021.

Anubhai P, 'Sickness in Indian Textile Industry: Causes and Remedies' (1988) 23 Economic and Political Weekly 147 <https://www.epw.in/journal/1988/48/review-industry-and-management-uncategorised/sickness-indian-textile-industry-causes> accessed 20 February 2021.

Athalye A, 'Kota Doria - Weaving India through International Brocade' (2018) Technology of Fibres and Textile Processing <https://doi.org/10.32474/LTTFD.2018.02.000131> accessed 10 December 2020.

Attri A, 'Handloom Industries in Himachal Pradesh: An Overview' (2017) International Journal of Advanced Research and Development <http://www.advancedjournal.com/archives/2017/vol2/issue5/2-5-31> accessed 15 December 2020.

Bahl N and Gautam K, 'Geographical Indication: Pochampally Ikat' All India Artisans and Craftworkers Welfare Association <http://docplayer.net/29031011-Geographical-indication-pochampally-ikat.html> accessed 10 December 2020.

Barjolle D, Sylvander B and Thévenod-Mottet E, 'Public Policies and Geographical Indications' (2011) CAB International <https://www.researchgate.net/publication/282498953_Public_policies_and_geographical_indications> accessed 21 January 2021.

Bearad L and Marchenay P, 'From Localised Products to Geographical Indications' (January 2008) CNRS Ressources des terroirs 64 <https://www.ethno-terroirs.cnrs.fr/spip.php?page=article&id_article=153&lang=fr> accessed 15 January 2021.

Beddig C, 'Cluster Development Policy Rooted in the Collective Efficiency Approach: An Effective Poverty Alleviation Tool in the Indian Handloom Sector? Case Studies: The Varanasi and Chanderi Handloom Clusters (2007–08)' (2008) The Graduate Institute, Geneva <https://www.scribd.com/document/254608224/Cluster-Development-Policy-in-Indian-Handloom-Cl-BeddigDec-09> accessed 15 January 2021.

Belapurkar R, 'Paithani Saree: Woven Histories of Maharashtra' (*Sahapedia*, 16 July 2018) <https://www.sahapedia.org/paithani-saree-woven-histories-of-maharashtra> accessed 10 October 2020.

Belletti G, Marescotti A, Penker M, Quiñones-Ruiz X and Scaramuzzi S, 'Why Early Collective Action Pays Off: Evidence From Setting Protected Geographical Indications' (2016) 32 Cambridge University Press 179 <https://www.cambridge.org/core/journals/renewable-agriculture-and-food-systems/article/why-early-collective-action-pays-off-evidence-from-setting-protected-geographical-indications/C177715D352C7C35211291686FC292AB > accessed 10 August 2020.

Belletti G, Marescotti A, Sanz-Cañada J and Vakoufaris H, 'Linking Protection of Geographical Indications to the Environment: Evidence from the European Union Olive-Oil Sector' (2015) Land Use Policy <https://doi.org/10.1016/j.landusepol.2015.05.003> accessed 30 May 2020.

Belwal M, Kaliappan S and Sigamany V, 'Geographical Indication: An Exploratory Examination on GI Tagging Indian Food in Opening Avenues to Develop Culinary/Gastronomic Tourism' (2018) IOSR Journal of Environmental Science, Toxicology and Food Technology <https://www.iosrjournals.org/iosr-jestft/papers/Vol12-%20Issue%2010/Version-1/J1210016068.pdf> accessed 21 July 2020.

Bernués A, Olaizola A and Corcoran K, 'Labelling Information Demanded by European Consumers and Relationships with Purchasing Motives, Quality and Safety of Meat' (2003) Meat Science <https://doi.org/10.1016/S0309-1740(02)00327-3> accessed 21 July 2020.

Bocedi G, Desimoni F and Mendelson R, 'Protecting Geographical Indications in Emerging Economies (Brazil, Russia, India and China - BRICs Countries): A Practical Manual for Producers' Groups' Organisation for an International Geographical Indications Network <https://www.aop-igp.ch/fileadmin/Dokumente/AOP-IGP_im_internationalen_Umfeld/BRICS_protecting-GI_12.pdf> accessed 01 July 2020.

Bramley C, Biénabe E and Kirsten J, 'The Economics of Geographical Indications: Towards a Conceptual Framework for Geographical Indication Research in Developing Countries' (2009) The Economics of Intellectual Property <http://www.wipo.int/ip-development/en/economics/pdf/wo_1012_e_ch_4.pdf> accessed 05 July 2020.

Calboli I and Gervais D, 'The Socio-Economic Aspects of Geographical Indications of Origin' (2016) <https://www.wipo.int/edocs/mdocs/geoind/en/wipo_geo_bud_15/wipo_geo_bud_15_9-annex1.pdf> accessed 20 July 2020.

Candilhon J J, Lecoent A and Vandecandelaere E, 'Quality Linked to Geographical Origins and Geographical Indications: Lesson Learned from Six Case Studies in Asia' FAO, RAP Publication 2010/04 <http://www.fao.org/3/i1592e/i1592e00.pdf> accessed 12 July 2020.

Chakrabarti G, 'Geographical Indications: Ambiguity in Legal Provisions in India' (2019) 2 Delhi Journal of Contemporary Law <http://lc2.du.ac.in/DJCL2/2.%20Gargi%20Chakrabarti.pdf> accessed 30 July 2020.

Chatterjee A and Jain N, 'A Study of the Socio-Economic Conditions of the Handloom Weavers of Kota and Bundi District in Rajasthan' (2020) TEST Magazine <http://www.testmagzine.biz/index.php/testmagzine/article/view/8713> accessed 26 September 2020.

Chaudhary K, 'Kota Doria Article GC 16' (Green Fashion 2016 'Empowering Khadi and Handlooms through Design Intervention, MSU, Baroda, India,

November, 2018) <https://www.researchgate.net/publication/329091719_Kota_Doria_Article_GC_16> accessed 22 August 2020.

Choe Y C, Park J, Chung M and Moon J, 'Effect of the Food Traceability System for Building Trust: Price Premium and Buying Behavior' (2009) Information Systems Frontiers <https://doi.org/10.1007/s10796-008-9134-z> accessed 20 July 2020.

Choudhary S and Raju K D, 'Geographical Indications in Odisha: A Leading Destination of Traditional Handlooms' (2013) Odisha Review <http://magazines.odisha.gov.in/Orissareview/2013/apr/engpdf/april-or-2013.pdf> accessed 15 August 2020.

Commission of the European Communities, 'Protection of Geographical Indications in 160 Countries around the World: Part II' (2007) Geographical Indications and TRIPs: 10 Years Later...A Roadmap for EU GI Holders to Gain Protection in Other WTO Members <http://trade.ec.europa.eu/doclib/docs/2007/june/tradoc_135089.pdf> accessed 18 August 2020.

Das K, 'Prospects and Challenges of Geographical Indications in India' (2010) The Journal of World Intellectual Property <https://doi.org/10.1111/j.1747-1796.2009.00363.x> accessed 02 September 2020.

Das K, 'Socioeconomic Implications of Protecting Geographical Indications in India' (1 August 2009) India Habitat Centre - Research and Information System for Developing Countries <https://www.researchgate.net/publication/228247372_Socioeconomic_Implications_of_Protecting_Geographical_Indications_in_India> accessed 7 August 2020.

Deepika J, Devi G M and Lakshmi V V, 'Assessment of Socio-Economic Status of Pochampally Ikat Handloom Weavers' (2019) International Journal of Current Microbiology and Applied Sciences <https://www.researchgate.net/publication/337043835_Assessment_of_Socio-Economic_Status_of_Pochampally_Ikat_Handloom_Weavers> accessed 20 August 2020.

Dimara E and Skuras D, 'Consumer Evaluations of Product Certification, Geographic Association and Traceability in Greece' (2003) European Journal of Marketing <https://doi.org/10.1108/03090560310465099> accessed 25 July 2020.

Donthu N, Lee S and Yoo B, 'An Examination of Selected Marketing Mix Elements and Brand Equity' (2000) 28(2) Journal of the Academy of Marketing Science 195 <https://doi.org/10.1177/0092070300282002> accessed 20 July 2020.

Duncan J, Medina F and Parasecoli F, 'Geographic Indications: Socio-Cultural, Political and Economic Considerations' (2012) Universitat Oberta de Catalunya, UOC Open Learning Resources <http://hdl.handle.net/10609/51181> accessed 15 July 2020.

Elena R-D, Javier B-E F and Esmeralda C-A, 'A Cross-Cultural Analysis of Perceived Product Quality, Perceived Risk and Purchase Intention in E-commerce Platforms' (2019) Journal of Enterprise Information Management <https://doi.org/10.1108/JEIM-06-2019-0150> accessed 12 July 2020.

Elliott G R and Cameron R C 'Consumer Perception of Product Quality and the Country-of-Origin Effect' (1994) Journal of International Marketing <www.jstor.org/stable/25048542> accessed 15 July 2020.

Erlanger S, 'Vive le Terroir' (2013) *New York Times* <https://www.nytimes.com/2013/09/01/sunday-review/vive-le-terroir.html> accessed 18 July 2020.

Farley C, 'The Protection of Geographical Indications in the Inter-American Convention' (2014) Articles in Law Reviews & Other Academic Journals <https://digitalcommons.wcl.american.edu/facsch_lawrev/721> accessed 18 July 2020.

Finlay D, Kneafsey M and Zhao X, 'The Effectiveness of Contemporary Geographical Indications (GIs) Schemes in Enhancing the Quality of Chinese Agrifoods – Experiences from the Field' (2014) 36 Journal of Rural Studies 77–86 <https://doi.org/10.1016/j.jrurstud.2014.06.012> accessed 28 July 2020

Flodgren J, 'Geographical Indications and Trademarks: Synergies and Conflicts in the International Market' (2009) <https://www.origin-gi.com/images/stories/PDFs/English/OriGIn_publications/News/johan_flodgren_essay.pdf> accessed 14 July 2020.

Frewer L and Van R W, 'Consumer Perceptions of Food Quality and Safety and Their Relation to Traceability' (2008) 110(10) British Food Journal 1034–1046 <https://doi.org/10.1108/00070700810906642> accessed 14 July 2020.

Giovannucci D, Josling T E, Kerr W A, O'Connor B and Yeung M T, 'Guide to Geographical Indications: Linking Products and Their Origins' (2009) International Trade Centre <https://www.origin-gi.com/images/stories/PDFs/English/E-Library/geographical_indications.pdf> accessed 20 July 2020.

Giraud G, Halawany-Darson R, Menozzi D and Mora C, 'Motives towards Traceable Food Choice: A Comparison between French and Italian Consumers' (2015) 49 Food Control 40–48 <https://doi.org/10.1016/j.foodcont.2013.09.006> accessed 14 July 2020.

Gogoi J, 'Proprietorship of GI in India with Special Focus on the State of Assam' (2020) 25 Journal of Intellectual Property Rights <http://nopr.niscair.res.in/handle/123456789/55612> accessed 17 August 2020.

Görlach B, Keefe H, Leipprand A, Riccher M and Schlegel S, 'Impacts of The IPR Rules on Sustainable Development' (November 2006) Queen Mary University of England <https://cordis.europa.eu/docs/results/503/503613/124857281-6_en.pdf> accessed 17 August 2020.

Harnetty P, 'Deindustrialization Revisited: The Handloom Weavers of the Central Provinces of India, c. I800–1947' (1991) 25(3) Modern Asian Studies 455 <https://www.jstor.org/stable/pdf/312614.pdf?refreqid=excelsior%3Ad79369a5b3364caa4f30b3f46bdb6c27> accessed 2 March 2021.

Intensive Handloom Development Programme, Government of Gujarat <http://cottage.gujarat.gov.in/Home-2425665B5D2D-214079-2824725E2572-28247221713D> accessed 18 January 2021.

Joshi S, 'A Brief History of Handloom Reservation Act' (*Network of Rural Agrarian Studies* 2016) 1 <http://ruralagrarianstudies.org/wp-content/uploads/2016/03/Paper.pdf> accessed 1 November 2020.

Kizos T, Koshaka R, Penker M, Piatti C, Vogl C and Uchiyama Y, 'The Governance of Geographical Indications: Experiences of Practical Implementation of Selected Case Studies in Austria, Italy Greece and Japan' (2017) British Food Journal 2863 <https://www.emerald.com/insight/content/doi/10.1108/BFJ-01-2017-0037/full/html> accessed 17 September 2020.

Konde V and Kulkarni V, 'Pre- and Post- Geographical Indications Registration Measures for Handicrafts in India' (November 2011) 16 Journal of Intellectual Property Rights 463–469 <http://nopr.niscair.res.in/bitstream/123456789/13056/1/JIPR%2016%286%29%20463-469.pdf> accessed 17 September 2020.

Medeiros M, Passador C and Passador J, 'Implications of Geographical Indications: A Comprehensive Review of Papers Listed in CAPES' Journal Database' (2016) 13 Innovation and Management Review 315 <https://www.sciencedirect.com/science/article/pii/S1809203916310713?via%3Dihub> accessed 18 August 2020.

Mir Y A and Darzi M A, 'Kashmir Pashmina - A Journey of Standardization through Geographical Indication' (2017) 3(5) IJAR <https://www.allresearchjournal.com/archives/2017/vol3issue5/PartA/3-4-149-517.pdf> accessed 20 October 2020.

Mishra P, Khare A K and Kothari V R, 'Indian Traditional Textiles & Geographical Indications' (2013) Textile Review Magazine 2013 <www.fibre2fashion.com>.

Monten L, 'Geographical Indications of Origin: Should They Be Protected and Why? An Analysis of the Issue from the U.S. and E.U. Perspectives' (May 2010) 22 Santa Clara High Technology Law Journal 2 <https://papers.ssrn.com/sol3/papers.cfm?abstract_id=1597091> accessed 12 July 2020.

Nair M D, 'TRIPS, WTO and IPR: Geographical Indication Protection in India' (2011) 16 Journal of Intellectual Property Rights 429–430 <http://nopr.niscair.res.in/bitstream/123456789/12694/1/JIPR%2016%285%29%20429-430.pdf> accessed 12 July 2020.

Nazlida M, Normalisa M I and Shiem L V, 'Docs the Country of Origin of a Halal Logo Matter? The Case of Packaged Food Purchases' (2017) 27(4) Review of International Business and Strategy 484–500 <https://doi.org/10.1108/RIBS-06-2017-0049> accessed 12 July 2020.

Okhedui R, 'The International Intellectual Property Roots of Geographical Indications' (2007) 82 Chicago-Kent Law Review 1329 <https://scholarship.kentlaw.iit.edu/cgi/viewcontent.cgi?article=3621&context=cklawreview> accessed 02 July 2020.

Raniwala P, 'What Makes the Gujarati Patola Sari a Pricless Heirloom?' (*Vogue India*, 22 March 2019) <https://www.vogue.in/content/gujarati-patola-sarees-history-significance-weaving-process> accessed 30 December 2020.

Raustiala K and Munzer S, 'The Global Struggle over Geographic Indications' (2007) 18 The European Journal of International Law 337 <https://academic.oup.com/ejil/article/18/2/337/361981> accessed 9 December 2020.

Ravindran S and Mathew A, 'The Protection of Geographical Indications in India – Case Study on Darjeeling Tea' (2009) International Property Rights Index <http://nbcgib.uesc.br/nit/ig/app/papers/1035442708158048.pdf> accessed 12 July 2020.

Reynolds A, 'Patan Patola, the Cloth of Kings' (*Lost with Purpose*, 5 January 2021) <https://www.lostwithpurpose.com/patan-patola/> accessed 26 December 2021.

Sawhney A P S, Price J B and Calamari T A, 'A Successful Weaving Trial with a Size-Free Cotton Warp' (2004) 29 Indian Journal of Fibre and Textile Research 117 <http://www.niscair.res.in/sciencecommunication/researchjournals/rejour/ijftr/Fulltextsearch/2004/June%202004/IJFTR-Vol%2029-June%202004-pp%20117-121.htm> accessed 10 August 2020.

Sindhu M V, 'The Story of Patan Patola: A Fabric that Never Fades and One Family's Tryst with Keeping it Alive' (*Your Story*, 24 October 2016) <https://yourstory.com/2016/10/patan-patola-fabric> accessed 28 December 2021.

Soundarapandian M, National Bank for Agriculture and Rural Development, 'Growth and Prospects of Handloom Sector in India' (2002) ix <https://www.nabard.org/demo/auth/writereaddata/File/OC%2022.pdf> accessed 2 March 2021.

Srivastava S, 'Geographical Indications and Legal Framework in India' (2003) 38 EPW <https://www.epw.in/journal/2003/38/special-articles/geographical-indications-and-legal-framework-india.html> accessed 09 March 2021.

Textile Magazine, *Cotton Yarn Price Increase and Shortage: Reasons and Solution* (2010) <https://www.indiantextilemagazine.in/industry-news/cotton-yarn-price-increase-and-shortage-reasons-and-solution/> accessed 2 March 2021.

Tomáš S, 'Examining Attitudes toward Food Quality Labels: Evidence from Czechia' (2020) 26(3) Journal of Food Products Marketing 197–211 <https://doi.org/10.1080/10454446.2020.1745347> accessed 12 August 2020.

Verma S and Mishra N, 'Recognition and Marketing Opportunities of a "GI" Tag in Handloom Product: A Study of Banaras Brocades and Sarees'(2018) 23 Journal of Intellectual Property Rights 101–110 <http://nopr.niscair.res.in/bitstream/123456789/45333/1/JIPR%2023%282-3%29%20101-110.pdf> accessed 10 October 2020.

Vinayan S, 'Geographical Indications in India: Issues and Challenges–An Overview' (2017) 20(3/4) The Journal of World Intellectual Property 119–132 <https://doi.org/10.1111/jwip.12076> accessed 12 July 2020.

Vinayan S, 'Intellectual Property Rights and the Handloom Sector: Challenges in Implementation of Geographical Indications Act' (January, 2012) 17(1) Journal of Intellectual Property Rights 55–63 <https://www.researchgate.net/publication/280561722_Intellectual_Property_Rights_and_the_Handloom_Sector_Challenges_in_Implementation_of_Geographical_Indications_Act> accessed 12 July 2020.

Zeithaml V A, 'Consumer Perceptions of Price, Quality, and Value: A Means-End Model and Synthesis of Evidence' (1988) 52(3) Journal of Marketing 2–22 <https://doi.org/10.1177/002224298805200302> accessed 22 July 2020.

Books

Bramley C, Marie-Vivien D and Biénabe E (eds), *Considerations in Designing an Appropriate Legal Framework for GIs in Southern Countries* (Springer 2013).

Calboli I and Loon N (eds), *Geographical Indications at the Crossroads of Trade, Development and Culture* (Cambridge University Press 2017).

Dange T, *Intellectual Property and Traditional Knowledge in the Global Economy: Translating Geographical Indications for Development* (Routledge 2015).

Finger J M and Schuler P (eds), *Poor People's Knowledge Promoting Intellectual Property in Developing Countries* (World Bank and Oxford University Press 2004).

Fitzergerald P J, *Salmond on Jurisprudence* (12th edn, Indian Economy Reprint, Universal Law Publishing 2004).

Gangjee D S, *Relocating the Law of Geographical Indications* (Cambridge University Press 2012).

Gangjee D S (ed.), *Research Handbook on Intellectual Property and Geographical Indications* (Edward Elgar 2016).

Holland T, *The Elements of Jurisprudence* (13th edn, Indian Economy Reprint, Universal Law Publishing 2006).

Kapur A, *Made Only in India* (Routledge 2016).
Marie-Vivien D, *The Protection of Geographical Indications in India: A New Perspective on the French and European Experience* (SAGE Law 2015).
Maskus K, *Private Rights and Public Problems, The Global Economics of Intellectual Property in the 21st Century* (Peterson Institute Press 2012).
May S, Sidali K L, Spiller A and Tschofen B (eds), 'Taste – Power – Tradition. Placing Geographical Indications on an Interdisciplinary Agenda' in *Göttingen Studies in Cultural Property* (Universitätsverlag Göttingen 2017).
Narasaiah L and Krishna T, *Crisis of Handloom Industry* (Discovery Publishing House 1999).
Narayanan L and Vinayan S, *Regional Products and Rural Livelihoods* (Oxford University Publishing 2019).
Rout T K and Majh B (ed.), *WTO, TRIPS and Geographical Indications* (New Century Publications 2014).
Singh V, *The Law of Geographical Indications: Rising Above the Horizon* (Eastern Law House 2017).

Cases

Motilal Padmapat v State of Uttar Pradesh AIR 1979 SC 621, 118 ITR 326.
Parvej Aktar v Union of India and Ors. 1993 SCR (1) 803.

Conference Papers and Working Papers

Barjolle D, Paus M and Perret A, 'Impacts of Geographical Indications Review of Methods and Empirical Evidences' (2009) International Association of Agricultural Economists Conference, Beijing, China, August 16–22 <https://www.researchgate.net/publication/237476073_Impacts_of_Geographical_Indications_-_Review_of_Methods_and_Empirical_Evidences> accessed 20 September 2020.
Basole A, 'Authenticity, Innovation and the Geographical Indication in an Artisanal Industry: The Case of the Banarasi Sari', Department of Economics, University of Massachusetts Boston Working Paper 2014–09 <https://onlinelibrary.wiley.com/doi/abs/10.1111/jwip.12035> accessed 05 October 2020.
Biswas A and Kapil K, 'Geographical Indications in India: A Case Study of Kota Doria' CUTS Centre for International Trade, Economics and Environment Briefing Paper, GRANITE II-1/2010 Working Paper <http://demo.netcommlabs.net/citee/pdf/Briefing_Paper10-Geographical_Indications_in_India-A_Case_Study_of_Kota_Doria.pdf> accessed 20 February 2021.
Blakeney M, 'Geographical Indication and TRIPS' (November 2012) University of Western Australia, Research Paper No. 2012-09, <https://papers.ssrn.com/sol3/papers.cfm?abstract_id=2177435> accessed 12 August 2020.
Bramley C, 'A Review of the Socio-Economic Impact of Geographical Indications: Considerations for the Developing World' (2011) WIPO Worldwide Symposium on Geographical Indications, Lima, Peru, June 22–24 <http://193.5.93.81/edocs/mdocs/geoind/en/wipo_geo_lim_11/wipo_geo_lim_11_9.pdf> accessed 14 September 2020.

Calboli I, 'Expanding the Protection of Geographical Indictions of Origin under Trips: Old Debate or New Opportunity' (2006) Marquette Intellectual Property Law School Legal Studies Paper No. 06-19 <https://papers.ssrn.com/sol3/papers.cfm?abstract_id=893193> accessed 10 August 2020.

Calboli I, 'Of Markets, Culture, and Terroir: The Unique Economic and Culture-Related Benefits of Geographical Indications of Origin' in D Gervais (ed.), *Research Handbook in International Intellectual Property* (Edward Elgar 2014) <https://papers.ssrn.com/sol3/papers.cfm?abstract_id=2329566> accessed-20 August 2020.

Choudhury N, 'Socio-Economic Problems of Muga Silk Weavers of Sualkuchi Silk Industry' (2019) 8(9) International Journal of Scientific and Technology Research <http://www.ijstr.org/final-print/sep2019/Socio-economic-Problems-Of-Muga-Silk-Weavers-Of-Sualkuchi-Silk-Industry.pdf> accessed 12 October 2020.

Das K, 'Geographical Indications at the WTO: An Unfinished Agenda' (February 2010) Research and Information System for Developing Countries RIS-DP No.162 <https://papers.ssrn.com/sol3/papers.cfm?abstract_id=1597091> accessed 12 July 2020.

Das K, 'Protection of Geographical Indications: An Overview of Select Issues with Particular Reference to India' (2007) Centre for Trade and Development Working Paper-8 <https://papers.ssrn.com/sol3/papers.cfm?abstract_id=1587372> accessed 25 July 2020.

Export-Import Bank of India, 'Indian Handloom Industry: Potential and Prospects' (September 2018) Export Import Bank of India Working Paper No. 80 <https://www.eximbankindia.in/Assets/Dynamic/PDF/Publication-Resources/ResearchPapers/102file.pdf> accessed 10 December 2020.

Gangjee D S, 'Genericide: The Death of a Geographical Indication?' (January 2016), in D Gangjee (ed.), *Research Handbook on Intellectual Property and Geographical Indications* (Edward Elgar 2016) <https://ssrn.com/abstract=2923895> accessed 23 August 2020.

Gangjee D S, 'Proving Provenance? Geographical Indications Certification and Its Ambiguities' (February 25, 2017) World Development, 2017 <https://ssrn.com/abstract=2923898> accessed 21 September 2020.

International Bureau, 'Possible Solutions for Conflicts between Trademarks and Geographical Indications and for Conflicts between Homonymous Geographical Indications' (Meeting Organised by WIPO on June 8 2000 (SCT/5/3) <https://www.wipo.int/meetings/en/doc_details.jsp?doc_id=1410> accessed 12 July 2020.

Kaushik K V, Khanna A and Sah S, 'Indian Handloom Industry: Position Paper' (2019) Thought Arbitrage Research Institute for FICCI Ladies Organisation <http://www.ficciflo.com/wp-content/uploads/2019/03/Indian-Handloom-Industry-Final.pdf> accessed 12 June 2020.

KPMG Advisory Services Pvt Ltd, *Human Resources and Skill Requirements in the Handloom and Handicrafts Sector: Vol. 13* (2013–17, 2017–22) (New Delhi, India: NSDC, 2015).

Laumonier A, 'Some Key Points on How to Ensure Optimal Management and Protection of Geographical Indications' (International Seminar on Geographical Indications, Yangzhou, China, June 29–July 1, 2017) <https://www.wipo.int/edocs/mdocs/geoind/en/wipo_geo_yty_17/wipo_geo_yty_17_10-annex1.pdf> accessed 10 September 2020.

Meier-Ewert W, 'Geographical Indications in the WTO' (WIPO Worldwide GI Symposium 2019, Lisbon, Portugal, July 2019) <https://www.wipo.int/edocs/mdocs/sct/en/wipo_geo_lis_19/wipo_geo_lis_19_7.pdf> accessed 10 September 2020.

Pant R, 'Protecting and Promoting Traditional Knowledge in India: What Role for Geographical Indications?' (2015) International Institute for Environment and Development Working Paper: May 2015 < https://pubs.iied.org/16576IIED/> accessed 10 December 2020.

Patterson S R C, 'Weaving Traditions along the "Wool Road" in India' (Textile Society of America Symposium Proceedings, 2002).

Rich K, 'Trajectories of Value Chain Governance and Geographical Indications: Issues for Upgrading Handicraft Goods in India', CUTS Centre for International Trade, Economics and Environment Working Paper No. 1/2011 <https://www.cuts-citee.org/pdf/WP11-01.pdf> accessed 05 August 2020.

Rizo M, 'Update on Geographical Indications from WIPO' (Worldwide Symposium on Geographical Indications held at Lisbon Portugal, July 2019) <https://www.wipo.int/edocs/mdocs/sct/en/wipo_geo_lis_19/wipo_geo_lis_19_1.pdf07> accessed August 2020.

Saha S, 'Non-Agricultural GI's: A Strategic Issue' (International Conference on GI in The XXI Century at Bordeaux, organised by oriGIn & AREPO, 21 May 2013) <https://www.origingi.com/images/stories/PDFs/English/Event/International_Conference_Bordeaux/21> accessed 25 September 2020.

Government Documents

Department for Promotion of Industry and Internal Trade, *Guidelines for Permitting the Use of Geographical (GI) Logo and Tagline* (2019) <https://dipp.gov.in/sites/default/files/GI_Guideline_Finalised.pdf> accessed 1 March 2021.

Government of Gujarat, *Cluster Development Scheme* (2016) <http://cottage.gujarat.gov.in/Home-242566262A74-214079-2824725E2572-3F2E72> accessed 1 March 2021.

Government of Gujarat, *Cottage and Rural Industries Policy* (2016) <http://www.imd-gujarat.gov.in/cottage-and-rural-industries> accessed 1 February 2021.

Government of Gujarat, *Dattopant Thengadi Artisan Interest Subsidy Scheme* (2014) <http://www.cottage.gujarat.gov.in/Home-28247221713D-214079-2824725E2572-282472 accessed 18 January 2021.

Government of Gujarat, *Gramodyog Vikas Kendra* (2000) <http://www.imd-gujarat.gov.in/gramodyog-vikas-kendra> accessed 1 March 2021.

Government of Gujarat, *Jyoti Gramodyog Vikas Yojana* (2015) <http://www.imd-gujarat.gov.in/jyoti-gramodyog-vikas-yojana> accessed 18 January 2021.

Government of Gujarat, *Shri Vajpayee Bankable Yojana* (2011) <http://www.cottage.gujarat.gov.in/Home-5E25726C3B65-214079-2824725E2572-5E2572> accessed 18 January 2021.

Government of India, Ministry of Commerce and Industry, Department of Industrial Policy and Promotion (DIPP), *National Intellectual Property Rights Policy* 2016 (2016) <https://dipp.gov.in/sites/default/files/National_IPR_Policy_English.pdf> accessed 2 March 2021.

Government of India, Ministry of Statistics and Programme Implementation, Central Statistics Office, *Sixth Economic Census* (2013–14) <http://www.icssrdataservice.in/datarepository/index.php/catalog/146/study-description> accessed 20 February 2021.

Government of India, Ministry of Textiles, *Annual Report* (2018–19) <http://texmin.nic.in/sites/default/files/Textiles-AnnualReport2018-2019%28English%29.pdf> accessed 10 August 2020.

Government of India, Ministry of Textiles, *Fourth All India Handloom Census of India 2019–20* <http://handlooms.nic.in/writereaddata/3736.pdf> accessed 1 March 2021.

Government of India, Ministry of Textiles, Development Commission (Handlooms), National Council of Applied Economic Research, *Handloom Census of India 2009–10* <http://handlooms.nic.in/Writereaddata/Handloom%20report.pdf> accessed 1 March 2021.

Government of India, Ministry of Textiles, *Mahatma Gandhi Bunkar Bima Yojana* (2021) <https://pib.gov.in/PressReleasePage.aspx?PRID=1607362 > accessed 4 March 2021.

Government of India, Ministry of Textiles, *Procedure for IPR Protection through Geographical Indication (GI) Act, 1999* (June 2009) <http://www.textilescommittee.nic.in/publication/procedure-ipr-protection-through-gi-act> accessed 20 September 2020.

Government of India, Ministry of Textiles, *Yarn Supply Scheme* (2018) <handlooms.nic.in> accessed 18 January 2021.

National Centre for Design & Product Development, *A Compendium of Indian Handicrafts and Handlooms Covered under Geographical Indications* (Ministry of Textiles, Government of India) <https://www.scribd.com/document/451001531/12222017102212GI-BOOK-FINAL-2-5-17-resized-pdf> accessed 12 November 2020.

Office of the Development Commissioner for Handlooms, Ministry of Textiles, Government of India, *Guidelines for Implementation of National Handloom Development Programme (NHDP) during the Period from April 2017 to March 2020 – reg., No.13/5/2016-DCH/NHDP/Cluster* (2017) <http://handlooms.nic.in/writereaddata/2634.>pdf accessed 1 March 2021.

Office of the Development Commissioner for Handlooms, Ministry of Textiles, Government of India, State-Wise Details of Handloom Clusters Sanction under IHCDS/IHDS/CHCDS/CHDS/NHDP/NERTPS during 2006–07 to 2015–16 (as on 31.03.2016) <handlooms.nic.in>.

Planning Commission, *Approach and Salient Features of the Eleventh Five Year Plan* (2007) <http://mpplanningcommission.gov.in/fiveyearplan/VolumeIsep07/Chapter-4-salient%20features%20final.pdf> accessed 1 March 2021.

Reports

All India Artisans and Craftworkers Welfare Association, *National Handicrafts Policy Report* (Ministry of Textiles, Government of India) <https://www.aiacaonline.org/wp-content/uploads/2018/06/National-Handicrafts-Policy-Report_Full-version_Final.pdf> accessed 15 July 2020.

Bankers Institute of Rural Development (BIRD), *Lucknow Study Report on Problems and Prospects of Handloom Sector in Employment Generation in the Globally Competitive Environment* (2016) <http://www.birdlucknow.in/wp-content/uploads/2016/04/Study-Report-on-Probelms-Prospects-of-handloom-Sector-by-BIRD-Lucknow1.pdf> accessed 03 March 2021.

Central Silk Board, *Functioning of Central Silk Board & Performance of Indian Silk Industry* (2019) Ministry of Textiles, Government of India <http://ministryoftextiles.gov.in/sites/default/files/note-on-sericulture2017-18-ThirdQtr.pdf> accessed 20 December 2020.

CUTS Centre for International Trade, Economics & Environment Workshop Report (GRANITE) Phase II, *State Level workshop Report: Grassroots Reach out & Networking in India on Trade & Economics* (20 April 2010) <https://cuts-crc.org/pdf/Report-GRANITE-Phase-II.pdf> accessed 15 September 2020.

Digital Empowerment Foundation, 'Digital Cluster of People, Skills & Empowerment: Baseline Survey of Pochampally, Nalgonda District, Telangana' <http://dcdpindia.org/wp-content/uploads/2017/09/Pochampally-Report_Ed.pdf#:~:text=Baseline%20Survey%20of%20Pochampally%2C%20Nalgonda%20District%2C%20Telangana%20The,Vinoba%20Bhave%20visited%20Pochampally%20mandal%20in%20Nalgonda%20district> accessed 10 December 2020.

EPCH Country Study – USA, (2005) Export Promotion Council for Handicrafts <https://epch.in/projects/EPCH%20-%20USA%20COUNTRY%20REPORT%20%20Revised%20-%20June%202006.pdf#:~:text=EPCH%20Country%20Study%20%E2%80%93%20USA7%20d%29%20LEGAL%20SYSTEMS,legislative%20acts%3B%20accepts%20compulsory%20ICJ%20jurisdiction%20with%20reservations> accessed 10 December 2020.

Ernst and Young Pvt Ltd (prepared for Export Promotion Council for Handicrafts), *Report on Competitive Study on Handicrafts Sector in China* (May 2012) <https://epch.in/ChinaStudy/Report.pdf> accessed 15 September 2020.

Export Promotion Council for Handicrafts, 34th Annual Report 2019–20 <https://epch.in/electionofcoa/2020annualreport.pdf> accessed 10 November 2020.

Food and Agricultural Organisation of the United Nations, *Qualification: Setting Rules for GI Products* <http://www.fao.org/3/i1057e/i1057e04.pdf> accessed 25 September 2020.

Food and Agriculture Organisation of the United Nations, *Strengthening Sustainable Food Systems through Geographical Indications* <http://www.fao.org/3/a-i8737en.pdf> accessed 10 November 2020.

Frost and Sullivan, *Market Feasibility Study and Business Development Plan for the Handicrafts Sector* (August 2005) Submitted to Export Promotion Council For Handicrafts, New Delhi, India <https://epch.in/projects/Handicrafts%20Final%20Report_August,%202005.pdf> accessed 10 November 2020.

Ganguli P, 'Geographical Indications, Its Evolving Countors' (2009) WTC Research Study Report <https://www.wipo.int/edocs/mdocs/sme/en/wipo_smes_hyd_07/wipo_smes_hyd_07_www_91823.pdf> accessed 10 August 2020.

Geographical Indications and TRIPs: 10 Years Later… A Roadmap for EU GI Holders to Get Protection in Other WTO Members' (October 2003), O' Connor and Company (Financed by Commission of the European Communities) <https://trade.ec.europa.eu/doclib/docs/2007/june/tradoc_135088.pdf> accessed 16 August 2020.

Geographical Indications: Historical Background, Nature of Rights, Existing Systems for Protection and Obtaining Effective Protection in Other Countries' (March 2001) Meeting of Standing Committee on the Law of Trademarks, Industrial Designs and Geographical Indications (SCT/6) <https://www.wipo.int/edocs/mdocs/sct/en/sct_6/sct_6_3.pdf> accessed 16 August 2020.

Indian Patent Office, (2020) *Details of Registered Authorised Users as on July 31, 2020* <https://ipindia.gov.in/writereaddata/Portal/Images/pdf/Registered_GI_Authorised_User_Details_-_Till_Dates.pdf> accessed 10 August 2020.

Khamir and Vankars of Kachchh, eds, 'Sandhani: Weaving Transformations in Kachchh, India: Key Findings and Analysis' (August, 2019) Kalpavriksh <https://kalpavriksh.org/publication/sandhani-weaving-transformations-in-kachchh-india-key-findings-and-analysis/> accessed 10 August 2020.

Larson J, 'Relevance of Geographical Indications and Designations of Origin for the Sustainable Use of Genetic Resources' (2007) Global Facilitation Unit for Underutilized Species <http://www.nuscommunity.org/fileadmin/templates/nuscommunity.org/upload/documents/IFAD-EU_NUS_Project/IFAD-EU-CCAFS_Launch/gi_larson_lr.pdf> accessed 10 July 2020.

Muthukumar R, 'The Weavers of Kanchipuram: A Detailed Report about the Issues Faced by Weavers in Kanchipuram' (National School of Journalism and Public Discourse, 25 February 2020) <https://www.nsoj.in/stories/the-weavers-of-kanchipuram> accessed 14 October 2020.

Narayanan L and Vinayan S, 'GIs for Protecting Agro-Biodiversity and Promoting Rural Livelihoods: Status, Strategies and Way Forward' (2017) Gujarat Institute of Development Research Working Paper Series No. 240: January 2017, accessed 10 July 2020.

Narayanan L and Vinayan S, 'Infringements in GI Protected Products: How Do We Protect the Producers and the Consumers?' (2019) Gujarat Institute of Development Research Working Paper Series No. 256: April 2019 <https://gidr.ac.in/pdf/wp-256-3248.pdf> accessed 05 July 2020.

National Council on Applied Economic Research, (2006) *Examining Employment Figures in the Handloom Sector* (All India Artisans and Craftworkers Welfare Association) <https://www.aiacaonline.org/wp-content/uploads/2018/pdf/research-NCAER-study-employment-figures-handloom-sector.pdf> accessed 01 March 2021.

National Skill Development Corporation Human Resources and Skill Requirements in the Handlooms and Handicrafts Sector (2013–17, 2017–22) <https://nsdcindia.org/sites/default/files/Handlooms-Handicrafts.pdf> accessed 03 March 2021.

Niranjana S and Vinayan S, 'Report on Growth and Prospects of Handloom Industry' (2001) Planning Commission https://www.academia.edu/4792509/Growth_and_Prospects_of_the_Handloom_Industry accessed 10 December 2020.

NITI AAYOG, (2012) *Chapter 10, Handlooms and Handicrafts* <https://niti.gov.in/planningcommission.gov.in/docs/plans/mta/11th_mta/chapterwise/chap10_handloom.pdf> accessed 20 February 2021.

NITI AAYOG, (2018) *Handlooms- A Large Employment Generating Sector*, Report of the Working Group on Handlooms for the 12th Five Year Plan (2012–17) <https://niti.gov.in/planningcommission.gov.in/docs/aboutus/committee/wrkgrp12/wg_emp_planing.pdf> accessed 1 March 2021.

Office of the Controller General of Patents, Designs, Trademarks and Geographical Indications, Government of India, (2019) *Annual Report 2018–19* <https://dipp.gov.in/sites/default/files/annualReport_2018-19_E_0.pdf>

Rangnekar D, 'Geographical Indications (A Review of Proposals at the TRIPS Council: Extending Article 23 to Products other than Wines and Spirits)' International Centre for Trade and Sustainable Development (ICTSD) International Environment House <https://unctad.org/system/files/official-document/ictsd2003ipd4_en.pdf>- accessed 05 August 2020.

Rangnekar D, 'Demanding Stronger Protection for Geographical Indications: The Relationship between Local Knowledge, Information and Reputation' INTECH (2004).

Sarkar A K, 'Impact of Geographical Indication (GI) on Craftsmen of Varanasi in Uttar Pradesh' (April 2019) National Bank Staff College, Lucknow <http://www.nbsc.in/MediaGallery/Impact%20of%20Geographical%20Indication%20(GI)%20on%20Craftsmen%20of%20Varanasi%20in%20Uttar%20Pradesh.pdf> accessed 05 August 2020.

Sharma R and Kulhari H, 'Marketing of GI Products: Unlocking Their Commercial Potential' (2015) WTO Research Study <http://wtocentre.iift.ac.in/Papers/Marketing%20of%20GI%20Products%20Unlocking%20their%20Commercial%20Potential.pdf> accessed 25 September 2020.

Sharma S C, Impact Assessment and Mid-Term Evaluation of the Handloom Cluster of Chanderi (August–September 2005) United Nations Industrial Development Organisation <https://ilrtindia.org/downloads/Chanderi-Report-Final_28.pdf> accessed 20 December 2020.

The All-India Artisans and Craftworkers Welfare Association, (2006) *Examining Employment Figures in the Handloom Sector* <https://www.aiacaonline.org/wp-content/uploads/2018/08/research-NCAER-study-employment-figures-handloom-sector.pdf> accessed 1 March 2021.

UNCTAD Secretariat, 'Systems and National Experiences for Protecting Traditional Knowledge, Innovations and Practices' (UNCTAD, TD/BCOM.1/EM.13/2, 2000) at 6 <https://unctad.org/system/files/official-document/c1em13d2.en.pdf> accessed 24 June 2020.

Vandecandelaere E, Belletti G, Marescotti A and Arfini F, *Linking People, Places and Products: A Guide for Promoting Quality Linked to Geographical ORIGIN AND Sustainable Geographical Indications* (United Nations (FAO), January 2010).

Vasudev S, 'Ground Report- The Banaras Bind', *Livemint* https://www.livemint.com/Leisure/5h1lnyORjhtn9Pr0Z4wiXL/Ground-Report–The-Banaras-bind.html accessed 09 March 2021.

VSE Division, Planning Commission Government of India, *Report on the Steering Committee on Handloom and Handicrafts* (2012) <http://handicrafts.nic.in/CmsUpload/22342016043422str_handloom0305.pdf> accessed 01 August 2020.

Working Group on Handloom Sector, Planning Commission, Government of India, (2018) *Report for the 12TH Five Year Plan (2012–17)* <https://niti.gov.in/planningcommission.gov.in/docs/aboutus/committee/wrkgrp12/wg_handloom1101.pdf> accessed 12 November 2020.

World Intellectual Property Organisation, (2019) *World Intellectual Property Indicators 2019*, Geographical Indications (Chapter 5) <https://tind.wipo.int/record/40353> accessed 12 November 2020.

Theses

Diallo A, 'Evaluation of the Economic Impact of Geographical Indications: Three Case Studies' (Ph.D Thesis, Université Clermont Auvergne 2019).

Flodgren J, 'Geographical Indications in the 21st Century- What, When and How? A Critical Review of the Legal Framework for GI Protection and GI Related Trade in the International Community' (Master Thesis, Faculty of Law, University of Lund 2009).

Gangjee D S, 'Geographical Indication Protection for Handicrafts under TRIPS' (M.Phil Thesis, University Of Oxford 2002).

Hati (Ray) P, 'Protection of Geographical Indication with Special Reference to India' (DPhil Thesis, University of Burdwan 2015).

Mamidipudi A, 'Towards a Theory of Innovation in Handloom Weaving in India' (Doctor at Maastricht University Thesis, University of Maatstricht, 2016) <https://cris.maastrichtuniversity.nl/portal/files/4083287/c5295.pdf> accessed 01 August 2020.

Mehta D, 'The Uniqueness of Tangaliya Weaving of Gujarat' (M. A Thesis, National Institute of Fashion Technology, 2017).

Rovamo O, 'Monopolising Names: The Protection of Geographical Indications in the European Community' (Pro Graduation Thesis, Helsinki University 2006).

Williams R, 'Do Geographical Indications Promote Sustainable Rural Development' (Master Thesis, Lincoln University 2007).

Newspaper Articles

Bodh A, 'Kullu Shawl, Made in Ludhiana' (*Times of India*, 15 February 2015) <https://timesofindia.indiatimes.com/city/chandigarh/kullu-shawl-made-in-ludhiana/articleshow/46248839.cms> accessed 25 December 2020.

Chakravartty A, 'Golden Thread of Misery' (*Down To Earth*, 15 November 2016) <https://www.downtoearth.org.in/news/economy/golden-thread-of-misery-56195> accessed 12 October 2020.

'Govt. to Support Tangaliya Weavers: Smriti Irani' *Times of India* (Ahmedabad, 20 January 2017) <https://timesofindia.indiatimes.com/gujarat/govet-to-support-tangaliya-weavers-smriti-irani/articleshow/56684251.cms> accessed 01 February 2021.

Joshi K, 'Cash-Crunch Hit Weavers in MP Find It Tough to Run Households' (*Hindustan Times*, 14 December 2016) <https://www.hindustantimes.com/bhopal/cash-crunch-hit-weavers-in-mp-find-it-tough-to-run-households/story-dReamXZELtiit1WhzRUnpL.html> accessed 15 December 2020.

Manta D, 'Weavers Finding it Hard to Deal with the Sale of Fake Kullu Shawls' (*The Tribune*, 1 December 2018) <https://www.tribuneindia.com/news/archive/himachaltribune/weavers-finding-it-hard-to-deal-with-sale-of-fake-kullu-shawls-691631> accessed 25 December 2020.

Nair M, ‘Cloning the Chanderi’ *Times of India* (India, 21 June 2015) <https://timesofindia.indiatimes.com/home/sunday-times/deep-focus/Cloning-the-Chanderi/articleshow/47750085.cms> accessed 15 December 2020.

Rao M, ‘MP Weavers Hanging by a Chanderi Thread’ (*People’s Archive of Rural India*, 7 May 2020) <https://ruralindiaonline.org/en/articles/mp-weavers-hanging-by-a-chanderi-thread/> accessed 15 December 2020.

Rashid O, ‘WhatsApp Worsens Varanasi Weavers’ Woes’ *The Hindu* (Varanasi, 30 March 2014) <https://www.thehindu.com/news/national/other-states/whatsapp-worsens-varanasi-weavers-woes/article5851933.ece> accessed 24 February 2021.

Santhanam K, ‘Reviving Textile Traditions’ *The Hindu* (India, 16 February 2012) <https://www.thehindu.com/arts/crafts/reviving-textile-traditions/article2899650.ece> accessed 2 March 2021.

Sharma H, ‘Economic Slowdown: Madhya Pradesh Weavers Suffer due to Low Sale of Chanderi Sarees’ (*India Today*, 31 August 2019) <https://www.indiatoday.in/india/story/economic-slowdown-madhya-pradesh-weavers-suffer-due-to-low-sale-of-chanderi-sarees-1593743-2019-08-31> accessed 15 December 2020.

‘Smriti Irani Visits Tangalia Weavers of Surendranagar, Announces Society, Subsidy for Them’ *DeshGujarat* (Surendranagar, 19 January 2017) <https://www.deshgujarat.com/2017/01/19/smriti-irani-visits-tangalia-weavers-of-surendranagar-announces-society-subsidy-for-them/> accessed 01 February 2021.

Vincent P, ‘Boards that Gave Artisans a Voice Scrapped’ *The Telegraph* (India, 8 August,2020)<https://www.telegraphindia.com/india/all-india-handloom-board-and-the-all-india-handicrafts-board-scrapped/cid/1788527> accessed 2 March 2021.

Websites

‘Advisory Bodies’ (Ministry of Textiles, 2021) <http://texmin.nic.in/about-us/advisory-bodies> accessed 2 March 2021.

‘Craft of Gujarat’ <https://craftofgujarat.gujarat.gov.in/AwardWinners> accessed 20 August 2020.

‘Crafts of Kachcch’ (*Khamir*, 2021) <http://www.khamir.org/crafts/weaving> accessed 20 August 2020.

‘Details of Registered Authorised Users as on July 31, 2020’ (*Geographical Indications Registry*, 2020) <https://ipindia.gov.in/writereaddata/Portal/Images/pdf/Registered_GI_Authorised_User_Details_-_Till_Dates.pdf> accessed 1 March 2020.

‘Frequently Asked Questions, India Handloom Brand’ (Ministry of Textiles, Government of India, 2021) This document enlists all products eligible for registration under the IHB <http://www.indiahandloombrand.gov.in/downloads/FAQ_India_Handloom_Brand_English.pdf> accessed 18 January 2021.

‘Geographical Indications: Historical Background, Nature of Rights, Existing Systems for Protection and Obtaining Protection in Other Countries’ (World Intellectual Property Organization 2002) <https://www.wipo.int/edocs/mdocs/sct/en/sct_8/sct_8_4.pdf> accessed 05 August 2020.

George K, 'When the Tezpur University Came to GI Tagged Muga Silk of Assam's Rescue' (*SpicyIP*, 29 April 2015) <https://spicyip.com/2015/04/when-the-tezpur-university-came-to-gi-tagged-muga-silk-of-assams-rescue.html> accessed 12 October 2020.

Gogoi J, 'The Need to Look beyond Wines and Spirits: GI Law in India and the Woes of Muga Silk' (*SpicyIP*, 11 May 2019) <https://spicyip.com/2019/05/the-need-to-look-beyond-wines-and-spirits-gi-law-in-india-and-the-woes-of-muga-silk.html> accessed 12 October 2020.

'Indian Institute of Handloom Technology, Salem' Handloom Export Promotion Council <https://www.hepcindia.com/page/about_hepc> accessed 2 March 2021. <http://www.iihtsalem.edu.in/about-us/> accessed 2 March 2021.

'Key-Concepts of GIs' (*Organisation for an International Geographical Indications Network*) <https://www.origin-gi.com/your-gi-kit/key-concepts-of-gis.html> accessed January 12, 2021.

'List of Weavers' Service Centres' (*Office of Development Commissioner (Handlooms)*) <http://www.handlooms.nic.in/writereaddata/Address%20and%20contact%2028%20WSCs635725578191936271.pdf> accessed 2 March 2021.

'Manual of Geographical Indications Practice and Procedure' (*Office of The Controller General of Patents, Designs and Trademarks & Registrar of Geographical Indications*, 2011) <https://ipindia.gov.in/writereaddata/Portal/IPOGuidelinesManuals/1_31_1_manual-of-geographical-indications-practice-and-procedure.pdf> accessed 01 July 2020.

'Office of the Development Commissioner (Handlooms)' <www.handlooms.nic.in> accessed 2 March 2021.

'Our Story, Chanderiyaan' (Digital Empowerment Foundation, 2009) <https://dcdpindia.org/chanderiyaan/> accessed 20 December 2020.

'Powerloom Industry and Exports in India' (*India Brand Equity Foundation*) https://www.ibef.org/exports/powerloom-industry-in-india.aspx accessed 10 August 2020.

'Registered Users List' (Ministry of Textiles, Government of India, 2021) <https://www.indiahandloombrand.gov.in/Members/user_list/> accessed 18 January 2021.

Reiss S, 'Commentary on the Paris Convention for the Protection of Industrial Property' (*Lex-IP.com*) <http://lex-ip.com/Paris.pdf> accessed 01 August 2020.

'Traditional Knowledge and Intellectual Property – Background Brief' (World Intellectual Property Organization) <https://www.wipo.int/pressroom/en/briefs/tk_ip.html> accessed 09 March 2021.

United Nations Educational, Scientific and Cultural Organization, 'Iconic Saree Weaving Clusters of India' (Ref No. 5890 April 15, 2014) <https://whc.unesco.org/en/tentativelists/5890/> accessed 12 August 2020.

'Vankar Shamji Vishram' (*Border & Fall*, 2021) <http://www.borderandfall.com/vankar-shamji-vishram/> accessed 20 August 2020.

'Why Geographical Indications for Least Developed Countries (LDCs)?' (UNCTAD, 2015) <https://unctad.org/webflyer/why-geographical-indications-least-developed-countries#:~:text=Since%202010%20UNCTAD%20is%20supporting,through%20Geographical%20Indications%20(GIs).&text=GIs%20encourage%20the%20preservation%20of,know%2Dhow%20and%20natural%20resources> accessed 12 October 2020.

APPENDIX 1

Details of handlooms registered as Geographical Indications in India

Sr. No.	*Geographical Indications*	*State*	*Valid up to*
APRIL 2004–MARCH 2005			
1.	Pochampalli Ikat	Telangana	14-12-23
APRIL 2005–MARCH 2006			
2.	Salem Fabric	Tamil Nadu	11-02-14
3.	Chanderi Sarees	Madhya Pradesh	01-04-24
4.	Solapur Chaddar	Maharashtra	04-04-24
5.	Solapur Terry Towel	Maharashtra	19-05-24
6.	Kotpad Handloom fabric	Odisha	09-06-24
7.	Mysore Silk	Karnataka	21-07-24
8.	Kota Doria	Rajasthan	21-07-24
9.	Kancheepuram Silk	Tamil Nadu	06-10-24
10.	Bhavani Jamakkalam	Tamil Nadu	24-10-24
11.	Kullu Shawl	Himachal Pradesh	09-12-24
12.	Madurai Sangudi	Tamil Nadu	23-01-25
13.	Orissa Ikat	Odisha	31-01-25
APRIL 2007–MARCH 2008			
14.	Muga Silk of Assam	Assam	19-07-26
15.	Ilkal Sarees	Karnataka	15-10-26
16.	Navalgund Durries	Karnataka	25-07-26
17.	Molakalmuru Sarees	Karnataka	15-10-26
18.	Salem Silk known as Salem Venpattu	Tamil Nadu	15-05-27
19.	Kovai Kora Cotton Sarees	Tamil Nadu	24-04-27
20.	Arani Silk	Tamil Nadu	24-04-27
APRIL 2008–MARCH 2009			
21.	Kani Shawl	Jammu & Kashmir	12-02-26
22.	Kashmir Pashmina	Jammu & Kashmir	08-12-25
23.	Uppada Jamdani Sarees	Andhra Pradesh	09-04-28
APRIL 2009–MARCH 2010			
24.	Banaras Brocades and Sarees	Uttar Pradesh	03-07-27
25.	Tangaliya Shawl	Gujarat	08-06-18
26.	Santipore Saree	West Bengal	21-09-28

(*Continued*)

Sr. No.	*Geographical Indications*	*State*	*Valid up to*
27.	Cannanore Home Furnishings	Kerala	13-11-28
28.	Balaramapuram Sarees and Fine Cotton Fabrics	Kerala	18-01-29
APRIL 2010–MARCH 2011			
29.	Gadwal Sarees	Telangana	21-09-28
30.	Kinnauri Shawl	Himachal Pradesh	03-12-18
31.	Kasaragod Sarees	Kerala	10-05-29
32.	Kuthampully Sarees	Kerala	12-07-29
33.	Paithani Sarees and Fabrics	Maharashtra	04-01-29
34.	Champa Silk Saree And Fabrics	Chhattisgarh	24-05-29
35.	Khandua Saree and Fabrics	Odisha	11-09-28
APRIL 2011–MARCH 2012			
36.	Venkatagiri Sarees	Andhra Pradesh	12-11-29
37.	Kachchh Shawls	Gujarat	03-06-29
38.	Baluchari Saree	West Bengal	31-05-29
39.	Dhaniakhali Saree	West Bengal	01-07-29
40.	Chendamangalam Dhoties & Set Mundu	Kerala	17-11-13
41.	Gopalpur Tussar Fabrics	Odisha	14-04-19
42.	Siddipet Gollabama	Telangana	01-11-29
APRIL 2012–MARCH 2013			
43.	Maheshwar Sarees & Fabrics	Madhya Pradesh	07-02-30
44.	Dhalapathar Parda & Fabrics	Odisha	11-07-30
45.	Sambalpuri Bandha Saree & Fabrics	Odisha	12-07-30
46.	Bomkai Saree & Fabrics	Odisha	12-09-30
47.	Habaspuri Saree & Fabrics	Odisha	12-09-20
48.	Berhampur Patta (Phoda Kumbha) Saree & Joda	Odisha	12-09-30
49.	Bhagalpur Silk	Bihar	14-07-19
50.	Mangalagiri Sarees and Fabrics	Andhra Pradesh	25-02-30

(*Continued*)

Sr. No.	*Geographical Indications*	*State*	*Valid up to*
51.	Narayanpet Handloom Sarees	Telangana	01-08-30
52.	Agra Durrie	Uttar Pradesh	32-03-21
APRIL 2013–MARCH 2014			
53.	Patan Patola	Gujarat	09-03-21
54.	Dharmavaram Handloom Pattu Sarres And Paavadas	Andhra Pradesh	01-08-30
55.	Shaphee Lanphee	Manipur	NA
56.	Wangkhei Phee	Manipur	NA
57.	Moirang Phee	Manipur	NA
APRIL 2014–MARCH 2015			
58.	Mirzapur Handmade Dari	Uttar Pradesh	30-10-23
APRIL 2015–MARCH 2016			
59.	Guledgudd Khana	Karnataka	28-07-20
60.	Udupi Sarees	Karnataka	02-11-30
61.	Kuthampally Dhoties & Set Mundu	Kerala	10-02-23
APRIL 2016–MARCH 2017			
62.	Karvath Kati Sarees & Fabrics	Maharashtra	06-01-23
APRIL 2017–MARCH 2018			
63.	Chakshesang Shawl	Nagaland	31-12-25
64.	Warangal Durries	Telangana	05-03-25
APRIL 2018–MARCH 2019			
65.	Rajkot Patola	Gujarat	15-03-22
66.	Thirubuvanam Silk Sarees	Tamil Nadu	14-04-24
APRIL 2019–MARCH 2020			
67.	Pawndum	Mizoram	NA
68.	Ngotekherh	Mizoram	NA
69.	Hmaram	Mizoram	NA
70.	Tawlhlohpuan	Mizoram	19-06-27
71.	Mizo Puanchei	Mizoram	19-06-27
72.	Idu Mishmi Textiles	Arunachal Pradesh	08-10-28
73.	Kandangi Saree	Tamil Nadu	15-05-23
74.	Telia Rumal	Telangana	NA

Source: Prepared by authors

APPENDIX 2

Details of inspection bodies of registered handlooms in India

Sr. No.	*Geographical Indications*	*State*	*Inspection body*
APRIL 2004–MARCH 2005			
1.	Pochampalli Ikat	Telangana	The applicants have Stated that they are moving towards the establishment of an inspection structure in consultation with the following: • Textile Committee under MoT, GoI • Weavers' Service Centre, GoI • Government of Andhra Pradesh
APRIL 2005–MARCH 2006			
2.	Salem Fabric	Tamil Nadu	Textiles Committee, Government of India, Regional Office, Salem
3.	Chanderi Sarees	Madhya Pradesh	State Government of Madhya Pradesh with no specific distribution of roles and responsibilities
4.	Solapur Chaddar	Maharashtra	Textile Development Foundation
5.	Solapur Terry Towel	Maharashtra	Textile Development Foundation
6.	Kotpad Handloom Fabric	Odisha	• One experienced textile officer posted by Boyanika for quality maintenance • Technical Field officers, Zonal Assistant Director of Textiles Office of Directorate of Textiles, Government of Odisha • Weavers Service Centre, Bhubaneshwar and Textile Committee • Boyanika has taken the responsibility for the marketing of the product One textile designer of national repute is placed in the Kotapad Cluster for skill development
7.	Mysore Silk	Karnataka	Karnataka Silk Industries Corporation with no specific distribution of roles and responsibilities
8.	Kota Doria	Rajasthan	Kota Doria Development Hadauti Foundation with no specific distribution of roles and responsibilities
9.	Bhavani Jamakkalam	Tamil Nadu	Modalities of Inspection body is regulated and the quality of the product is being worked out
10.	Kancheepuram Silk	Tamil Nadu	State Government of Tamil Nadu with no specific distribution of roles and responsibilities

(*Continued*)

Sr. No.	*Geographical Indications*	*State*	*Inspection body*
11.	Kullu Shawl Himachal Pradesh		The inspection body comprises the following: • Co-ordinator, H. P. Patent Information Centre, State Council for Science, Technology and Environment, H. P. • General Manager, District Industries Centre, Kullu or his representative • Managing Director, Himbunkar, Bhunter, District Kullu • President, Kullu Shawl Weavers' Association, Kullu • Assistant Registrar, Co-operative Societies, Kullu • H.P. Handicraft and Handloom Corporation • In charge, Central Wool Development Board, Kullu • One expert in textile technology/design
12.	Madurai Sangudi	Tamil Nadu	The applicants have Stated that they are moving towards the establishment of an inspection structure in consultation with the following: Textile Committee under the Ministry of Textile, Government of India
13.	Orissa Ikat	Odisha	The applicants have Stated that they are moving towards the establishment of an inspection structure in consultation with the following: • Technical guidance from Weavers Service Centre, Bhubaneswar • Textile Committee, Bhubaneswar The external members from the following organizations will also be included: • District Rural Development Agency (DRDA) • National Handloom Development Corporation (NHDC)

APRIL 2007–MARCH 2008

14.	Muga Silk of Assam	Assam	The inspection body comprises the following: • Department of Sericulture, Government of Assam • Representative Committee • Central Silk Board of India • Weavers' Association • Weavers' Service Centre • ARTFED • District Industry Officer • Representative of Department of Sericulture • PIC/ ASTEC • Institute of Advanced Studies in Science and Technology, Asom Laboratory and Certification with no specific distribution of roles and responsibilities
15.	Ilkal Sarees	Karnataka	It is proposed by the Department of Handlooms and Textiles, Government of Karnataka to form a core team to ensure the standard, quality, integrity and consistency of goods. The team of members would comprise: • Dy Director Textiles, Department of Handlooms • Government of Karnataka, Bagalkote – Member Secretary • Dy Director, Weaver's Service Centre, Bangalore – Member • Central Silk Technological Research Institute, Bangalore – Member • Leading societies at Ilkal – Members – 2 Nos. • Karnataka Handloom Development Corporation, Ilkal – Member • National Institute of Fashion Technology, Bangalore – Member • A representative of master weavers

(Continued)

Sr. No.	*Geographical Indications*	*State*	*Inspection body*
16.	Navalgund Durries	Karnataka	The inspection body consisting of the following have been constituted for maintaining the quality of the product: • Officer-in-charge, O/o the Development Commissioner (Handicraft), Bangalore/Mysore • Director (Market Research), Textiles Committee, Ministry of Textiles, Mumbai • Representative of producers associations, prominent master artisans of the product
17.	Molakalmuru Sarees	Karnataka	It is proposed by the Department of Handlooms and Textiles, Government of Karnataka to form a core team towards ensuring the standards, quality, integrity and consistency of goods. The team of members would be: • Dy Director Textiles, Department of Handlooms, Government of Karnataka, Bagalkote – Member Secretary • Dy Director, Weavers Service Centre, Bangalore – Member • Central Silk Technological Research Institute, Bangalore – Member • A member from a leading society in Molakalmuru. • Karnataka Handloom Development Corporation, Ilkal town – Member
18.	Salem Silk known as Salem Venpattu	Tamil Nadu	A quality control body is being established by Department of Handlooms and Textiles, Government of Tamil Nadu, which is autonomous and consists of not less than ten members representing central and State government organizations and industries in order to control the quality and to maintain the quality of Salem Silks, known as Salem Venpattu.

19.	Kovai Kora Cotton Sarees	Tamil Nadu	A quality control body is being established by Department of Handlooms and Textiles, Government of Tamil Nadu, which is autonomous and consists of not less than ten members representing central and State government organizations and industries in order to control the quality and to maintain the quality of Kovai Kora Cotton Sarees.
20.	Arani Silk	Tamil Nadu	A quality control body is being established by Department of Handlooms and Textiles, Government of Tamil Nadu, which is autonomous and consists of not less than ten members representing central and State government organizations and industries in order to control the quality and to maintain the quality of Arani Silks.
APRIL 2008 – MARCH 2009			
21.	Kani Shawl	Jammu and Kashmir	The application is taking steps to set up a suitable and effective inspection body.
22.	Kashmir Pashmina	Jammu and Kashmir	The applicant is taking steps to set up a suitable and effective inspection body.
23.	Uppada Jamdani Sarees	Andhra Pradesh	Each product is made through the above-mentioned process and inspected by the master weavers using a counting glass, which is a special instrument used for this purpose. Based on the number of threads available per inch, the master weavers assess the quality of the goods. If the goods meet the required standards, then upon being satisfied as to the quality of the goods, the handicrafts seal is affixed to the goods. Therefore, each product, before going to the market, is subjected to inspection and certification by the master weavers.

(*Continued*)

Sr. No.	*Geographical Indications*	*State*	*Inspection body*
APRIL 2009 – MARCH 2010			
24.	Banaras Brocades and Sarees	Uttar Pradesh	The inspection body comprises the following: • The Department of Handlooms, Government of Uttar Pradesh • Development Commissioner (Handlooms), Government of India • The Weavers' Service Centre, Government of India, Banaras, which is also providing technical and design-related services to the weavers • Master weavers • The Textiles Committee, Ministry of Textiles, Government of India with no specific distribution of roles and responsibilities
25.	Tangaliya Shawls	Gujarat	The inspection body comprises craftsmen from Tangaliya, experts from the National Institute of Fashion Technology (NIFT), Gandhinagar and experts from the National Institute of Design, with no specific distribution of roles and responsibilities.
26.	Santipore Sarees	West Bengal	• Patent Information Centre, West Bengal State Council of Science and Technology, Department of Science and Technology, Government of West Bengal • Directorate of Handloom and Textile, Government of West Bengal
27.	Cannanore Home Furnishings	Kerala	Steps are being taken by the applicants to set up a suitable, independent, and effective inspection body involving external members.

28.	Balaramapuram Sarees and Fine Cotton Fabrics	Kerala	The Department of Handlooms and Textiles, Government of Kerala, and the Development Commissioner (Handlooms), Government of India are supporting the weavers in the quality control of the products. Besides the master weavers in the entrepreneurial sector, the weaver masters of the co-operative societies have their own quality control mechanism. During the processes of production, like winding and warping, creation of motifs, weaving, etc., these master weavers/weaving masters used to inspect the different predetermined parameters and the quality before permitting the final/finishing stage of production. However, providing the specifications for the quality inspection of the master artisans is difficult as it varies from one master weaver to another. The Textiles Committee, a statutory body under the Ministry of Textiles, Government of India, known all over the country for quality inspection and testing of different textiles and clothing products, is also actively participating in educating the weavers and other stakeholders about maintaining the quality and its importance, marketing strategies, brand building of the product, and 47 other development activities relating to the stakeholders of Balaramapuram Sarees and Fine Cotton Fabrics. Even the traders and exporters involved in the marketing of the unique traditional products are also specifying a specific level of quality while placing orders to the manufacturers on the basis of demand patterns in the market and subsequently inspecting the various stages of production and the final product before procurement. But in the present scenario, it has been decided that the Textiles Committee, Government of India, Mumbai, having a regional office at Kannur, along with the master weavers and the Department of Handlooms, Government of Kerala, will provide an inspection mechanism for maintaining the quality of the product in the post-GI registration scenario.

(*Continued*)

Sr. No.	*Geographical Indications*	*State*	*Inspection body*
APRIL 2010 – MARCH 2011			
29.	Gadwal Sarees	Telangana	Gadwal sarees are inspected for their quality by the master weaver. The master weaver is a person who has expert knowledge in all aspects relating to the process of making Gadwal sarees, which include the critical art of the visualization of their design, their layout, and the orientation and intricacy of the body, border and pallu of the saree. Only upon personal inspection by the master weaver are the sarees are made ready for the market. Further, steps are being taken by the applicants to set up a suitable, independent and effective inspection body involving external members.
30.	Kinnauri Shawl	Himachal Pradesh	The inspection body for the Kinnauri Shawl is proposed as follows: • Co-Ordinator, HP Patent Information Centre, State Council for Science, Technology and Environment, H.P. • General Manager, District Industries Centre, Kinnaur • President, Kinnauri Shawl Weavers/Producers Association • General Manager, H.P. Handicraft and Handloom Corporation, B-6, SDA Complex, Kasumpti, Shimla – 171009 • In charge, Central Wool Development Board at Kullu

31.	Kasaragod Sarees	Kerala	The Development Commissioner (Handlooms), Government of India and the Department of Handlooms and Textiles, Government of Kerala are supporting the weavers in quality control of the products. Besides, the weaving masters of the co- operative societies have their own quality control mechanism. During the processes of production like winding and warping, creation of motifs, weaving, etc., the weaving masters used to inspect the different predetermined parameters and the quality before permitting the final/finishing stage of production. The Textiles Committee, a statutory body under the Ministry of Textiles, Government of India, known all over the country for quality inspection and testing of different textiles and clothing products, is also actively participating in educating the weavers and other stakeholders about maintaining quality and its importance, marketing strategies, the brand building of the product, and other development activities relating to the stakeholders of Kasaragod Sarees. Even the traders and exporters involved in the marketing of these unique traditional products are also specifying specific levels of quality while placing orders to the manufacturers on the basis of demand patterns in the market, and they subsequently inspect the various stages of production and the final product before procurement. But in the present scenario, it has been decided that the Textiles Committee, Government of India, Mumbai, having a regional office at Kannur, along with the Department of Handlooms, Government of Kerala will provide an inspection mechanism for maintaining the quality of the product in the post-GI registration scenario.

(*Continued*)

Sr. No.	*Geographical Indications*	*State*	*Inspection body*
32.	Kuthampully Sarees	Kerala	The Development Commissioner (Handlooms), Government of India and the Department of Handlooms and Textiles, Government of Kerala are supporting the weavers in quality control of the products. Besides, the weaving masters of the co- operative societies have their own quality control mechanism. During the process of production like winding and warping, creation of motifs, weaving, etc., the weaving masters used to inspect the different predetermined parameters and the quality before permitting the final/finishing stage of production. The Textiles Committee, a statutory body under the Ministry of Textiles, Government of India, known all over the country for quality inspection and testing of different textiles and clothing products, is also actively participating in educating the weavers and other stakeholders about maintaining quality and its importance, marketing strategies, brand building of the product, and other development activities relating to the stakeholders of Kuthampully Sarees. Even the traders and exporters involved in the marketing of these unique traditional products are also specifying specific levels of quality while placing orders to the manufacturers on the basis of demand patterns in the market, and they subsequently inspect the various stages of production and the final product before procurement. But in the present scenario, it has been decided that the Textiles Committee, Government of India, Mumbai, having a regional office at Kannur, along with the Department of Handlooms, Government of Kerala will provide inspection mechanism for maintaining quality of the product in the post-GI registration scenario.

33.	Paithani Sarees and Fabrics	Maharashtra	The inspection body comprises the following: • The Department of Powerloom, Handloom and Textiles, Government of Maharashtra • Development Commissioner (Handlooms), Government of India • Maharashtra Handloom Development Corporation • Maharashtra State Small Scale Industrial Development Corporation (MSSIDC) • A mix of artisans, experts from Ministry of Textiles and traders of Paithani are suggested to be added with no specific distribution of roles and responsibilities
34.	Champa Silk Saree and Fabrics	Chhattisgarh	The inspection body proposed for Champa Silk Saree and Fabrics would be as follows: • Department of Handlooms and Textile, Government of Chhattisgarh • Central and State Silk Board • Weaver's Service Centre • Consortium of producers, manufacturers and exporters • Textile Committee
35.	Khandua Saree and Fabrics	Odisha	Steps are being taken by the applicants to set up a suitable, independent and effective inspection body involving external members.
APRIL 2011 – MARCH 2012			
36.	Venkatagiri Sarees	Andhra Pradesh	Usually, the master weavers identify flaws in Venkatagiri sarees by touch. The quality is assessed by the nature of the work done and then the product is sent to the showrooms for display. Inspection would be done by Venkatagiri Handloom Sarees Apex Society to ensure that every production unit maintains quality standards.

(Continued)

Sr. No.	*Geographical Indications*	*State*	*Inspection body*
37.	Kachchh Shawls	Gujarat	An inspection structure will be established comprising the master artisans, experts from the handloom sector, designers, members of government and non- government organizations etc.
38.	Baluchari Saree	West Bengal	Inspection Committee Body, Department of Micro and Small Scale Enterprise and Textiles, Government of West Bengal
39.	Dhaniakhali Saree	West Bengal	• Patent Information Centre, West Bengal State Council of Science and Technology, Government of West Bengal • Directorate of Textiles/Handlooms. Spinning Mills, Silk Weaving and Handloom based Handicrafts Division), Government of West Bengal • Dhaniakhali Union T.S.S.. Ltd. • Gurap T.S.S. Ltd. • Somaspur Union C.W.S. Ltd. • Chanditala I No. BL P.W.C.S. Ltd. • Chhototajpur T.S.S. Ltd. • Chanditala I No. TB. T.S.S. Ltd. • Chanditala I No. Bl. TH. T.S.S. Ltd • Gangadharpur Anchal T.S.S. Ltd. • Janai W.C.S. Ltd. • Kharsarai Madhyampara T.S.S. Ltd • Kharsarai T.S.S. Ltd.

			• Kharsarai Dakshinpara T.S.S. Ltd. • Begarnpur Anchal T.S.S. Ltd • Pararrbua Sahabazar A.C.W.S. Ltd. • Begampur Handloom C.S. Ltd. • Jangipara Block P.W.C.S. Ltd. • Jangipara Thana Tantbihin T.S.S Ltd. • Naskardanga W.C.S. Ltd. • Pursurah Block P.W.C.S. Lld. • Rajbalhat Uttarsi l para T.S.S. Ltd. • Raja Rammohan Roy T.S.S. Ltd. • Daspur C.W.S. Ltd. • Daspur Adarsha T.S.S. Ltd. • Gultia Tantsilpa T.S.S. Ltd. • Gopalour T.S.S. Lrd. 2s. Ha;ip;r w.c.s. Lrd. • Haripal Block P.W.C.S. Ltd. • Haripal T.S.S. Ltd. 3l. Ichhapur T.S.S. Ltd. • Rajbalhat Madhyapara B.S.S.S. Ltd • Bilarapalpara T.S.S. Ltd. • Bora T.S.S. Ltd. • Atghara T.S.S. Ltd. • Silpara Bayan T.S.S. Ltd. • Rashipdur Union WCS Ltd.
40.	Chendamangalam Dhoties and Set Mundu	Kerala	NA

(Continued)

Sr. No.	*Geographical Indications*	*State*	*Inspection body*
41.	Gopalpur Tussar Fabrics	Odisha	The Department of Handlooms, Government of Orissa, Development Commissioner (Handlooms), Government of India, having an office at Bhubaneswar, is involved in quality control of the products. Besides, the master artisans of the product have their own method of quality control. During the processes of production, like preparation of yarn, dyeing, winding and warping, creation of motifs, weaving, etc., the master weavers used to inspect the different predetermined parameters and quality before permitting the final/finishing stage of production. However, providing the specification of the quality inspection of the master weavers is difficult as it varies from one master weaver to other. Since the majority of the support service providers are women in the case of this product, special care has been taken to protect their interests and for their economic support while undertaking developmental activities. Even the traders and exporters involved in the marketing of this unique product are also specifying specific levels of quality while providing orders to the manufacturers on the basis of demand patterns in the market, and they subsequently inspect the various stages of production and final product before procurement. Hence, in this scenario, it has been decided that Department of Handlooms, Government of Orissa along with the master weavers, with the support of Institute of Socio-Economic Research and Training (ISERT), Cuttack, a civil society organization working for the betterment of the artisan community, will provide inspection mechanism for maintaining quality of the product in the post-GI registration scenario.

42.	Siddipet Gollabama	Telangana	Inspection and quality control are undertaken in the first instance by the master artisans, who employ high standards of quality control. Subsequently, the final product is inspected by the APCO Regional Manager to add another layer of quality control and inspection. Apart from the above prevailing two-tier inspection system, the Weaver Service Centre and additional director handlooms act in an advisory capacity to the master weavers.
APRIL 2012 – MARCH 2013			
43.	Maheshwar Sarees and Fabrics	Madhya Pradesh	Presently the State Government of Madhya Pradesh is involved in quality control of the Maheshwar Sarees and Fabric and all of its products. The Directorate of Handloom, Government of Madhya Pradesh also stamping the quality products against usual charges. The Directorate of Handloom, Government of Madhya Pradesh vide its orders dated May 22 1998 has laid down specific rules in this respect and they issue cards to the producer/weavers who apply to them to verify the quality and specifications. The office of Assistant Director of Handloom and Training Centre, Department of Handlooms, Government of Madhya Pradesh, Maheshwar shall act as inspecting agency. The applicants further affirms to abide by all the rules, regulations and orders so issued by the Madhya Pradesh Government and by the aforesaid inspecting agency in regulating the standards and specifications for Maheshwar Sarees and Fabrics.

(Continued)

Sr. No.	*Geographical Indications*	*State*	*Inspection body*
44.	Dhalapathar Parda and Fabrics	Odisha	It is proposed by the Department of Handlooms and Textiles, Government of Orissa to form a core team to ensure the standards, quality, integrity and consistency of goods. The team of members would be: • Representative of the Director of Textiles, Department of Textiles and Handlooms, Government of Orissa – Member Secretary • Deputy Director, Weavers Service Centre, Bhubaneswar – Member • Managing Director, Orissa State Handloom WCS Ltd.(BOYANIKA) – Member • Nominee from NHDC – Member • ADT, Kurda – Member • Nominee from Textiles Committee – Bhubaneswar – Member
45.	Sambalpuri Bandha Saree and Fabrics	Odisha	It is proposed by the Department of Handlooms and Textiles, Government of Orissa to form a core team to ensure the standards, quality, integrity and consistency of goods. The team of members would be: • Managing Director, Orissa State Handloom WCS Ltd.(BOYANIKA) – Chairman • Deputy Director, Weavers Service Cenffe, Bhubaneswar – Member • Managing Director, Sambalpuri Bastralaya – Member • Nominee from NHDC – Member 5– ADT – Burgarh – Member • Nominee from Textiles Committee – Bhubaneswar – Member

46.	Bomkai Saree and Fabrics	Odisha	It is proposed by the Department of Handlooms and Textiles, Government of Orissa to form a core team to ensure the standards, quality, integrity and consistency of goods. The team of members would be: • Managing Director, Sambalpuri Bastralaya –Chairman • Deputy Director, Weavers Service Centre, Bhubaneswar – Member • Managing Director, Orissa State Handloom WCS Ltd. (BOYANIKA) – Member • Nominee from NHDC – Member • Deputy Director, Textiles, Sonepur – Member • Nominee from Textiles Committee – Bhubaneswar – Member
47.	Habaspuri Saree and Fabrics	Odisha	It is proposed by the Department of Handlooms and Textiles, Government of Orissa to form a core team to ensure the standards, quality, integrity and consistency of goods. The team of members would be: • Director of Textiles, Department of Handlooms, Government of Orissa – Chairman • Deputy Director, Weavers Service Centre, Bhubaneswar – Member • Managing Director, Orissa State Handloom WCS Ltd.(BOYANIKA) Member • Managing Director, Sambalpuri Bastralaya – Member • Nominee from NHDC – Member 6 –ADT – Kalahandi – Member • Nominee from Textiles Committee – Bhubaneswar – Member

(*Continued*)

Sr. No.	*Geographical Indications*	*State*	*Inspection body*
48.	Berhampur Patta (Phoda Kumbha) Saree and Joda	Odisha	It is proposed by the Department of Handlooms and Textiles, Government of Orissa to form a core team to ensure the standards, quality, integrity and consistency of goods. The team of members would be: • Managing Director, Orissa State Handloom WCS Ltd. (BOYANIKA) – Member Secretary • Deputy Director, Weavers Service Centre, Bhubaneswar – Member • Nominee from NHDC – Member 4 – ADT, Berhampur – Member • Nominee from Textiles Committee – Bhubaneswar – Member
49.	Bhagalpur Silk	Bihar	An inspection body consisting of the following organizations has been constituted. These organizations are working for development of Bhagalpur silk. The organizations are: • Bhagalpur Tussar Silk Development Samiti • Bhagalpur Regional Handloom Weavers Cooperative Union Ltd. • Weavers Service Centre (WSC) • Asian Society for Entrepreneurship Education and Development (ASEED) • Central Silk Board • Directorate of Handlooms DOH (Industry Department Government of Bihar) • Indian Silk Export Promotion Council Textiles Committee

50.	Mangalagiri Sarees and Fabrics	Andhra Pradesh	Inspection and quality control are undertaken in the first instance by the master artisans, who employ high standards of quality control. The master weavers are confident of identifying flaws by touch. A Read and Pick mechanism is followed to ensure the quality of the textile woven. Subsequent to inspection by master artisans, the product is inspected by the APCO Regional Manager to add another layer of quality control and Inspection. Apart from the above prevailing two-tier inspection system, the Weaver Service Centre and additional director handlooms act in an advisory capacity to the master weavers. The weavers and societies concerned are confident and conscious of the kind of yarn used as the all raw materials are sourced from the same place.
51.	Narayanpet Handloom Sarees	Telangana	• Central Silk Board – responsible for quality of silk and zari • APCO – inspects quality of sarees procured from weavers' co-operative societies (EPI and PPI) • Authorized User of Silk Mark Organization of India • Member of Handloom Mark • Inspection and quality control are undertaken in the first instance by the master artisans at the first instance, who employ high standards of quality control. The master weavers are confident of identifying flaws by touch. A Read and Pick mechanism is followed to ensure the quality of the textile woven. • Subsequent to inspection by master artisans, the final product is inspected by the APCO Regional Manager to add another layer of quality control and inspection. Apart from the above prevailing two-tier inspection system, the Weaver Service Centre and additional director handlooms act in an advisory capacity to the master weavers. • Weavers and societies concerned are confident and conscious of the kind of yarn used as all raw materials are sourced from the same place.

(*Continued*)

Sr. No.	*Geographical Indications*	*State*	*Inspection body*
52.	Agra Durrie	Uttar Pradesh	An inspection body consisting of the following members has been constituted: • Director, Department of Handlooms and Textiles, Government of Uttar Pradesh • Joint Export Commissioner, Export Promotion Bureau, Government of Uttar Pradesh • Director (Market Research), Textiles Committee, Government of India • Two master artisans • O/o Development Commissioner of Handicraft, Government of India, New Delhi
APRIL 2013 – MARCH 2014			
53.	Patan Patola	Gujarat	The inspection body comprises the following two-tier inspection system: • Initial inspection by expert artisans • Inspection by inspection committee consisting of two members of the association and one expert independent agency as appointed from time to time, with no specific distribution of roles and responsibilities
54.	Dharmavaram Handloom Pattu Sarees And Paavadas	Andhra Pradesh	It has been proposed to have a five-member team as inspection body for the GI Dharmavaram Handloom Pattu sarees and Pavadas. The members are: • One member from the Textile Committee • One senior official from the Central Silk Board, local asst. director, Handlooms, Anantpur Dist. • One master weaver president/vice president of the society.

55.	Shaphee Lanphee	Manipur	The inspection committee is an independent and neutral body which is capable of regulating quality and the use of Geographical Indications in respect of the Moirang Pheejin, consisting of following members: • One representative from the Department of Handlooms and Textiles – not lower than the rank of deputy director • One representative from Manipur State Weavers Apex Society • One representative from the Department of Commerce, Manipur University • One representative from the Weavers Service Centre, Manipur • One representative from the Primary Weavers Service Cooperative Society • One national/State-awarded artisan of Shaphee Lanphee • One artisan of Shaphee Lanphee • One representative from the Indian Institute of Entrepreneurship • One representative from the Mutua Museum, Imphal
56.	Wangkhei Phee	Manipur	Same as above
57.	Moirang Phee	Manipur	Same as above
APRIL 2014 – MARCH 2015			
58.	Mirzapur Handmade Dari	Uttar Pradesh	To regulate the use of GI in the territory, it is proposed that the inspection committee shall consist of the following members: • The Department of Industries, Government of Uttar Pradesh • O/o Development Commissioner (Handicraft), Government of India, having an office at Varanasi • One representative from the Indian Institute of Carpet Technology, Bhadohi • One representative from the Human Welfare Association • One national/State award winner - Mirzapur Handmade Dari • One Mirzapur Handmade Dari - Master Weaver/Shilp Guru • One representative from Pooja Handloom Silk Utpadan Sahkari Samiti Limited

(*Continued*)

Sr. No.	*Geographical Indications*	*State*	*Inspection body*
APRIL 2015 – MARCH 2016			
59.	Guledgudd Khana	Karnataka	• The Deputy Director, Handlooms and Textile Department, Zilla Panchayath, Navangar, Bagalkot • The Managing Director, Cauvery Handlooms, Karnataka State Co-operative Handloom Weavers Federation Ltd., No.49, Model House Street, Basavangaudi, Bengaluru – 560004 • The Assistant Director, Handlooms and Textile Department, Zilla Panchayath, Navanagar, Bagalkot • The Secretary, Guledgudd Handloom Weavers Production and Marketing Cooperative Society Limited, Ward No. 5, Bhavanipet, Guledgudd, Taluk Badami, District Bagalkot – 587203 • The Secretary, Shri Sanganabasaveshwara Handloom Weavers Co-operative Society Limited, Guledgudd, Taluk Badami, District Bagalkot – 587203 • The Secretary, Shri Mookeshwari Karimagga Reshme Khanagala Utpadak Sahakari Sangh, Ni., Guledgudd, Taluk Badami, District Bagalkot – 587203 • The Secretary, Shri Saleshwar Kaimagga Nekarar Sahakari Sanga, Niyamit, Guledgudd, Taluk Badami, District Bagalkot – 587203 • The Secretary, Shri Shivashankara Handloom Weavers Co-operative Society Limited, Ward No.5, Bhavanipet, Guledgudd, Taluk Badami, District Bagalkot – 587203 • The Secretary, Shri Mankandeshwara Handloom Weavers Co-operative Society Limited, Guledgudd, Taluk Badami, District Bagalkot – 587203 • The Secretary, Shri Shivappaiah Handloom Weavers Co-operative Society Limited, Nagarkhanpet, Guledgudd, Taluk Badami, District Bagalkot – 587203

60.	Udupi Sarees	Karnataka	• Even the co-operative societies involved in the production and marketing of the unique traditional products are also stipulating specific levels of quality while placing orders to the weavers on the basis of demand patterns in the market, and they subsequently inspect the various stages of production and final product before procurement. Besides this, the weaving masters in the co-operative societies have their own quality control mechanism. During the processes of production, like winding and warping, creation of butas, weaving, etc., the weaving masters used to inspect the different predetermined parameters and the quality before permitting final/finishing stage of production. • The Assistant Director, Handlooms and Textile Department, Zilla Panchayath, Udupi • The Assistant Director, Handlooms and Textile Department, Zilla Panchayath, Dakshina Kannada, Mangalore • The Managing Director Cauvery Handlooms, Karnataka State Co-operative Handloom Weavers Federation Ltd., No.49, Model House Street, Basavanagudi, Bengaluru – 560004 • The Managing Director, Padupanambur Primary Weavers Service Co-operative Society Limited, Haleangadi, Dakshina Kannada – 574146. GI Journal No. 77 23 November 30, 2015 • The Managing Director, Udupi Primary Weavers Service Co-operative Society Limited, Sanskrit College Road, Udupi – 576101 • The Managing Director, Shivalli Primary Weavers Service Co-operative Society Limited, Malpe Road, Adiudupi, Udupi – 576103 • The Managing Director, Brahmawara

(*Continued*)

Sr. No.	*Geographical Indications*	*State*	*Inspection body*
			• Primary Weavers Service Co-operative Society Limited, Brahmawara, Udupi District – 576213 • The Managing Director, Basrur Primary Weavers Service Co-operative Society Limited, Basrur, Kundapur Taluk, Udupi District – 576211 • The Managing Director, Talipady Primary Weavers Service Co-operative Society Limited, Kinnigoli Dakshina Kannada District – 574150 • The Managing Director, Mangalore Primary Weavers Service Co-operative Society Limited, Shibrikere, Mangalore Taluk, Dakshina Kannada District. • 574164
61.	Kuthampally Dhoties and Set Mundu	Kerala	1. The Department of Handlooms and Textiles, Government of Kerala 2. Development Commissioner (Handlooms), Government of India are supporting the weavers in quality control of the products 3. Besides the master weavers in the entrepreneurial sector, the weaving masters in the co-operative societies have their own quality control mechanism. During the processes of production, like winding, creation of motifs, weaving, etc., these master weavers/weaving masters used to inspect the different predetermined parameters and the quality before permitting the final/finishing stage of production. However, providing the specifications for the quality inspection of the master artisans is difficult as it varies from one master weaver to another.

4. The Textiles Committee, a statutory body under the Ministry of Textiles, Government of India, known all over the country for quality inspection and testing of different textiles and clothing products, is also actively participating in educating the weavers and other stakeholders about maintaining the quality and its importance, marketing strategies, brand building, and other development activities relating to the stakeholders of Kuthampully Dhoties and Set Mundu.

Even the traders and exporters involved in the marketing of the unique traditional products are also insisting on specific levels of quality while placing orders to the manufacturers on the basis of demand patterns in the market, and they subsequently inspect the various stages of production and the final product before procurement. But in the present scenario, it has been decided that the Textiles Committee, Government of India, Mumbai, having regional offices at Kannur and Coimbatore, along with the master weavers and the Department of Handlooms, Government of Kerala, will provide an inspection mechanism for maintaining the quality of the product in the post-GI registration scenario.

(*Continued*)

Sr. No.	*Geographical Indications*	*State*	*Inspection body*
APRIL 2016 – MARCH 2017			
62.	Karvath Kati Sarees and Fabrics	Maharashtra	• The Department of Powerloom, Handloom and Textiles, Government of Maharashtra Weavers Service Centre, Nagpur, Development Commissioner (Handlooms), Government of India • Maharashtra Handloom Development Corporation, Nagpur • Moreover, the master artisans of the product have their own method of quality control. During the processes of production, like dyeing, winding and warping, creation of motifs, weaving, etc., the master weavers used to inspect the different predetermined parameters and quality before permitting the final/finishing stage of production. However, providing the specifications for the quality inspection by the master artisans is difficult as it varies from one master weaver to other. • At present, the Textiles Committee, a statutory body under the Ministry of Textiles, Government of India, which is known all over the country for quality inspection and testing of different textiles and clothing products, is also actively participating in educating the weavers and other stakeholders about quality control and its importance, marketing strategies, brand building and other development activities relating to the stakeholders of Karvath Kati Sarees and Fabrics. Even the traders involved in the marketing of the unique product are also specifying specific levels of quality while placing orders to the manufacturers on the basis of demand patterns in the market, and they subsequently inspect the various stages of production and the final product before procurement.

APRIL 2017 – MARCH 2018

63.	Chakshesang Shawl	Nagaland	The inspection and quality control body has the following members: • Representative from Department of Industry and Commerce, Government of Nagaland • Representative from Department of Art and Culture, Government of Nagaland • Representative from Chakhesang cultural organization • Representative from Chakhesang public organization • Representative from the Science and Technology Council, Government of Nagaland • Further, the representative from the Science and Technology Council shall be the member secretary for the said inspection and quality control body.

(*Continued*)

Sr. No.	*Geographical Indications*	*State*	*Inspection body*
64.	Warangal Durries	Telangana	The quality of Warangal cotton durries is inspected by the weavers themselves, as they are the best judge of the craft. The weavers ensure that the quality is maintained from the stage of cotton selection through each stage of bleaching, dyeing, starching, warp and weft preparation and weaving to obtain the final product. It is proposed to create an inspection body comprising an official from each of the following bodies: 1. The Andhra Pradesh Handicrafts Development Corporation Ltd. 2. The Shatranji Hand-Loom Weavers' Co-operative Production and Sales Society Ltd. 3. Kakatiya Shatranji Handloom Weavers Co-operative Production and Sales Society Ltd. 4. Poornananda Shatranji Handloom Weavers Co-operative Production and Sales Society Ltd. 5. Master weavers and local NGOs will provide a standard quality mechanism so as to regulate the standard quality and parameters of the durries from time to time.
APRIL 2018 – MARCH 2019			
65.	Rajkot Patola	Gujarat	The inspection body comprises expert artisans and the Rajkot District Weavers Association with no specific distribution of roles and responsibilities.

66.	Thirubuvanam Silk Sarees	Tamil Nadu	The Department of Handlooms and Textiles would establish an inspection body, a statutory body consisting of a minimum of eight persons, under the guidance of central and State government to protect and secure the quality of Thirubuvanam Silk: • One person from each society • One person from the Department of Handlooms and Textiles • Two persons from Government of India • One person from an NGO in the territory of jurisdiction of the manufacturing area
APRIL 2019 – MARCH 2020			
67.	Pawndum	Mizoram	The inspection structure is formed by the State Government of Mizoram vide Notification No.D.28016/1/2015-AC dated 26 October, 2018, consisting of the following members: • Chairman: Secretary to Government of Mizoram, Art and Culture Department • Member Secretary: Director, Art and Culture Department • C. Members: • Director, Commerce and Industries Department. • Scientific Officer, Patent Information Centre, Mizoram Science, Technology and Innovation Council. • Chairman, Mizoram Handloom and Handicraft Cooperative Society Ltd. • Representative from Mizo Puan Producer

(*Continued*)

Sr. No.	Geographical Indications	State	Inspection body
			• President, Mizoram Upa Pawl General Headquarters • President, Central Young Mizo Association • President, MizoHmeichheInsuihkhawm Pawl General Headquarters • Expert in Mizo traditional textiles (to be nominated). The Committee shall monitor, review and make suggestions on the action to be taken by the concerned Departments and also maintain the quality post-registration of the Geographical Indication regarding Mizo Traditional Puan viz. (1) Puanchei, (2) Pawndum, (3) Hmaram, (4) Ngotekherh, (5) Tawlhlohpuan, etc.
68.	Ngotekherh	Mizoram	Same as above
69.	Hmaram	Mizoram	Same as above
70.	Tawlhlohpuan	Mizoram	Same as above
71.	Mizo Puanchei	Mizoram	Same as above
72.	Idu Mishmi Textiles	Arunachal Pradesh	To regulate the use of GI in the geographical area, a committee is being formulated consisting of following members; • One person from the Directorate of Textiles, Department of Industries, Arunachal Pradesh • One person from Department of Research, Government of Arunachal Pradesh • One person from Jawahar Lal Nehru State Museum, Itanagar • One person from Institute of Tribal Studies, Rajiv Gandhi University, Itanagar • One person from RIWATCH, Roing, Arunachal Pradesh • Two representatives from IMCLS, Idu Mishmi textile producer's group

73.	Kandangi Saree	Tamil Nadu	Representatives of the Department of Handlooms and Textiles, Government of Tamil Nadu along with experts, local artisans, NGOs, textile analysts and GI attorneys will shortly create an inspection body to strictly regulate the standard quality and parameters of the Kandangi cotton saree. This body would function independently.
74.	Telia Rumal	Telangana	The inspection body consists of the below mentioned persons to maintain the quality of the products. 1. One representative from the Craft Council of Telangana 2. One representative from the Craft Council of India 3. One representative from the Department of Handlooms, Government of Telangana 4. One Representative from the Consortium of Puttapaka Handloom Cluster – IHDS 5. Three producers of Telia Rumal. This inspection body shall act independently to ensure that quality checks are made on the goods and will check the quality, manufacturing and mechanism of the goods.

Source: Prepared by authors

INDEX

Page numbers in **bold** indicate a table on the corresponding page

For Product Safety Concerns and Information please contact our EU
representative GPSR@taylorandfrancis.com
Taylor & Francis Verlag GmbH, Kaufingerstraße 24, 80331 München, Germany

www.ingramcontent.com/pod-product-compliance
Ingram Content Group UK Ltd.
Pitfield, Milton Keynes, MK11 3LW, UK
UKHW022043061126
477531UK00009B/511
9781032187761